Violence

in the Workplace

Preventing, Assessing, and Managing Threats at Work

Carol W. Wilkinson, MD, MSPH, Editor

Government Institutes
Rockville, MD

Government Institutes, Inc., 4 Research Place, Rockville, Maryland 20850, USA.
Phone: (301) 921-2300
Fax: (301) 921-0373
Email: giinfo@govinst.com
Internet address: http://www.govinst.com

02 01 00 99   5   4   3   2

The reader should not rely on this publication to address specific questions that apply to a particular set of facts. The author and publisher make no representation or warranty, express or implied, as to the completeness, correctness, or utility of the information in this publication. In addition, the author and publisher assume no liability of any kind whatsoever resulting from the use of or reliance upon the contents of this book.

Library of Congress Cataloging-in-Publication Data

Wilkinson, Carol W.
        Violence in the workplace : preventing, assessing, and managing threats at work / by Carol W. Wilkinson.
                p.   cm.
        Includes index.
        ISBN: 0-86587-542-1
        1. Violence in the workplace. 2. Employee crimes--Prevention.
3. Employees--Psychology. I. Title.
        HF5549.5.E43W54   1998
        658.4 '73--dc21
                                        98-13592
                                        CIP

Printed in the United States of America

To my parents,
who worked so hard
and
gave me so much

Contents

Introduction
Carol W. Wilkinson xxiii

Chapter One
Violence in the Workplace: Scope of the Problem and Risk Factors
E. Lynn Jenkins 1

Chapter Two
Prevention Strategies and Research Needs
E. Lynn Jenkins 21

Chapter Three
The Potential for Violence among Employees with Psychiatric Disorders
Kenneth Tardiff 33

Chapter Four

Chapter Five

Chapter Six

Chapter Seven

Chapter Eight

Chapter Nine

Chapter Ten

Chapter Eleven

Chapter Twelve

Chapter Thirteen

Chapter Fourteen

Chapter Fifteen

List of Tables

List of Figures

List of Checklists

Foreword

As I sat at my keyboard deciding how to launch a foreword for this fine collection of papers on workplace violence, a news bulletin came over the radio interrupting the theme song from *Titanic*. A reportedly deranged man, back to work at the Connecticut State Lottery following a stress-related leave, had gone on a deadly rampage, killing four of his superiors before turning the gun on himself. The details of this latest tragedy seemed all too familiar. Sadly, the irony of my writing task seemed somehow more surprising than the event itself.

For the American worker, the past ten years have certainly not been kind. Although unemployment has dropped to below the five percent mark, underemployment is increasingly the norm, with many middle-income, manufacturing jobs being replaced by lower paying positions in the service industry. In the process, the economic pie has shrunk to just about the size of a poptart,

In response to cut-throat competition, some unhappy workers have sought remedies through the law. But more and more, embittered and vengeful workers have settled matters outside of court...with fighting words and a loaded gun.

To many casual observers, the problem of workplace violence is often equated with disgruntled postal workers. The term "going postal" has become a codeword for workplace massacres, and there is even a new computer game, simply called *Postal*, with the theme of going berserk in public places. But as this book clearly indicates, the problem of workplace violence extends well beyond the confines of local postal facilities.

Nationally, about four people are murdered every month at the hands of a co-worker or former co-worker who is bent on revenge. And for every tragic instance of workplace homicide, thousands of workers are assaulted or threatened by an associate on the job.

In response to rising levels of violence in the American workplace, a wide range of books and pamphlets, seminars and consultants have surfaced to help companies large and small cope with the growing threat of violence on the job. Some experts focus on security concerns, others on promoting effective EAP strategies. Even others recommend processes to enhance channels of communication so as to alert management about problem workers before they explode.

While all these approaches are useful and important, the overriding goal should be to make civility and human decency as critical a goal as profit. Companies need to upgrade and humanize the way in which they deal with all employees every day rather than just to focus narrowly on how to respond to the one who may have uttered threats.

As this book points out, the problem of workplace violence is broader than just the so-called "co-worker from hell." To a greater extent, customers and clients in hospitals, law firms, and other public and private worksites are expressing their displeasure in the most explosive way. Here, too, corporate America seems to be moving in the wrong direction. Rather than seeking to become more people-minded and service-oriented, disgruntled clients and customers confront frustrating automated phone systems as well as poorly-trained and uninspired customer relations staffs.

In today's corporate environment, it is increasingly more difficult to find someone in charge who has the ability, the authority, and the desire to make things right. Apparently, these days the customer is not always right...unless, of course, he is packing an AK47.

James Alan Fox, Ph.D.
Dean
College of Criminology
Northeastern University

About the Authors

Carol W. Wilkinson, MD, MSPH

Dr. Wilkinson is Regional Medical Director at IBM. During her ten years there she has been involved in the medical aspects of workplace threat assessment and violence prevention. Before coming to IBM, she worked for the New Jersey State Health Department, Time Inc., and Mt. Sinai Medical Center. At Mt. Sinai she studied cases that involved police officers killed in the line of duty. She received her undergraduate degree from Harvard University, her medical degree from Cornell University, and a Master of Public Health degree from Columbia University. She is board certified in internal medicine and occupational medicine. She enjoys the challenge of working on problems in which multiple disciplines interface, such as workplace violence prevention. Her particular areas of expertise and interest in occupational medicine include workers' compensation, ergonomics, and Internet medical information, in addition to the assessment, prevention, and management of threats at work.

Timothy P. Dineen, PhD

Timothy P. Dineen is a clinical psychologist who specializes in applications that involve an understanding of both psychology and organizational behavior. Born and raised in New York City, he completed both his undergradute and graduate education at Columbia University. In addition to his private practice, Dr. Dineen has consulted with a number of companies both nationally and internationally. These consultation assignments have involved working with human resource and medical departments on a variety of issues related to mental health, including coping with violent behavior in the workplace. He has helped to develop strategies designed to reduce violent behavior on the part of employees during periods of crisis or organizational stress. He has also given seminars to occupational health staff and to management groups on recognizing, preventing, and, when necessary, responding to violence in the workplace. His responsibilities have included assisting management in recognizing and planning for the impact of rapid change on organization members and working with medical personnel in assessing, diagnosing, and monitoring treatment of troubled employees.

Kenneth R. Grover, PhD

Ken Grover has been involved in law enforcement and corporate security for more than thirty years. He is presently Vice President of Corporate Security for Darden Restaurants and currently serves as President of the National Food Service Security Council. He has also been president of a national consulting firm specializing in workplace violence issues. Dr. Grover's previous roles include Chief of Police, Crime Prevention Bureau Commander, Associate Dean of Criminal Justice, and Police Academy Director. Dr. Grover has also served as Director of Security for the Marriott Corporation and is the author of numerous articles and books on law enforcement and private security.

Benjamin W. Hahn, JD

In his twenty years of legal practice, Benjamin W. Hahn has represented private and public employers in a wide variety of employment and labor matters. His litigation experience has focused on employment discrimination and wrongful discharge cases. He also has litigated many employee fraud and misconduct matters. Mr. Hahn frequently advises clients and conducts training in such management issues as sexual harassment, workplace violence, substance abuse and drug testing, and physical and mental disability. He has often worked with forensic psychiatrists on employee psychological disorders and actual and potential workplace violence. He received his Bachelor of Arts in economics from Stanford University, with distinction, and his Juris Doctor from Stanford Law School. Mr. Hahn is a member of Phi Beta Kappa. He is a member of the District of Columbia, Maryland, New York, and Texas bars, as well as the bars of the United States Supreme Court and numerous federal district and appellate courts. Mr. Hahn conducts his national legal practice from Annapolis, Maryland.

James Hardeman, MSW, MPA

During Jim Hardeman's fourteen-year employment at Polaroid Corporation in Cambridge, Massachusetts, he became Corporate Employee Assistance Program Manager and the principle designer of Polaroid's workplace violence procedures, protocols, and guidelines. (Polaroid has become internationally known for its workplace violence safety practices.) He has five years experience as a correctional administrator and two years as a forensic therapist. He is currently on the faculty of the Boston College Graduate School of Social Work and is a Ph.D. candidate in social welfare policy at Brandeis University. The former Air Force captain is also the founder of a battered women's shelter and a batterer's program. Jim has received Polaroid's Community Service Award and Black Achiever Award, as well as the Massachusetts NASW (National Association of Social Workers) Outstanding Contribution Award and Greatest Contribution to Social Work Practice.

John T. Horn, MS

As the head of Kroll's Corporate Security group since 1989, Mr. Horn has managed and worked on hundreds of security and crisis management assignments for many of the world's largest and best known corporations. His responsibilities include providing clients with security services for assuring the protection of personnel, assets, and facilities. He conducts assessments and analyses of company security organizations, participates in disaster management planning and development, and provides counsel to companies facing threats, harassment, and extortion situations. Prior to joining Kroll, Mr. Horn was Director of Security at United Technologies Corporation where he was responsible for the firm's worldwide security operations. There he managed and conducted investigations of internal fraud, industrial espionage, theft, and conflict of interest. Mr. Horn has been designated a Certified Fraud Examiner (CFE) by the National Association of Certified Fraud Examiners and a Certified Protection Professional (CPP) by the American Society for Industrial Security (ASIS). Mr. Horn holds a BA in political science from the University of Pittsburgh and a Masters Degree in organizational behavior from the University of Hartford.

E. Lynn Jenkins, MA

Ms. Jenkins earned her B.A. degree in psychology from West Virginia University (WVU) in 1987 and her M.A. in applied social research, also from WVU, in 1988. Ms. Jenkins has been with the National Institute for Occupational Safety and Health (NIOSH) since 1990. She served for four years as the Chief of the Injury Surveillance Section, guiding the collection and analysis of data on all kinds of workplace injuries. Since February 1996, she has been in the NIOSH Office of the Director as a Senior Scientist. Ms. Jenkins' primary area of research in recent years has been workplace violence, but she has also published research on the topics of occupational injuries among women and the use of various coding systems in the analysis of workplace injuries.

Marilyn Knight, MSW

Marilyn Knight, M.S.W. is an internationally recognized speaker, trainer, and consultant in the areas of crisis management planning, post-incident response, workplace violence prevention and organizational change. She is the President and CEO of the Incident Management Team, Inc. and Director of the Center for Workplace Violence Prevention in Southfield, Michigan. She has assisted with conducting risk assessments for potential of violence and has responded in the aftermath of such crisis events as the terrorist bombing in Oklahoma City, airline disasters, line of duty deaths of law enforcement and emergency services personnel, Postal Service shooting incidents, and many other industrial accidents and acts of violence in many different types of industry. Ms. Knight is a sworn Special Deputy of the Wayne County Sheriff's Department (Metropolitan Detroit) and has assisted in training law enforcement and emergency response personnel in advanced hostage negotiations, critical incident response, and workplace violence prevention.

John W. Kyle, JD

John W. Kyle is an attorney concentrating his practice in employment and labor law matters on behalf of employers. Before joining the nationally recognized firm of Littler Mendelson, Mr. Kyle enjoyed a distinguished career as an attorney and investigator with key federal labor agencies, including the National Labor Relations Board and the Office of Federal Contracts Compliance Programs. He has many years of experience in providing advice, counsel, training, and representation in a wide variety of private and public sector labor and employment law matters. He has frequently advised and represented employers in matters concerning abusive, disruptive, or violent behavior in the workplace. He litigates regularly in the federal and state courts and is a frequent lecturer to business and employer groups. Mr. Kyle received his Juris Doctor from the University of Baltimore School of Law. He now maintains a practice in Columbia, Maryland and is a member of the Maryland and District of Columbia bars.

Warren F. Miller, ARM, ALCM

Warren Miller has worked actively with customers to protect profits by preventing losses throughout his twenty years as an insurance professional. Since joining Kemper Insurance Companies in 1977, he has specialized in risk management, promoting education and training as the keys to improving workplace safety and health. Mr. Miller's primary roles have been as a risk control consultant for customers with multiple locations and varied operations and as the developer of casualty, property, and liability risk management seminars for producers and their clients. Most recently, Mr. Miller has been instrumental in building resources to address the growing threat of violence in the workplace. Specific contributions in this area include developing videos for disaster response, educational and training seminars, consulting on preparedness and violence prevention, and professional writing and speaking on risk management and violence prevention. Mr. Miller received a BS degree in fire protection and safety technology from Empire State College-SUNY and earned his Associate in Risk Management (ARM) and Associate in Loss Control Management (ALCM) designation from the Insurance Institute of America.

Peter D. Olenen, MD

Dr. Olenen is a graduate of the Albert Einstein College of Medicine. He has been associated with IBM since 1981. He presently serves as the Physician Program Manager at the IBM East Fishkill site. He is board certified in occupational medicine. He has many years experience dealing with difficult and threatening employees. He developed the medical component of the Separation Management Plan for an unprecedented layoff. He was actively involved in management training, consultation, and employee evaluation prior to and during the layoffs.

Robert Pater, MA

Robert Pater is Director of Strategic Safety Associates, a Portland, Oregon-based safety training company specializing in programs that reduce injuries, boost motivation, and heighten productivity, utilizing principles from certain martial arts. Clients have included a number of national and multinational companies. He is also the author of *The Black-Belt Manager*, published in five languages. Robert has an MA in industrial psychology. He has presented throughout the United States for the National Safety Council and various other organizations.

Robert W. Russell, BS

Rob Russell has over twenty years of management experience in manufacturing, banking, and retail organizations. He has been a private consultant since 1984, specializing in the design and presentation of programs to increase organizational safety and enhance interpersonal relations. He has worked on safety and leadership programs with many public and private organizations. In 1990, the State of Oregon named him their External Consultant of the Year. He graduated from Oregon State University in 1961 with a degree in business administration and a minor in industrial metals. He teaches university classes in training, design, and dealing with difficult people. He is an active member of ASTD (American Society for Training and Development) having served on that organization's Western Region Council and as a past President of the Portland, Oregon Chapter.

Tom Scaletta, MD

Tom Scaletta, M.D. is an emergency physician and the Chairman of the Department of Emergency Medicine at West Suburban Hospital Medical Center in Oak Park, Illinois. He is assistant professor of emergency medicine at Rush College of Medicine and the former associate director of the emergency department at Cook County Hospital. Dr. Scaletta has lectured nationally and authored several textbook chapters on medical workplace violence prevention. He served as a reviewer for texts on hospital security published by the Joint Commission on Accreditation of Healthcare Organizations. Dr. Scaletta represents the nonprofit organization, Physician for a Violence-Free Society, for initiatives relating to the management of medical workplace violence.

Kenneth Tardiff, MD, MPH

Kenneth Tardiff, M.D., M.P.H. was born in New Orleans. He received his M.D. degree from Tulane Medical School, his residency training in psychiatry at the Massachusetts General Hospital, and a Master of Public Health degree from Harvard School of Public Health. He is Professor of Psychiatry and Public Health at Cornell University Medical College and an attending psychiatrist at the New York Hospital in New York City. He has published over 150 books, chapters, and scientific papers, mostly on violence and suicide. He has served as a consultant to healthcare institutions and companies on the management of potentially violent persons. He has served as an expert witness in civil and criminal cases.

Kenneth L. Wolf, PhD

Kenneth L. Wolf, Ph.D., is Director of the Incident Management Team, Inc., an international crisis management and security company in Southfield, Michigan. He has been a violence management and crisis response consultant to a number of government and large private corporations.. He has consulted on worksite violence, threat assessment, and case management of potentially violent individuals for numerous Fortune 500 Companies. Dr. Wolf has assisted in writing corporate national critical incident response procedures and has assisted with crisis management response following the post office mass shootings. On behalf of the American Society on Industrial Security (ASIS), Dr. Wolf gave testimony on worksite violence before congressional committees of the United States Senate and House in Washington, D.C. on November 2, 1994. He is a fully licensed clinical psychologist.

Acknowledgments

A book such as this has had many beginnings. I want to express my appreciation to those people who made this book possible. Thanks to Dr. Phil Landrigan who first got me involved in violence research when he suggested I use public health analytic tools to study cases of police officers killed in the line of duty. Thanks to Jim Daly, from Human Resources, when he asked me to advise him about managing a threatening and possibly violent employee, challenging me to learn more about this field. Thanks to Organizational Resources Counselors who requested I put together a presentation on our corporate experience in violence prevention. Thanks to Dr. Pat Hagendorn for volunteering me to organize a course on workplace violence prevention for occupational physicians. And lastly, thanks to Alex Padro and lunch at Ceasars Palace, when he encouraged me to take the plunge and do this book.

I also want to thank Isabelle Swift for generously sharing her knowledge about book publishing. Thanks to Angela O'Neil, my secretary, for her attention to details and her ongoing efforts to keep me organized. My thanks also to a number of people at IBM for their encouragement and support. I want to thank the many colleagues, patients, and employees who, directly or indirectly, helped me better understand this complex problem. My thanks to my contributors for their expertise, time, and effort, without which this book could not have happened.

Finally, thanks to my daughter Claire for helping me out by having the computer intelligence of youth. And thanks to my husband Jack for his ongoing love, understanding, and support.

Introduction

Carol W. Wilkinson, MD, MSPH

The field of workplace violence prevention relies on the blending of experience, knowledge, and judgment. Effective workplace violence prevention requires the collaboration of persons from multiple disciplines, each of whom has a unique contribution to solving the problem. As a result, each specialist benefits from the perspective of the others. The purpose of this book is to bring together those various perspectives and ranges of expertise that contribute to the prevention of workplace violence. These include the fields of law, security, training, research, psychiatry, and risk management. In addition, this book highlights the risk of violence with layoffs as well as the violence risk for the healthcare profession and service industry. Finally, it recognizes the contribution of domestic conflict to violence at work.

This book is intended for those people whose responsibilities may require them to address threats and violence in the workplace, including the human resource specialist, line management, the education and training department, the legal specialist, security personnel, and the occupational health professional. A resource for companies developing violence prevention policies and programs, this book can assist them in dealing with potentially violent employees. The book should be valuable for the specialist trying to understand the issues in areas where he or she may not be knowledgeable. Occupational health professionals, doctors, and nurses will find this book useful both in assessing the violent potential of an employee as well as understanding the perspective of others in addressing the problem. Generalists will benefit from the detailed description of this problem.

Ultimately, this book cannot replace experience and knowledge applied to specific situations. What it will do is provide an overview and general guidelines. An organization still must design and implement a violence prevention program based on its particular needs. In the process it will still need to identify resources based on what is appropriate and available.

One of the challenges in approaching workplace violence prevention is that, although businesses may from time to time deal with threats and hostilities, these rarely progress to overt acts of violence. Therefore, one is faced with the challenge of needing to be prepared for what is an unlikely event, but one in which the stakes are high. In some work environments, such as in the health care and service industries, the risks of violence are at times accepted as part of the job and therefore appropriate training and other interventions may not be implemented. Increasingly, it is being recognized that there are interventions that can reduce the risk of violence in all work places whether high risk or low.

This book is a resource to assist both employees and employers in reaching this goal of a safer workplace. In this book, I bring together chapters written by specialists from their own perspectives and experiences. Inevitably, there will be some overlap from chapter to chapter because the contributors are looking at the same problem from different perspectives. As the reader progresses through the book, he or she should have a richer and more detailed understanding than might have been obtained from a single author or from a single specialty.

First, what do we know about violence in the workplace? Lynn Jenkins, from NIOSH, reviews the data on workplace violence, indicating the knowledge, the gaps, and the unanswered questions. Despite the greater publicity associated with killings done by disgruntled employees, robbery is by far the most common reason for workplace homicide. In 1994, there were 1,071 homicides at work and 80% of these involved robberies. Therefore, the violence-risk profile of work places will vary depending on the nature of the work and the availability of money or other valuables. The study of nonfatal violence is complicated by problems of case definition and incomplete reporting. It is estimated that there are 1,000 assaults for every workplace homicide. We know that nonfatal workplace violence has different characteristics from violence in fatal cases. Only about 8% of nonfatal assaults are associated with robberies, compared with over 80% of workplace homicides. The numbers of men and women assaulted are nearly equal, whereas there are four times as many men murdered at work as women. Lastly, though threats are the most common expression of violence at work, they are the least studied. Threats are indicators of possible violence and make employees feel unsafe at work. Much of violence prevention in the workplace is the assessment and management of threats. Despite the statistics, there have been too few studies of violence prevention interventions to assess their effectiveness. Therefore, much of workplace violence prevention is still based on a combination of experience and common sense.

What are the psychiatric dimensions of workplace violence? Dr. Tardiff, with years of experience studying, consulting, and writing on violence, discusses how different psychiatric conditions may manifest themselves in violence at work, the contribution of other risk factors such as drugs and alcohol, and the components of a short-term violence assessment. Many violent acts are predominantly criminal acts, particularly those associated with robbery for money or other goods of value. Other violent acts arise from a disturbed mind, a distorted world view, and impaired relationships. These are the more problematic cases. Such people are often acting based on feelings and concerns we may not understand or be aware of. It is useful to have identified a local resource to assist in violence assessment. Each case is unique in its antecedents, manifestations, and management. The better one understands the specifics, the better one can decide how to handle each case.

A corporation can easily be lulled into complacency about workplace violence, believing that "it can never happen here." Unfortunately, there are no such guarantees. Program development reduces the likelihood of having a violent event and minimizes the devastation should an event occur. It is preferable to learn about workplace violence prevention during the development of a program rather than in the heat of crisis. The time to build executive support, define policy, and find local resources is before the need arises. Dr. Ken Wolfe, from the Center for Workplace Violence Prevention, provides an overview of program development and threat management. Threats are the early warning system for violence prevention programs. Though not all threats progress to violence, most violent episodes are preceded by threats. It is important to set limits consistently, assess them promptly and to address threats directly. The risk of ignoring threats is that the employee may continue to make threats and even escalate their severity and/or frequency.

When threats are not addressed, co-workers feel unsafe at work, and the possibility of violence at work increases.

Security is a key player in workplace violence prevention. The security staff has the law enforcement background and contacts; they are responsible for assessing and maintaining a secure workplace, and they will be called upon at the time of crisis. John Horn, from Kroll Associates, points out in his chapter on the role of security in preventing violence that the nature of the response will depend on the risk profile of the business and the resources and skills available within the company. An organization needs to recognize what its staff can and cannot do and to obtain additional expertise as needed.

John Kyle and Benjamin Hahn, from the law firm of Littler, Mendelson, Fastiff, Tichy & Mathiason, remind the reader of the need to consider legal issues in program development and implementation. The employer needs to balance the responsibility for maintaining a safe workplace with an individual's rights and freedom. Similarly, they must consider their responsibilities to the community and customers. The authors have laid out a framework describing a number of scenarios, but a detailed citation of case law is beyond the scope of this book. These chapters are not meant to be a replacement for legal advice but to sensitize the reader to the legal implications of policies, practices, and actions.

Another resource as one develops a violence prevention program is the insurance risk manager, as described by Warren Miller from Kemper National Insurance Company. A well-developed workplace violence prevention program can be an important component in reducing the risk of violence to employees, customers, and the community. One of the consequences of a good program may be the potential for reducing insurance costs to the business. Risk management consists of reviewing and identifying exposures and then developing appropriate responses and interventions. These may include facility modifications, security training for service employees, and guidelines for employees who work in high risk areas and at night. Risk management is not a cookbook approach, but rather it is tailored to the particular business and risks.

Domestic violence can spill over into work. Jim Hardeman, the Employee Assistance Program manager at Polaroid, shares his knowledge and experience about domestic violence. He brings the insight that the employee who has the risk of being violent at work may already be violent at home, that patterns of behavior seen at work may well have been seen at home, and that the stresses at home and/or work are potential precipitators for increasing the risk of violence. Hardeman shares the details of a Polaroid case which highlights the business need for a violence prevention program. In addition, he includes Polaroid material for domestic violence which covers responsibilities of management, guidelines for providing assistance, and suggestions on intervention.

In his chapter on preventing violence in the healthcare environment, Dr. Tom Scaletta makes the point that until recently there has been a denial about the risk of violence for healthcare professionals. As a result, there may not be systems in place to track violent incidents at work, discouraging professionals from reporting episodes and increasing the tendency to "blame the victim." This approach tends to minimize rather than legitimize the risk and makes it difficult to get the resources needed to protect healthcare workers. In the long run, this is a short-sighted perspective since the cost of remediation after an incident is often several times greater than the cost preventing the initial incident.

Kenneth Grover, Ph.D., contributed the chapter on violence prevention in service industries. The service industry is faced with the challenge of protecting vastly different environments, so the solutions must be fitted to the particular risks and opportunities. Effective violence prevention is more than a series of regulations. By a careful examination of each establishment, its neighborhood, and its risk profile, one can design a safer workplace. Safety is a combination of environmental conditions and human interventions. For example, the lock on the back door does not help if the staff needs to go back and forth regularly through that door and, consequently, leaves the door ajar. A number of efforts are under way to collect and communicate the service industry experience in violence prevention for customers and employees. The challenge is to transfer the knowledge from the larger organizations, which have the experience and resources, to the smaller establishments with more limited resources.

Without training one does not have a full workplace violence prevention program. Training complements other interventions such as establishing corporate policy and improving physical security. People can only be as good as their training. Their ability to respond effectively when faced with threats will depend on how well they have learned to recognize potential problems and the organizational response in place to support them in dealing with these problems. Violence prevention is an area that is unfamiliar to most people, and it can be uncomfortable if not frightening. In a threatening situation, a person's instinctive reactions are unpredictable and may be counterproductive. Training increases a person's understanding and awareness of what is happening, what are possible behaviors, and how best to proceed. In addition to imparting knowledge and skills, training communicates a company's values and its commitment to a safe workplace. Training is invaluable in reducing the chance that a threatening situation might worsen. It is an investment in an organization's well-being and provides insurance to maintaining that well-being if a crisis occurs. The chapter by Pater and Russell covers many of these dimensions of training, starting with the identification of common organizational barriers to implementing training and suggestions on how to overcome them. It is a guide that can be used, either in evaluating existing programs or in implementing new ones.

The possibility of violence associated with a job action such as layoff is a real concern for employers. Media coverage dramatizes situations where an employee has returned to "get even" after a job loss. It is difficult to predict how an employee will react to the news of being laid off. Some employees are more fragile and more at risk at the time of a job layoff. They might have pressures at home, financial worries and emotional or social stressors. They might have had prior experience with job termination and their prospects for re-employment may be bleak. Some of them might have patterns of reacting violently to difficult situations. The combination of anger, shame, and despair could be lethal. Violent acts at work are desperate acts. Drs. Dineen and Olenen review the problem of violence prevention during layoffs. The goal in a layoff is to minimize the likelihood of violence through a process that allows the employee to leave with dignity. It helps for communication to be reasonable and respectful and to have resources available to support employees' emotional needs. When managers are informed and involved in the process, they are better able to identify at-risk employees, to acknowledge the employees' distress, to be sensitive to nuances of threats, and to assist the employee in moving on from the separation to the next step of considering alternatives and other employment options. Fortunately, the collective nature of a layoff means that employees are not alone, and this collectiveness can provide support for the employees as they deal with their feelings and their futures.

Ultimately, despite all efforts, an organization may be faced with having to deal with a violent episode at work—one which may injure and even kill people. We have learned from experience that there are good and bad ways to respond to such traumatic events. Therefore, organizations and their representatives can make choices that reduce the pain, anger, and panic and contribute to the recovery of involved family, friends, and co-workers. Critical incident response uses this experience to structure an effective response. It is a combination of a proactive communication plan and structured support for the victims. At such a time, there is need for compassionate, informed, and regular communication. This communication process provides reassurance, dispels rumors, and updates everyone on information as it becomes available. Victim support is very important. Victims need to know that the emotional turmoil they are experiencing is normal. They need to be able to grieve, relive the event, and get solace from others that were involved. These are important parts of the recovery process. They need to come to terms with the event and their feelings before they can return to the everyday routine. Violence can shatter the safety of the workplace; without help in recovery, there is a greater likelihood that dysfunction at home and work will persist to the point of long-term disability.

In conclusion, this book should assist one in the process of understanding a complicated and challenging problem and making decisions that contribute to a safer workplace. We believe planning is preferable to reacting. It allows for identification and development of resources. The challenge of threat assessment is in maximizing information available, recognizing the inevitable gaps, and synthesizing what information is available in order to implement a response that reduces the possibility of workplace violence. One needs to find a balance between doing too much and doing too little. There is the risk of making a situation worse either by doing nothing or by doing the *wrong* thing. In the final analysis, effective violence prevention is a combination of rationality tempered with intuition. The threatening person may be driven by events and concerns we neither know nor understand. Experienced professionals in this field understand the complexity of the issues and the challenge of trying to figure out the full picture when pieces are missing and unobtainable. They are familiar with the dilemma of applying rationality to what are usually desperate and irrational people. We need their help in the process both of assessing specific situations and developing programs. With the expertise presented here, this book will prove a useful resource to anyone who must deal with the issue of workplace violence.

Chapter One

- ❏ Reasons for studying workplace violence
- ❏ Magnitude of fatal and nonfatal attacks at work
- ❏ Demographics of homicides at work
- ❏ How nonfatal attacks at work differ from fatal attacks
- ❏ Why it is difficult to study nonfatal attacks
- ❏ Cost of workplace violence in lost workdays and wages

Violence
in the Workplace
Scope of the Problem
and Risk Factors

E. Lynn Jenkins, MA

Case Study

The editor of the Daily Times *in a small midwestern town was concerned about the increase in violence. An angry employee at the fabricating plant in the neighboring town had come to work with a shotgun and threatened the shift manager. Last night, at about 2 A.M., the attendant at a service station was killed during a robbery. Saturday night a week ago, the bartender at his favorite restaurant was shot and wounded while trying to break up a fight between two customers. The editor asked his reporter to do a piece on the risks of being killed on the job.*

Introduction

Recently, violence in the workplace has received considerable attention in the popular press and among safety and health professionals. Much of the reason for this attention is the reporting of data by the National Institute for Occupational Safety and Health (NIOSH) and others regarding the magnitude of this problem in American workplaces. Unfortunately, sensational acts of co-worker violence (which form only a small part of the problem) are often emphasized by the media to the exclusion of the almost daily killings of taxicab drivers, convenience store clerks and other retail workers, security guards, and police officers. These deaths often go virtually unnoticed, yet their numbers are staggering: 1,071 workplace homicides occurred in 1994. These homicides included 179 supervisors or proprietors in retail sales, 105 cashiers, 86 taxicab drivers, 49 managers in restaurants or hotels, 70 police officers or detectives, and 76 security guards [BLS 1995]. An additional one million workers were assaulted each year. These figures indicate that an average of 20 workers are murdered and 18,000 are assaulted each week while at work or on duty. Death or injury should not be an inevitable result of one's chosen occupation, nor should these staggering figures be accepted as a cost of doing business in our society. This chapter reviews what is known about fatal and nonfatal violence in the workplace to determine the focus needed for prevention and research.

Definition of Workplace Violence

Defining workplace violence has generated considerable discussion. Some would include in the definition any language or actions that make one person uncomfortable in the workplace; others would include threats and harassment; and all would include any bodily injury inflicted by one person on another. Thus the spectrum of workplace violence ranges from offensive language to homicide, and a reasonable working definition of workplace violence is as follows: *violent acts, including physical assaults and threats of assault, directed toward persons at work or on duty.* Most studies to date have focused primarily on physical injuries, since they are clearly defined and easily measured. But this chapter examines data from multiple sources and acknowledges differences in definitions and coverage to learn as much as possible from these varied efforts.

The circumstances of workplace violence also vary and may include robbery-associated violence; violence by disgruntled clients, customers, patients, inmates, etc.; violence by co-workers, employees, or employers; and domestic violence that finds its way into the workplace. These circumstances all appear to be related to the level of violence in communities and in society in general. Thus the question arises: why study workplace violence separately from the larger universe of all violence? Several reasons exist for focusing specifically on workplace violence.

Reasons To Study Workplace Violence

✧ Violence is a substantial contributor to death and injury on the job. NIOSH data indicate that homicide has become the second leading cause of occupational-injury death, exceeded only by motor-vehicle-related deaths [Jenkins 1996]. Estimates of nonfatal workplace assaults vary dramatically, but a reasonable estimate from the National Crime Victimization Survey is that approximately one million people are assaulted while at work or on duty each year. This figure represents 15% of the acts of violence experienced by U.S. residents aged 12 or older [Bachman 1994].

✧ The circumstances of workplace violence differ significantly from those of all homicides. For example, 75% of all workplace homicides in 1993 were robbery related; but in the general population, only 9% of homicides were robbery-related, and only 19% were committed in conjunction with any kind of felony (robbery, rape, arson, etc.) [FBI 1994]. Furthermore, 47% of all murder victims in 1993 were related to or acquainted with their assailants [FBI 1994], whereas the majority of workplace homicides (because they are robbery-related) are believed to occur among persons not known to one another. Only 17% of female victims of workplace homicides were killed by a spouse or former spouse [Windau and Toscano 1994], whereas 29% of the female homicide victims in the general population were killed by a current or former husband or boyfriend [FBI 1994].

✧ Workplace violence is not distributed randomly across all workplaces but is clustered in particular occupational settings. More than half (56%) of workplace homicides occurred in retail trade and service industries. Homicide is the leading cause of death in these industries as well as in finance, insurance, and real estate. Eighty-five percent of nonfatal assaults in the workplace occur in service and retail trade industries [BLS 1994d]. As the U.S.

economy continues to shift toward the service sectors, fatal and nonfatal workplace violence will be an increasingly important occupational safety and health issue.

✧ The risk of workplace violence is associated with specific workplace factors such as dealing with the public, the exchange of money, and the delivery of services or goods. Consequently, great potential exists for workplace-specific prevention efforts such as bullet-resistant barriers and enclosures in taxicabs, convenience stores, gas stations, emergency departments, and other areas where workers come in direct contact with the public; locked drop safes and other cash-handling procedures in retail establishments; and threat-assessment policies in all types of workplaces.

✧ Long-term efforts to reduce the level of violence in U.S. society must address a variety of social issues such as education, poverty, and environmental justice. However, short-term efforts must address the pervasive nature of violence in our society and the need to protect workers. We cannot wait to address workplace violence as a social issue alone but must take immediate action to address it as a serious occupational safety and health issue.

Magnitude and Demographics of Workplace Homicide

NIOSH Data

Data from the National Traumatic Occupational Fatalities (NTOF) surveillance system indicate that 9,937 workplace homicides occurred during the 13-year period from 1980 through 1992, with an average workplace homicide rate of 0.70/100,000 workers (Table 1.1) [NIOSH 1995]. During the 1980s, workplace homicides decreased; but in the 1990s, the numbers began to increase, surpassing machine-related deaths and approaching the number of workplace motor-vehicle-related deaths (Figure 1.1). Although the 1992 figure was lower than that for 1991, it exceeded the 1990 figure and did not include 1992 data for New York City and the State of Connecticut. NTOF is an ongoing, death-certificate-based census of traumatic occupational fatalities in the United States, with data from all 50 states and the District of Columbia. NTOF includes information for all workers aged 16 or older who died from an injury or poisoning and for whom the certifier noted a positive response to the injury-at-work item on the death certificate. For additional discussion of the NTOF system and the limitations of death certificates for the study of workplace homicide, see Castillo and Jenkins [1994].

Gender, Age, Race, and Method of Homicide

The majority (80%) of workplace homicides during 1980–92 occurred among male workers. The leading cause of occupational injury death varied by gen-

Year	Number	Rate†
1980	929	.96
1981	944	.94
1982	859	.86
1983	721	.72
1984	660	.63
1985	751	.70
1986	672	.61
1987	649	.58
1988	699	.61
1989	696	.59
1990	725	.61
1991	875	.75
1992	757	.64
Total	**9,937**	**.70**

Source: NIOSH [1995].
* Data not available for New York City and Connecticut.
† Per 100,000 workers.

Table 1.1: Workplace homicides in the United States, 1980–92*

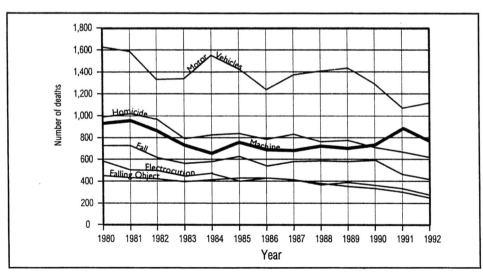

Figure 1.1: Leading causes of occupational-injury deaths in the United States, 1980–1992. Data were not available for New York City and Connecticut. (Source: Jenkins, 1996)

der, with homicides accounting for 11% of all occupational injury deaths among male workers and 42% among female workers [NIOSH 1995]. The majority of female homicide vicims were employed in retail trade (46%) and service (22%) industries (Table 1.2). A large number of male homicide victims were employed not only in retail trade (36%) and service (16%) industries but in public administration (11%) and transportation/communication/public utilities (11%) (Table 1.2). Although homicide is the leading cause of occupational injury death among female workers,

	Homicides (% of total)	
Industry	Male workers	Female workers
Retail trade	36.1	45.5
Services	16.0	22.2
Public administration	10.5	2.9
Transportation/communi-cation/public utilities	10.6	3.8
Manufacturing	7.0	4.9
Construction	4.1	0.6
Agriculture/forestry/ fishing	2.7	0.6
Finance/insurance/ real estate	2.4	6.8
Wholesale trade	1.7	1.1
Mining	0.6	0.1
Not classified	8.5	11.7

Source: NIOSH [1995].
* Data for New York City and Connecticut were not available for 1992.
† Percentages add to more than 100% because of rounding.

Table 1.2: Workplace homicides by industry and gender, United States 1980–92*

male workers have more than three times the risk of work-related homicide (Table 1.3).

The age of workplace homicide victims ranged from 16 (the youngest reported in NTOF) to 93 during 1980–92. The largest number of workplace homicides occurred among workers aged 25 to 34, whereas the rate of workplace homicide increased with age (Table 1.3). The highest rates of workplace homicide occurred among workers aged 65 and older; the rates for these workers were more than twice those for workers aged 55 to 64 (Table 1.3). This pattern held true for both male and female workers.

Although the majority of workplace homicide victims were white (73%), black workers (1.39/100,000) and workers of other races (1.87/100,000) had the highest rates, per 100,000 workers, of work-related homicide (Table 1.4).

Between 1980 and 1992, 76% (7,590) of work-related homicides were committed with firearms, another 12% (1,231) resulted from wounds inflicted by cutting

Age group	Male workers		Female workers		All workers	
	Number	Rate†	Number	Rate†	Number	Rate†
16-19	242	0.55	102	0.25	344	0.41
20-24	796	.87	285	.35	1,081	.62
25-34	2,020	.89	591	.33	2,611	.65
35-44	1,841	.99	423	.28	2,265	.68
45-54	1,344	1.04	293	.29	1,637	.71
55-64	1,055	1.22	191	.31	1,246	.84
65+	620	2.59	115	.71	735	1.83
Total‡	7,935	—	2,001	—	9,937	—
Average	—	1.01	—	.32	—	.70

Source: NIOSH [1995].
* Data from New York City and Connecticut were not available for 1992.
† Rates are per 100,000 workers.
‡ Totals include victims for whom age data were missing

Table 1.3: Workplace homicides by age group and gender, United States 1980–92*

or piercing instruments, and the remaining 11% (1,116) were the result of strangulation and other means.

Industry and Occupation

During the 13-year period 1980–92, the greatest number of homicides, accounting for nearly half of the total, occurred in the retail trade (3,774) and service industries (1,713), whereas the highest rates per 100,000 workers occurred in retail trades (1.6), public administration (1.3), and transportation/communication/public utilities (0.94) (Table 1.5).

At the more detailed levels of industry (Table 1.6), the largest number of deaths from 1990 to 1992 occurred in grocery stores (330), eating and drinking places (262), taxicab services (138), and justice/

Race/ethnicity of victims	Number	% of total	Rate†
White (includes Hispanic)	7,239	72.8	0.59
Black	1,938	19.5	1.39
Other	760	7.6	1.87

Source: NIOSH [1995].
* Data for New York City and Connecticut were not available for 1992.
† Per 100,000 workers.

Table 1.4: Workplace homicides by race, United States 1980–92*

public-order establishments (137). Taxicab services had the highest rate of work-related homicide during the three-year period 1990–92 (41.4/ 100,000). This rate was nearly 60 times the national average rate of work-related homicides (0.70/100,000). This figure was followed by rates for liquor stores (7.5), detective/protective services (7.0), gas service stations (4.8), and jewelry stores (4.7) (Table 1.8). The rates show an increase from the previously published rates for 1980–89 for taxicab ser-

Industry	Number	% of total	Rate†
Retail trade	3,774	38.0	1.60
Public administration	889	8.9	1.30
Transportation/communication/public utilities	917	9.2	0.94
Agriculture/forestry/ fishing	222	2.2	0.50
Mining	45	0.5	0.40
Service	1,713	17.2	0.38
Construction	335	3.4	.37
Finance/insurance/ real estate	327	3.3	.35
Wholesale trade	155	1.6	.27
Manufacturing	650	6.5	.24
Not classified	910	9.1	—

Source: NIOSH [1995].
* Data for New York City and Connecticut were not available for 1992.
† Per 100,000 workers.

Table 1.5: Workplace homicides by industry, United States 1980–92*

Industry	1980–89		1990–92	
	Number	Rate†	Number	Rate†
Taxicab services	287	26.9	138	41.4
Liquor stores	115	8.0	30	7.5
Gas service stations	304	5.6	68	4.8
Detective/protective services	152	5.0	86	7.0
Justice/public order	640	3.4	137	2.2
Grocery stores	806	3.2	330	3.8
Jewelry stores	56	3.2	26	4.7
Hotels/motels	153	1.5	33	0.8
Barber shops	14	1.5	4	—
Eating/drinking places	734	1.5	262	1.5

Source: NIOSH [1995] (data for 1980-89 from Castillo and Jenkins [1994]).
* Data for New York City and Connecticut were not available for 1992.
† Rates are per 100,000 workers.
— Rate was not calculated because of the instability of rates based on small numbers.

Table 1.6: Workplace homicides in high-risk industries, United States

Occupation	1983–89		1990–92	
	Number	Rate‡	Number	Rate‡
Taxicab driver/chauffeur	197	15.1	140	22.7
Sheriff/bailiff	73	10.9	36	10.7
Police/ detective/public service	267	9.0	86	6.1
Hotel clerk	29	5.1	6	2.0
Gas station/garage worker	83	4.5	37	5.9
Security guard	160	3.6	115	5.5
Stock handler/bagger	189	3.1	95	3.5
Supervisor/proprietor, sales	662	2.8	372	3.3
Supervisor, police and detective	12	2.2	0	—
Barber	14	2.2	4	—
Bartender	49	2.1	20	2.3
Correctional institution officer	19	1.5	3	—
Salesperson (motor vehicle/ boat)	21	1.1	17	2.0
Salesperson (other commodities)	98	1.0	73	1.7
Sales counter clerk	13	1.2	18	3.1
Fire fighter	18	1.4	8	1.3
Logging occupation	4	—	6	2.3
Butcher/meatcutter	11	.6	12	1.5

Source: NIOSH [1995] (data for 1983-89 from Castillo and Jenkins [1994]).
* High-risk occupations have workplace homicide rates that are twice the average rate during one or both time periods.
† Data for New York City and Connecticut were not available for 1992.
‡ Rates are per 100,000 workers.
— Rate was not calculated because of the instability of rates based on small numbers.

Table 1.7: Workplace homicides in high-risk* occupations, United States

vices, detective/protective services, grocery stores, and jewelry stores. Rates decreased in liquor stores, gasoline service stations, justice/public-order establishments, and hotels/motels; they remained the same in eating and drinking places.

When detailed occupations were analyzed for 1990–92 (Table 1.7), the highest homicide rates were found for taxicab drivers/chauffeurs (22.7), sheriffs/bailiffs (10.7), police and detectives-public service (6.1), gas station/garage workers (5.9), and security guards (5.5). Compared with previously published data for the seven-year period 1983–89, these data indicate that rates increased more than two and a half times for sales counter clerks and nearly two times for motor vehicle and boat sales workers and sales workers in other commodities (including workers in jewelry, food, sporting goods, book, coin, and other retail stores). Homicide rates for taxicab drivers and security guards were one and a half times higher during the early 1990s than during 1983–89. However, some rates decreased: for 1990–92; the rate for hotel clerks was less than half the 1983–89 rate, and the rate for public sector police and detectives was two-thirds the 1983–89 rate. During 1990–92, an extraordinary number of homicides (372) occurred among sales supervisors and proprietors. These positions had twice the number of deaths of those in any other single category during both periods.

| | Homicides (% of total)* | | |
| | 1992 | 1993 | 1994 |
Circumstance	(1,004)	(1,063)	(1,071)
Robbery and other crime	82	75	73
Business dispute/work associate	9	10	9
Co-worker/former co-worker	4	6	5
Customer/client	5	4	4
Police in line of duty	6	6	7
Security guard in line of duty	†	5	7
Personal dispute/acquaintance	4	4	4

Source: BLS [1994b, 1995], Windau and Toscano [1994].
* Percentages add to more than 100% because of rounding.
† This category was not included in 1992.

Table 1.8: Circumstances of workplace homicides, United States

Bureau of Labor Statistics Data

Information from the Bureau of Labor Statistics (BLS) Census of Fatal Occupational Injuries (CFOI) Program identifies the same high-risk demographic and occupational groups as NIOSH NTOF data and allows description of the circumstances of workplace homicides for the period 1992–94. According to the BLS data, 73% to 82% of the homicides occurred during a robbery or other crime, whereas only 9% to 10% were attributed to business disputes, and only 4% to 6% were attributed specifically to co-workers or former employees (Table 1.8). A shift occurred in the robbery and other crimes category with the creation of the new security guard in-line-of-duty category, but the distribution of the circumstances has remained fairly stable during the three years in which data have been collected. The CFOI system uses multiple sources, including administrative documents from federal and state agencies (e.g., death certificates, medical examiner records, workers' compensation reports, and regulatory agency reports) as well as news reports and follow-up questionnaires to business establishments [Windau and Toscano 1994].

The BLS described a number of the robberies as occurring while workers were locking up at night or making money drops or pickups, but these were not specifically quantified. Also, homicide appeared to be primarily an urban problem, with eight of the largest metropolitan areas accounting for nearly half of the workplace homicides in 1993 [Toscano and Weber 1995]. The self-employed accounted for 24% to 27% of the homicides documented by the CFOI program for 1992–94, whereas this group accounted for only about 9% of the workforce during those years [BLS 1993, 1994b, 1995].

Problems of Workplace Homicide

Despite differences in data collection and the resulting total number of homicides reported by the NTOF and CFOI fatality surveillance systems, the ranking of high-risk industries and occupations is consistent, with taxicab drivers/chauffeurs, law enforcement and security personnel, and retail trade workers experiencing the greatest risks and the largest numbers of workplace homicides. Findings about the distributions by demographic characteristics are also remarkably similar [Windau and Toscano 1994; Toscano and Weber 1995; Castillo and Jenkins 1994].

Differences in leading causes of occupational-injury death by gender can be attributed at least in part to variations in employment patterns [Jenkins 1994]. For example, homicide is the leading cause of occupational injury death for female workers because they are exposed less frequently than male workers to hazards such as heavy machinery and work at elevations. The same is also true for differences among industries in leading causes of death. Workers in retail trade, services, and finance/insurance/real estate are not exposed to the same kinds of hazards as workers in construction, agriculture/forestry/ fishing, mining, or transportation/communication/public utilities. These factors are extremely important to the future direction of occupational safety and health as employment patterns shift from traditional heavy industry to retail trade and service sectors. Workplace homicide must be addressed to continue the trends of decreasing numbers and rates of occupational injury deaths [Jenkins et al. 1993; Stout et al. 1996].

Elevated rates of workplace homicide among workers aged 65 and older may be attributable to a number of factors, including a decreased ability to survive injury or the perception that such workers are "softer" targets [Jenkins et al. 1992].

The percentage of work-related homicides attributed to firearms (76%) is slightly higher than that found in the general population, where 71% of the 1993 murders with victims aged 18 or older were committed with firearms [FBI 1994].

Changes in the risk of workplace homicide in specific industry and occupation groups between the 1980s and the early 1990s may be attributable to a number of factors, including increased recognition and recording of cases as work-related, changes in training or other work practices, increased levels of crime in certain settings, and the distribution of resources in response to perceived levels of crime. The shift in risk for public police officers and private security guards is particularly noteworthy, as the data indicate a decline in rates among public police officers and a dramatic increase among private security guards. We do not know the extent to which these findings are attributable to efforts among public police forces to reduce risks through training and use of protective equipment, the employment of private security guards by businesses and communities that had previously relied solely on public safety personnel, and the level of training and background of private security officers. However, further research is warranted.

The circumstances of workplace homicides differ substantially from those portrayed by the media and from homicides in the general population. For the most part, workplace homicides are not the result of disgruntled workers who take out their frustrations on co-workers or supervisors, or of intimate partners and other relatives who kill loved ones in the course of a dispute; rather, they are mostly robbery-related crimes.

Nonfatal Assaults in the Workplace

Victimization Studies

Limited information is available in the criminal justice and public health literature regarding the nature and magnitude of nonfatal workplace violence. The criminology literature contains a few victimization studies that include designation of victimizations that occurred at work. Using the 1982 Victim Risk Supplement to the National Crime Victimization Survey, Lynch [1987] employed log linear modeling to examine workplace victimizations with regard to demographic variables as well as features of the workplace. Features of the workplace included exposure to and public access to the workplace, local travel, overnight trips, perceived dangerousness of the neighborhood and the workplace, and the frequency with which money was handled on the job. These analyses indicated that the risk of workplace victimization was related more to the task performed than to the demographic characteristics of the person performing the job. Factors related to an increased risk for workplace victimization included routine face-to-face contact with large numbers of people, the handling of money, and jobs that required routine travel or that did not have a single worksite. Using a 1983 crime survey in the metropolitan Washington, DC area, Collins and Cox [1987] found results similar to those of Lynch—the delivery of passengers or goods and dealing with the public were the factors associated with an increased risk for workplace assault. State-specific studies of workplace assaults using workers' compensation data have also been conducted, as have industry- and occupation-specific studies. A summary of these appears in Castillo [1994].

Estimated Magnitude of the Problem

Annual Survey of Occupational Injuries and Illnesses

A number of recent estimates have been made of the current magnitude of nonfatal assaults in U.S. workplaces. The first comes from the BLS Annual Survey of Occupational Injuries and Illnesses (ASOII). The ASOII is an annual survey of approximately 250,000 private establishments. This survey excludes the self-employed, small farmers, and government workers. These data indicate that 22,400 workplace assaults occurred in 1992. These assaults represented 1% of all cases involving days away from work [BLS 1994d]. Unlike homicides, nonfatal workplace assaults are distributed almost equally between men (44%) and women (56%). The majority of the nonfatal assaults reported in the ASOII occurred in the service (64%) and retail

Industry	Violent acts resulting in days away from work (% of total)
Services	64
Nursing homes	27
Social services	13
Hospitals	11
Other services	13
Retail trades	21
Grocery stores	6
Eating and drinking places	5
Other retail	10
Transportation/communication/ public utilities	4
Finance/insurance/real estate	4
Other	4
Manufacturing	3

Source: BLS [1994d].

Table 1.9: Violent acts resulting in days away from work (1992, by industry)

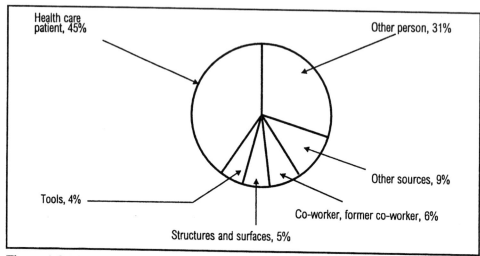

Figure 1.2: Violent acts resulting in days away from work, by source of injury, United States 1992. (Source: BLS [1994a])

trade (21%) industries. Of those in services, 27% occurred in nursing homes, 13% in social services, and 11% in hospitals. In retail trade, 6% occurred in grocery stores, and another 5% occurred in eating and drinking places (Table 1.9). The source of injury in 45% of the cases was a health care patient (Figure 1.2), with another 31% described as other person and 6% as co-worker or former co-worker. The BLS coding system requires that the object or substance that directly inflicted the injury be coded as the source of the injury. Thus 5% of the assaults are coded as structures and surfaces (these are likely events where workers were pushed into walls or to floors), and another 4% are categorized in the system as tools (these include events in which knives or other weapons were used). Furthermore, nearly half (47%) of the recorded workplace

Type of violent act	Number of cases	Median days away from work
Hitting, kicking, beating	10,425	5
Squeezing, pinching, scratching, twisting	2,457	4
Biting	901	3
Stabbing	598	28
Shooting	560	30
All other specified acts (e.g., rape, threats)	5,157	5

Source: BLS [1994c].

Table 1.10: Violent acts resulting in days away from work (Private industry, 1992)

assaults were described as incidents involving hitting, kicking, or beating; there were also cases of squeezing, pinching, scratching, biting, stabbing, and shooting, as well as rapes and threats of violence (Table 1.10). The median days away from work as the result of an assault was 5, but this figure varied by type of assault.

Type of crime	Average annual number	
	Victims	Injuries
Simple assault	615,160	89,572
Aggravated assault	264,174	48,180
Robbery	79,109	17,904
Rape*	13,068	3,438
Total	971,517	159,094

Source: Bachman [1994].
* Injuries are those in addition to the rape.

Table 1.11: Crimes of violence against persons at work or on duty, 1987–92

Northwestern National Life Insurance Company

Another estimate of the magnitude of nonfatal workplace assaults comes from a survey by the Northwestern National Life Insurance Company, which indicates that 2.2 million workplace assaults (defined as physical attacks) occurred between July 1992 and July 1993 [Northwestern National Life 1993]. This estimate and the findings from this survey must be used with caution, as the estimate for assaults was based on only 3% of the sample of 600, or 15 workers who reported having been attacked. In addition, the respondents to this survey did not accurately represent the actual distribution of the workforce [Castillo 1994].

National Crime Victimization Survey

A final estimate of assaults in the workplace comes from the National Crime Victimization Survey (NCVS), an annual, national, household-based survey of more than 100,000 individuals aged 12 or older. NCVS data for 1987-92 indicate that each year, nearly one million persons were assaulted while at work or on duty (Table 1.11); this fig-

Victim-offender relationship	% of workplace victimizations	
	Male workers	Female workers
Stranger	58	40
Acquaintance	30	35
Well-known person	10	19
Relative	1	1
Intimate (spouse, ex-spouse)	1	5

Source: Bachman [1994].

Table 1.12: Workplace victimizations by victim-offender relationship and gender, United States 1987–92

ure represents 15% of the 6.5 million acts of violence experienced by Americans [Bachman 1994]. Sixteen percent of workplace victimizations resulted in injuries.

Bureau of Justice Statistics

When the Bureau of Justice Statistics (BJS) analyzed the relationship of the victim to the offender for these events by gender, female workers appeared to be more likely to be attacked by someone they knew, although only 5% of victimizations were attributed to an intimate—defined as a husband, ex-husband, boyfriend, or ex-boyfriend (Table 1.12). A customer, client, or patient with whom the victim had an ongoing professional relationship would probably have been coded in the "acquaintance" or "well-known" categories, so these findings by gender may be misleading and may reflect the distribution of the workforce in service sectors more than real gender differences in victimization.

BJS also analyzed workplace victimizations by type of work setting and found that 61% occurred in private companies, 30% occurred among government employees, and 8% of the victims were self-employed [Bachman 1994]. BJS points out in its report that government workers make up only 18% of the workforce and thus appear to be suffering a disproportionate share of the attacks; it should also be noted that risk factors such as dealing with the public and delivery of services are common among government employees. In addition, all local, state, and federal police are included in this category.

Reporting Assaults

When individuals in the NCVS were asked whether this workplace victimization was reported to the police, 56% indicated that it was not. For 40% of respondents, the reason cited for not reporting to the police was that the event was believed to be a minor or private matter. Another 27% did not report to the police because the incident was reported to another official such as a company security guard [Bachman 1994].

Lost Workdays and Wages

The NCVS also solicits information about days away from work and lost wages due to the victimization. As a result of workplace victimizations, approximately half a million workers lost 1.75 million days of work annually (an average of 3.5 days per crime) and victims lost more than $55 million in wages, not including days covered by sick or annual leave. As a result of the 16% of victimizations in which injuries were incurred, 876,800 workdays were lost annually and $16 million were lost in wages, not including days covered by sick or annual leave [Bachman 1994].

Conclusion

Violence is a substantial contributor to occupational injury and death, and homicide has become the second leading cause of occupational injury death. Each week, an average of 20 workers are murdered and 18,000 are assaulted while at work or on duty. Nonfatal assaults result in millions of lost workdays and cost workers millions of dollars in lost wages. Workplace violence is clustered in certain occupational settings. The retail trade and service industries account for more than half of workplace homicides and 85% of nonfatal workplace assaults. Taxicab drivers have the highest risk of workplace homicides of any occupational group. Workers in health care, community services, and retail settings are at increased risk of nonfatal assaults.

Nonfatal assaults in the workplace clearly affect many workers and employers. Although groups at high risk for workplace homicide and nonfatal workplace assaults share similar characteristics, such as interaction with the public and the handling of money, there are also clear differences. For example, groups such as health care workers are not at elevated risk of workplace homicide, but they are at greatly increased risk of nonfatal assaults. Castillo [1994] suggests that some of the distinctions between fatal and nonfatal workplace assaults can be attributed to differences between robbery-related violence and violence resulting from the anger or frustration of customers, clients, or co-workers, with robbery-related violence being more likely to result in a fatal outcome. The premeditated use of firearms to facilitate robberies is also likely to influence the lethality of assaults in the workplace.

References

Bachman, R. "Violence and theft in the workplace." In: *U.S. Department of Justice Crime Data Brief*. Washington, DC: U.S. Government Printing Office, NCJ-148199. 1994

BLS. *Employment and Earnings*. Washington, DC: U.S. Department of Labor, Bureau of Labor Statistics, January 1993 issue.

BLS. *Annual Survey of Occupational Injuries and Illnesses*. Washington, DC: U.S. Department of Labor, Bureau of Labor Statistics. (Unpublished database). 1994a.

BLS. "National census of fatal occupational injuries, 1993." Washington, DC: U.S. Department of Labor, Bureau of Labor Statistics, *BLS News*, USDL-94-384. 1994b.

BLS. "Violence in the workplace comes under closer scrutiny." *Issues in labor statistics*. Washington, DC: U.S. Department of Labor, Bureau of Labor Statistics, Summary 94-10. 1994c.

BLS. "Work injuries and illnesses by selected characteristics, 1992." Washington, DC: U.S. Department of Labor, Bureau of Labor Statistics. 1994d.

BLS. "National census of fatal occupational injuries, 1994." Washington, DC: U.S. Department of Labor, *BLS News*, USDL-95-288. 1995.

Castillo, D.N. "Nonfatal violence in the workplace: directions for future research." In: *Questions and Answers in Lethal and Non-lethal Violence: Proceedings of the Third Annual Workshop of the Homicide Research Working Group*. Washington, DC: National Institute of Justice. 1994.

Castillo, D.N., Jenkins, E.L. "Industries and occupations at high risk for work-related homicide." *J Occup Med* 36:125-132. 1994.

Collins, J.J., Cox, B.G. "Job activities and personal crime victimization: implications for theory." *Soc Sci Res* 16:345-360. 1987.

FBI. "Uniform crime reports for the United States, 1993." Washington, DC: U.S. Department of Justice, Federal Bureau of Investigation. 1994.

Jenkins, E.L. "Occupational injury deaths among females: the U.S. experience for the decade 1980 to 1989." *Ann Epidemiol* 4(2): 146û151. 1994.

Jenkins, E.L. "Workplace homicide: industries and occupations at high risk." *Occup Med State of Art Reviews* 11(2):219-225. 1996.

Jenkins, E.L., Layne LA, Kisner SM. "Homicide in the workplace: the U.S. experience, 1980-1988." *AAOHN J* 40:215-218. 1992.

Jenkins, E.L., Kisner SM, Fosbroke DE, Layne LA, Stout NA, Castillo DN et al. "Fatal injuries to workers in the United States, 1980-1989: a decade of surveillance; national profile." Washington, DC: U.S. Government Printing Office, DHHS (NIOSH) Publication No. 93-108. 1993.

Lynch, J.P. "Routine activity and victimization at work." *J Quantitative Criminol* 3: 283-300. 1987.

NIOSH. "NIOSH Alert: request for assistance in preventing homicide in the workplace." Cincinnati, OH: U.S. Department of Health and Human Services, Public Health Service, Centers for Disease Control and Prevention, National Institute for Occupational Safety and Health, DHHS (NIOSH) Publication No. 93-109. 1993.

NIOSH. "National Traumatic Occupational Fatalities (NTOF) Surveillance System." Morgantown, WV: U.S. Department of Health and Human Services, Public Health Service, Centers for Disease Control and Prevention, National Institute for Occupational Safety and Health. Unpublished database. 1995.

Northwestern National Life. "Fear and violence in the workplace: a survey documenting the experience of American workers." Minneapolis, MN: Northwestern National Life. 1993.

Stout, N.A., Jenkins, E.L., Pizatella, T.J. "Occupational injury mortality rates in the United States: changes from 1980 to 1989." *Am J Public Health* 86:73-77. 1996.

Toscano, G., Weber, W. "Violence in the workplace. Compensation and working conditions." Washington, DC: U.S. Department of Labor, Bureau of Labor Statistics. 1995.

Windau, J., Toscano, G. "Workplace homicides in 1992. Compensation and working conditions," February 1994. Washington, DC: U.S. Department of Labor, Bureau of Labor Statistics. 1994.

Chapter Two

- ❑ Risk factors for workplace assault

- ❑ How environmental design can reduce the risk of workplace attack

- ❑ How to identify staffing practices, policies, and procedures which reduce the risk of potentially dangerous situations

- ❑ Components of a workplace prevention program

- ❑ Directions for future research by government and industry

Prevention Strategies
and
Research Needs

E. Lynn Jenkins, MA

Case Study

At a workplace violence training seminar, a supervisor wanted to know if a fight in the parking lot after the shift was over should be considered as a case of workplace violence. He started out by saying "you could see it coming all shift. The two employees were back and forth at each other all night with verbal insults and threats. It did not take much for it to break out into a serious fight as they went out to their cars." The company policy did not allow fights on the premises and both employees were fired. His fellow supervisors immediately confronted him with why he had allowed the situation to build to that point. They felt he should have intervened early so that the whole situation might have been avoided and the two employees might not have lost their jobs.

Introduction

The purpose of this chapter is to determine the focus needed for prevention and research efforts. This chapter also summarizes issues to be addressed when dealing with workplace violence in various settings such as offices, factories, warehouses, hospitals, convenience stores, and taxicabs. Risk factors for workplace violence include dealing with the public, the exchange of money, and the delivery of services or goods. Prevention strategies for minimizing the risk of workplace violence include, but are not limited to, cash-handling policies, physical separation of workers from customers, good lighting, security devices, escort services, and employee training. A workplace violence prevention program should include a system for documenting incidents, procedures to be taken in the event of incidents, and open communication between employers and workers. Although no definitive strategy will ever be appropriate for all workplaces, we must begin to change the way work is done in certain settings to minimize or remove the risk of workplace violence. We must also change the way we think about workplace violence by shifting the emphasis from reactionary approaches to prevention, and by embracing workplace violence as an occupational safety and health issue. This chapter examines these issues and proposes new strategies for prevention.

Prevention Strategies

Risk Factors

A number of factors may increase a worker's risk for workplace assault, and they have been described in previous research [Collins and Cox 1987; Davis 1987; Davis et al. 1987; Kraus 1987; Lynch 1987; NIOSH 1993; Castillo and Jenkins 1994]. These factors include those shown in Checklist 2.1.

Environmental Designs

Commonly implemented cash-handling policies in retail settings include procedures such as using locked drop safes, carrying small amounts of cash, and posting signs and printing notices that limited cash is available. It may also be useful to explore the feasibility of cashless transactions in taxicabs and retail settings through the use of machines that accommodate automatic teller account cards or debit

---

Checklist 2.1

Risk Factors for Workplace Assault

✔ Contact with the public

✔ Exchange of money

✔ Delivery of passengers, goods, or services

✔ Having a mobile workplace such as a taxicab or police cruiser

✔ Working with unstable or volatile persons in health care, social service, or criminal justice settings

✔ Working alone or in small numbers

✔ Working late at night or during early morning hours

✔ Working in high-crime areas

✔ Guarding valuable property or possessions

✔ Working in community-based settings

---

cards. These approaches could be used in any setting where cash is currently exchanged between workers and customers.

Physical separation of workers from customers, clients, and the general public through the use of bullet-resistant barriers or enclosures has been proposed for retail settings such as gas stations and convenience stores, hospital emergency departments, and social service agency claims areas. The height and depth of counters (with or without bullet-resistant barriers) are also important considerations in protecting workers, since they introduce physical distance between workers and potential attackers. Consideration must nonetheless be given to the continued ease of conducting business; a safety device that increases frustration for workers, customers, clients, or patients may be self-defeating.

Visibility and lighting are also important environmental design considerations. Making high-risk areas visible to more people and installing good external lighting should decrease the risk of workplace assaults [NIOSH 1993].

Access to and egress from the workplace are also important areas to assess. The number of entrances and exits, the ease with which non employees can gain access to work areas because doors are unlocked, and the number of areas where potential attackers can hide are issues that should be addressed. This issue has implications for the design of buildings and parking areas, landscaping and the placement of garbage areas, outdoor refrigeration areas, and other storage facilities that workers must use during a work shift.

Numerous security devices may reduce the risk of assaults against workers and facilitate the identification and apprehension of perpetrators. These include closed-circuit cameras, alarms, two-way mirrors, card-key access systems, panic-bar doors locked from the outside only, and trouble lights or geographic locating devices in taxicabs and other mobile workplaces.

Personal protective equipment such as body armor has been used effectively by public safety personnel to mitigate the effects of workplace violence. For example, the lives of more than 1,800 police officers have been saved by Kevlar® vests [Brierley 1996].

Administrative Controls

Staffing plans and work practices (such as escorting patients and prohibiting unsupervised movement within and between clinic areas) are included in the California Occupational Safety and Health Administration Guidelines for the Security and Safety of Health Care and Community Service Workers [State of California 1993]. Increasing the number of staff on duty may also be appropriate in any number of service and retail settings. The use of security guards or receptionists to screen persons entering the workplace and to control access to actual work areas has also been suggested by security experts.

Work practices and staffing patterns during the opening and closing of establishments and during money drops and pickups should be carefully reviewed for the increased risk of assault they pose to workers. These practices include having workers take out garbage, dispose of grease, store food or other items in external storage areas, and transport or store money.

Policies and procedures for assessing and reporting threats allow employers to track and assess threats and violent incidents in the workplace. Such policies clearly indicate a zero tolerance of workplace violence and provide mechanisms by which incidents can be reported and handled. In addition, such information allows employers to assess whether prevention strategies are appropriate and effective. These policies should also include guidance on recognizing the potential for violence, methods for defusing or de-escalating potentially violent situations, and instruction about the use of security devices and protective equipment. Procedures for obtaining medical care and psychological support following violent incidents should also be addressed. Training and education efforts are clearly needed to accompany such policies.

Behavioral Strategies

Training employees in nonviolent response and conflict resolution has been suggested to reduce the risk that volatile situations will escalate to physical violence. Also critical is training that addresses hazards associated with specific tasks or work sites and relevant prevention strategies. Training should not be regarded as the sole prevention strategy but as a component in a comprehensive approach to reducing workplace violence. To increase vigilance and compliance with stated violence prevention policies, training should emphasize the appropriate use and maintenance of protective equipment, adherence to administrative controls, and increased knowledge and awareness of the risk of workplace violence.

Program Development

The first priority in developing a workplace violence prevention policy is to establish a system for documenting violent incidents in the workplace. Such data are essential for assessing the nature and magnitude of workplace violence in a given workplace and for quantifying risk. These data can be used to assess the need for action to reduce the risks for workplace violence and to implement a reasonable intervention strategy. An existing intervention strategy may be identified within an industry or in similar industries, or new and unique strategies may be needed to address the risks in a given workplace or setting. Implementation of the reporting system, a workplace violence prevention policy, and specific prevention strategies should be publicized company-wide, and appropriate training sessions should be scheduled. The demonstrated commitment of management is crucial to the success of the program. The success and appropriateness of intervention strategies can be monitored and adjusted with continued data collection.

Threat Assessment Team

A written workplace violence policy should clearly indicate a zero tolerance for violence at work, whether the violence originates inside or outside the workplace. Just as workplaces have developed mechanisms for reporting and dealing with sexual harassment, they must also develop threat assessment teams to which threats and violent incidents can be reported. These teams should include representatives from human resources, security, employee assistance, unions, workers, management, and perhaps legal and public relations departments. The mission of this team is to assess threats of violence—e.g., to determine how specific a threat is, whether the person threatening the worker has the means for carrying out the threat, etc.—and to determine what steps are necessary to prevent the threat from being carried out. This team should also be charged with periodic reviews of violent incidents to identify ways in which similar incidents can be prevented in the future. Note that when violence or the threat of violence occurs among co-workers, firing the perpetrator may or may not be the most appropriate way to reduce the risk for additional or future violence. The employer may want to retain some control over the perpetrator and require or provide counseling or other care, if appropriate. The violence prevention policy should explicitly state the consequences of making threats or committing acts of violence in the workplace.

Response Team

A comprehensive workplace violence prevention policy and program should also include procedures to be taken in the event of a violent incident in the workplace. This policy should explicitly state how the response team is to be assembled and who is responsible for immediate care of the victim(s), reestablishing work areas and processes, and organizing and carrying out stress debriefing sessions with victims, their co-workers, and perhaps the families of victims and co-workers. Employee assistance programs, human resource professionals, and local mental health and emergency service personnel can offer assistance in developing these strategies.

Responding to an Immediate Threat of Workplace Violence

For a situation that poses an immediate threat of workplace violence, all legal, human resource, employee assistance, community mental health, security, and law enforcement resources should be used to develop a response. The risk of injury to all workers should be minimized. If a threat has been made that refers to particular times and places, or if the potential offender is knowledgeable about workplace procedures and time frames, patterns may need to be shifted. It may be advisable to change or even stagger departure times and implement a buddy system or an escort by security guard for leaving the building and getting to parking areas. The threat should not be ignored in the hope that it will resolve itself or out of fear of triggering an outburst from the person who has lodged the threat. If someone poses a danger to himself or others, appropriate authorities should be notified and action should be taken.

Dealing with the Consequences of Workplace Violence

Much discussion has also centered around the role of stress in workplace violence. The most important thing to remember is that stress can be both a cause and an effect of workplace violence. That is, high levels of stress may lead to violence in the workplace, but a violent incident in the workplace will most certainly lead to stress, perhaps even to post-traumatic stress disorder. The data from the National Crime Victimization Survey [Bachman 1994] present compelling evidence—more than a million workdays lost as a result of workplace assaults each year—of the need to be aware of the impact of workplace violence. Employers should therefore be sensitive to the effects of workplace violence and provide an environment that promotes open communication. They should also have in place an established procedure for reporting and responding to violence. Appropriate referrals to employee assistance programs or other local mental health services may be necessary for critical-incident stress debriefing sessions.

Current Efforts and Future Directions: Research and Prevention

Although we are beginning to have descriptive information about workplace violence, a number of questions remain to be answered before we will fully understand why violence takes place at work and what preventive strategies will be more effective. For example what factors in the job and environment increase workers' risk of violence? What are precipitating events and how do a victim's actions decrease or increase the risk. What safety measures will reduce the risk of violence? In addition to guiding future research, these same questions should be addressed in developing violence prevention strategies for specific workplaces.

Checklist 2.2

Questions for Workplace Violence Assessment

✔ What are the specific tasks and environments that place workers at greatest risk?

✔ What factors influence the lethality of violent incidents?

✔ What are the relationships of workplace assault victims to offenders?

✔ Are there identifiable precipitating events?

✔ Were there any safety measures in place?

✔ What were the actions of the victim and did they influence the outcome of the attack?

✔ What are the most effective prevention strategies?

A number of these questions were raised in 1990 at a workshop convened by NIOSH. They continue to require attention through the collaborative research and prevention efforts of public health, human resource, and criminal justice professionals. Other recommendations were made by a panel of experts in interpersonal violence on directions for NIOSH in this area [NIOSH 1992]. These recommendations have been implemented or initiated and include the following:

✧ Improve the quality of death certificate data

✧ Compare findings from NTOF, the National Center for Health Statistics, and the Federal Bureau of Investigation

✧ Conduct evaluation research to determine the effectiveness of various prevention strategies

✧ Disseminate information on workplace homicide risk

✧ Examine possibilities for collection and analysis of data on nonfatal workplace violence

✧ Increase collaboration between public health and criminal justice agencies

In the fall of 1993, NIOSH released an alert on preventing homicide in the workplace [NIOSH 1993] and encouraged employers, workers, unions, and others with a vested interest to look at their workplaces and take immediate action to reduce the risk for workplace homicide. In related efforts, NIOSH responded to numerous requests from the media, resulting in print, radio, and television coverage of the data and the NIOSH prevention message: Although no single intervention strategy is appropriate for all workplaces and no definitive strategies can be recommended at this time, immediate action should be taken to reduce the toll of workplace homicide on our nation's workforce. This message still holds true and applies not only to workplace homicide, but to all workplace violence. Clearly, violence is pervasive in U.S. workplaces, accounting for 1,071 homicides in 1994 and approximately a million nonfatal assaults each year. Research and prevention efforts must be actively pursued in order to reduce the risk of workplace violence for the Nation's workers. The murder of an average of 20 workers each week is unacceptable and should not be considered the cost of doing business in our society.

Conclusion

This chapter discussed preventive strategies for fatal and nonfatal violence in the workplace and it also summarized issues to be addressed when dealing with workplace violence in various settings such as offices, factories, warehouses, hospitals, convenience stores, and taxicabs. Violence is a substantial contributor to occupational injury and death, and homicide has become the second leading cause of occupational-injury death. Each week, an average of 20 workers are murdered and 18,000 are assaulted while at work or on duty. Nonfatal assaults result in millions of lost workdays and cost workers millions of dollars in lost wages.

Workplace violence is clustered in certain occupational settings. For example, the retail trade and service industries account for more than half of workplace homicides and 85% of nonfatal workplace assaults. Taxicab drivers have the highest risk of workplace homicides of any occupational group. Workers in health care, community services, and retail settings are at increased risk of nonfatal assaults.

Risk factors for workplace violence include dealing with the public, the exchange of money, and the delivery of services or goods. Prevention strategies for minimizing the risk of workplace violence include, but are not limited to, cash-handling policies, physical separation of workers from customers, good lighting, security devices, escort services, and employee training. A workplace violence prevention program should include a system for documenting incidents, procedures to be taken in the event of incidents, and open communication between employers and workers. Although no definitive prevention strategy is appropriate for all workplaces, all workers and employers should assess the risks for violence in their workplaces and take appropriate action to reduce those risks.

References

Bachman, R. "Violence and theft in the workplace." In: *U.S. Department of Justice Crime Data Brief*. Washington, DC: U.S. Government Printing Office, NCJ-148199. 1994.

BLS. *Employment and Earnings*. Washington, DC: U.S. Department of Labor, Bureau of Labor Statistics, January 1993.

BLS. "Annual survey of occupational injuries and illnesses." Washington, DC: U.S. Department of Labor, Bureau of Labor Statistics. (Unpublished database). 1994a.

BLS. "National census of fatal occupational injuries, 1993." Washington, DC: U.S. Department of Labor, Bureau of Labor Statistics, *BLS News*, USDL-94-384. 1994b.

BLS. "Violence in the workplace comes under closer scrutiny." *Issues in labor statistics*. Washington, DC: U.S. Department of Labor, Bureau of Labor Statistics, Summary 94-10. 1994c.

Brierley, B. Personal communication on February 7, 1996, between B. Brierley of the IACP/Dupont Kevlar Survivors' Club and Lynn Jenkins, Division of Safety Research, National Institute for Occupational Safety and Health, Centers for Disease Control and Prevention, Public Health Service, U.S. Department of Health and Human Services. 1996.

Castillo, D.N., Jenkins, E.L. "Industries and occupations at high risk for work-related homicide." *J Occup Med* 36:125-132. 1994.

Collins, J.J., Cox, B.G. "Job activities and personal crime victimization: implications for theory." *Soc Sci Res* 16:345-360. 1987.

Davis, H. "Workplace homicides of Texas males." *Am J Public Health* 77:1290-1293. 1987.

Davis, J., Honchar, P.A., Suarez, L. "Fatal occupational injuries of women, Texas 1975-1984." *Am J Public Health* 77:1524-1527. 1987.

Lynch, J.P. "Routine activity and victimization at work." *J Quantitative Criminol* 3: 283-300. 1987.

Kraus, J.F. "Homicide while at work: persons, industries, and occupations at high risk." *Am J Public Health* 77:1285-1289.

NIOSH. "Homicide in U.S. workplaces: a strategy for prevention and research." Morgantown, WV: U.S. Department of Health and Human Services, Public Health Service, Centers for Disease Control, National Institute for Occupational Safety and Health, DHHS (NIOSH) Publication No. 92-103. 1992.

NIOSH. "NIOSH Alert: request for assistance in preventing homicide in the workplace." Cincinnati, OH: U.S. Department of Health and Human Services, Public Health Service, Centers for Disease Control and Prevention, National Institute for Occupational Safety and Health, DHHS (NIOSH) Publication No. 93-109. 1993.

State of California. "Guidelines for security and safety of health care and community service workers." Sacramento, CA: Division of Occupational Safety and Health, Department of Industrial Relations. 1993.

Chapter Three

- ❑ Short-term assessment of violence potential
- ❑ Factors to consider for psychiatric referral
- ❑ Distinguishing characteristics of psychiatric diagnoses associated with violence
- ❑ Contribution of alcohol and drug abuse to violence
- ❑ How to respond to threats

The Potential for Violence among Employees with Psychiatric Disorders

Kenneth Tardiff, MD, MPH

Case Study

A 32-year-old white man manifested schizophrenia while in the army and received a medical discharge. His core pathology involved paranoid delusions about spies trying to overthrow the United States government. He believed that he was a counterspy. He was seen on a monthly basis at the V.A. clinic and was maintained on Haldol, which he regularly took. He worked installing carpets for a small business. One day he stabbed the owner of the business with a knife. On questioning he admitted that he stopped the Haldol and believed that his boss was a spy.

Introduction

The assessment of a person's potential for violence in a work setting is made for two time periods: short term and long term. Knowing if an employee poses a risk of violence in the near future (days or a week) helps the administration in a decision to remove the person before violence occurs. This could be a suspension during which time the person would receive treatment if he/she has a psychiatric disorder associated with a potential for violence. One would want to determine potential for violence in the long term as well as the near future if one is deciding how to respond to a threat of violence by an employee or former employee. Often the threat is made toward a supervisor or staff in human resources who have disciplined an employee. The following guidelines for the assessment of potential for violence are structured along clinical lines from the perspective of a psychiatrist. Since the person in the workplace responsible for deciding what should be done is unlikely to be a psychiatrist, a referral to a psychiatrist would be prudent. These guidelines should help in the decision as to whether a referral is indicated.

Assessment of Violence Potential: Analogy to Short-Term Suicide Potential

A well-trained psychiatrist or other mental health professional should be able to predict a person's short-term violence potential using assessment techniques analogous to the short-term predictors of suicide potential. Short-term is defined as a period of a few days or a week at most. Beyond that time, there is an opportunity for many intervening factors to change the risk of violence. These intervening factors may include noncompliance with medication, resumption of drinking or substance use, threats of divorce by a spouse, and other stressors. As with prediction of suicide, one focuses on the clinical aspects of the evaluation, namely psychopathology, but one must take into consideration demographic, historical, and environmental factors that may be related to an increased risk of violence.

In making a decision about violence potential, one should interview the employee as well as other employees, police, and other persons with information about the person and any past violent incidents to guard against the employee's minimizing dangerousness. One should review old charts for previous episodes of treatment, arrest records, and other records of judicial proceedings if available. Breach of confidentiality is warranted if the person may pose a danger to others and evaluation of this potential is needed. Some, such as those with paranoid delusions, may be reluctant to divulge thoughts of violence, so the clinicians must listen carefully and follow-up on any hints of violence that may surface during the interview.

Violence Prediction Model

If there are thoughts of violence, the degree of formulation of the ideas or plan of violence must be assessed. A well-formulated or detailed plan should make the clinician concerned about the risk of violence that a person poses. This includes details about where and when and how the person will attack the victim as well as knowledge about the potential victim's personal life such as daily schedules and address. For example, vague thoughts of "getting even" with the boss are not as serious, all other things being equal, as thoughts of ambushing the boss as he enters his car at his house before he drives to work.

Intent to Harm

If a person has thoughts of harming someone, it is important to assess his or her intent to harm others. Just because thoughts of violence recur in a person's mind may not be sufficient to warrant action by the clinician. For example, a young man was having obsessive thoughts and images of stabbing his father. These thoughts were frightening to him and he had no intent or desire to act on these thoughts.

Victim Availability

Availability of a potential victim is important. This refers to daily vulnerability of the victim as well as geographic distance. For example, a victim living in an doorman apartment in the city is generally safer than one living in a house in the suburbs. A breach by someone who violates a restraining order can be handled more efficiently, for example, by calling the police and hospitalizing the person. Geography plays a part in assessment of risk of violence to a potential victim. For example, a schizophrenic employee threatening his former boss who lives on the opposite coast will probably not be able to arrange transportation to reach the potential victim. The risk of an attack in that case would be less than when the threatened person works adjacent to the person making threats.

Weapon Availability

Availability of a weapon is a major consideration, perhaps not as to whether violence will occur, but to the lethality of the violence. The person should be asked, if there is a concern about violence if there is a gun in the household, whether they have other access to guns, or how they would go about buying a gun.

History of Violence

A history of violence or other impulsive behaviors by the person is a major factor in the prediction of violence. Past violence predicts future violence (1-6). Episodes of past violence, for example the most recent episode, must be dissected in a detailed, concrete manner by the clinician. This includes details of the time and place of the violence, who was present, who said what to whom, what the violent person saw, what the violent person remembers, what family members or staff remember, why the person was violent (e.g., delusions or anger), and what could have been done to avoid the violent confrontation. Often there is a pattern of escalation of violence. The pattern and theme of the violence are repetitive, for example, fights with co-workers around issues of respect, race, politics, etc.

The "history" of violence should be treated as any other medical symptom, for example, chest pain. This includes the date of onset, frequency, place (targets), and severity. Severity is measured by degree of injury to the victim(s) from pushing, to punching, to causing injuries such as bruises, to causing injuries such as broken bones, lacerations, internal injuries or even death. The history of violence should include the presence of other clinical phenomena, such as disorientation, amnesia, and guilt after the violent episode. Finally, the history of violence should include prior evaluations—for example, psychological testing or imaging—and treatment—for example, hospitalization, medications, and response to treatment.

Psychiatric Diagnoses with Increased Risk of Violence

Personality Disorders

A personality disorder is an enduring pattern of behavior that deviates markedly from the expectations of the person's culture. A personality disorder is stable over time, inflexible, and leads to impairment and maladjustment. A personality disor-

---

Checklist 3.1

Psychiatric Risk Factors for Violence

✔ Noncompliance with medication

✔ Resumption of drinking or drug use

✔ Personal stressors such as threats of divorce or job loss

✔ Well formulated plan

✔ Specific knowledge about the potential victem's personal life

✔ Intent or desire for violence

✔ Availability of a potential victem

✔ Availability of a weapon

✔ History of violence or other impulsive behavior

✔ Pattern of prior violence: date of onset, frequency, target, place and severity

✔ Prior evaluations and treatment

✔ Demographics:
  • young
  • male
  • social environment with greater acceptance of violence

✔ Other organic mental disorders

---

der begins in childhood or adolescence and continues into adulthood. The personality disorders most likely to be associated with violence or threats of violence are the antisocial, borderline, and paranoid personality disorders.(7,8)

Antisocial Personality

A person with antisocial personality has a pattern of disregard for, and violation of, the rights of others. There is a failure to conform to social norms with respect to the law. Violence manifested by persons with antisocial personality disorder is just one of many antisocial behaviors. These patients repeatedly get into physical fights and violence involving their spouses, children, and individuals outside of the family. A number of other antisocial behaviors include destroying property, harassing others, stealing, engaging in illegal occupations, driving in a reckless or intoxicated manner, and being involved in promiscuous relationships. The person often lies, does not honor financial obligations, and is unable to sustain consistent employment. Alcohol and substance abuse are often a problem. The violence toward others and other aspects of antisocial behavior are not accompanied by remorse or guilt. Violence is often accompanied by little display of emotion and seems cold-blooded. Issues of self-esteem and/or revenge frequently underlie the violence. Although the person may appear friendly, attractive, and engaging, manipulation and deceit are common.

Case Vignette

A 25-year-old white man worked in a large grocery store. In high school, he was disciplined for numerous infractions. He managed to graduate and began work after high school. He had a history of frequent job changes. He was arrested several times for driving while intoxicated with alcohol, once for driving 90 miles an hour at night with his headlights off. His supervisor in the grocery store began to suspect that he was stealing items at work. One day he confronted the employee, who immediately flew into a rage. He picked up a pipe which was lying around and struck the supervisor on the head. He would have continued to strike the supervisor, but other employees were able to restrain him.

Borderline Personality

A person with borderline personality has a pervasive pattern of instability of interpersonal relationships, emotions, and self-image with marked impulsivity. In addition to exhibiting frequent displays of anger and recurrent physical violence toward others, the person with borderline personality disorder manifests other behavioral problems between the violent episodes. There is often a wide range of impulsive behaviors, including suicidal or self-mutilating behaviors, excessive spending, indiscreet sexual behavior, drug abuse, shoplifting, and reckless driving. In addition, there is a marked and persistent identity problem manifested by uncertainty about self-image, sexual orientation, career goals, and other values. There are often manipulative attempts to obtain caring from others. Violence is characteristically in response to feelings of abandonment or rejection by someone from whom the person wants love, caring, or merely attention. Violence is accompanied by intense emotional displays and emotional instability.

Case Vignette

A 36-year-old white female lawyer was working over the weekend with a male client in a large law firm. She was highly thought of by her colleagues for her work although she came in late on a number of Mondays. Since the client's wife was out of town, the lawyer and he went to dinner. She invited him to her apartment afterwards for coffee and they had sexual intercourse. The next day, the client called her and apologized, wanting to sever the relationship. The lawyer continued to call the client at his work and home, but he refused her calls. One night, the lawyer went to the client's home and began shooting through a picture window. The client called the police, but the lawyer killed herself before they arrived.

Paranoid Personality

The person with paranoid personality is suspicious and distrustful of others. These persons assume that people will exploit, harm, or deceive them even though there is no evidence of it. They are argumentative and they bear grudges and are unwilling to forgive. The person believes that people conspire against him or her, whether they be in government, other organizations, or members of a certain race or class. He/she may be racist or sexist and perceive others to be so. They may belong to militaristic organizations or be preoccupied with militaristic themes. They tend to be preoccupied and possess firearms. Episodic violence is not frequent in the past; however, threats of violence against others are frequent. Most people with paranoid personality will not be physically violent, but when violence does occur, it may be lethal.

Case Vignette

A 41-year-old African-American man worked in the mailroom of a large corporation. He would engage other employees in the mailroom in heated discussions of politics, often with themes of discrimination against minorities. While in one of these discussions, he slipped off a tall chair he was sitting on and hurt his back. He was placed on disability and had difficulty returning to work. He started to leave messages on the voice mail of his supervisor in the mailroom. He claimed that the supervisor was a racist and responsible for his condition. One day he appeared in the mailroom with a handgun. He shot the supervisor and two other employees before he was shot and killed by the police.

Intermittent Explosive Disorder

The key characteristic of this syndrome is the episodic recurrent outburst of aggression and violence that is grossly out of proportion to any precipitating factor or provocation. There is often remorse following this violent episode—e.g., the case of a husband who has attacked his wife, a mother who has severely beaten a child, or an employee who has hit another worker. There is little evidence of other behavioral problems between these violent episodes. This is in distinction to the three personality disorders associated with violence: the borderline personality, the antisocial personality, and the paranoid personality disorder. Often the violent episode follows arguments where self-esteem is an issue.

Case Vignette

A 46-year-old white man worked at an insurance firm. Throughout his childhood and adolescence, he had constant feelings of inferiority despite his achievements in school. Despite his good performance at work, he persisted in fearing that he would be "discovered" and lose his job for incompetence. At home, he and his wife would have arguments about money. She accused him of not earning enough. On several occasions, she persisted until he hit her. She told him that she wanted a divorce. He begged her not to do so and promised he would not strike her again.

Alcohol Abuse

The ingestion of alcohol often may be associated with aggression and violence as a result of disinhibition or loss of control, particularly in the initial phase of intoxication. (9,10) Intoxication is accompanied by emotional instability and impaired judgment. The person may appear to have slurred speech, incoordination, unsteady gait, and a flushed face. Violent behavior can also be found in persons who drink small amounts of alcohol insufficient to cause intoxication in most people. This is known as the alcohol idiosyncratic intoxication.

Violence may be associated with alcohol withdrawal after cessation of prolonged, heavy ingestion of alcohol for two or three days. This is manifested by coarse tremor of the hands, tongue, or eyelids and at least one of the following: nausea or vomiting, weakness, anxiety, depressed mood or irritability, hallucinations (hearing voices or seeing things that are not there), headache, or insomnia. Violence may result from gross disorganization of behavior or in response to threatening auditory hallucinations.

Cocaine or Crack

Cocaine, particularly through the nasal route, initially produces a feeling of well-being. With continued use, particularly intravenously or smoked in the form of crack, the feeling of well-being turns to irritability, agitation, suspiciousness, and, frequently, violence. (11,12) With continued use, suspiciousness becomes paranoid ideation and, subsequently, paranoid delusional thinking. Thus violence results from delusional thinking as well as from the effect of cocaine through overall stimulation.

A person using cocaine has widening of the pupils, chills, nausea or vomiting, fast heart rate, and elevated blood pressure and may be perspiring and have hallucinations, particularly visual or tactile in nature. Unlike alcohol, cocaine withdrawal is not usually associated with violence but rather with depression. In some cases of prolonged use, cessation of cocaine use can result in profound impairment in thinking, suicidal behavior, irritability, and psychomotor agitation. Irritability, agitation, and, in some cases, paranoid ideation may result in violence. Intense craving for more cocaine when supplies have been exhausted may also lead to violence and/or stealing while the addict obtains cocaine or money for its purchase.

Amphetamines or Other Sympathomimetics

With intense or prolonged amphetamine use, a feeling of well-being and confidence turns to confusion, rambling, incoherence, paranoid ideation, and delusional thinking. With this there are agitation, fighting, and other forms of aggression and impaired social judgment. The person appears to have pupillary dilatation, may be perspiring, or may have chills, nausea and vomiting, fast heart rate, and elevated blood pressure. Amphetamine withdrawal, like cocaine withdrawal, is usually manifested by depression and problems with sleep, although there may be psychomotor agitation and paranoid ideation following prolonged heavy use of amphetamines or similar substances. The symptoms may persist more than 24 hours after cessation of use of amphetamines.

Hallucinogens

Hallucinogens, such as S-lysergic acid diethylamide (LSD), dimethyltryptamine (DMT), and mescaline may result in impaired judgment and paranoid ideation in addition to other perceptual changes so that one feels detached from one's mental processes or body. The external world may seem strange or unreal. Hallucinations, if present, are usually visual. The person may have marked anxiety and a fear of losing his or her mind; will appear with widening of the pupils, sweating, tremors, and incoordination; and may have a fast heart rate, and blurring of vision.

Violence may occur during intoxication with the above-mentioned hallucinogens, but it is not as common as in phencyclidine (PCP) intoxication. (13,14) Within one hour of oral use—five minutes if smoked or taken intravenously—PCP often produces marked violence, impulsivity, unpredictability, and grossly impaired judgment. There may be delusional thinking or delirium. The person may have trouble walking or speaking and manifest increased blood pressure or heart rate, numbness or diminished responsiveness to pain and muscle rigidity. The person may have seizures. There may be persistent psychopathology following PCP use; with other hallucinogens, except for occasional flashbacks, there is little residual psychopathology after limited use. Flashbacks are more often a source of great anxiety for the person rather than associated with violent behavior.

Inhalants

Inhalants are hydrocarbons found in substances such as gasoline, glue, paint, and paint thinners. These are often used by young children and early adolescents to produce intoxication, which may be characterized by belligerence and violence as well as impaired judgment. Chronic or heavy use of inhalants may produce neurologic signs such as incoordination, general muscle weakness, and retardation. The person may manifest, even with mild use, dizziness, incoordination, slurred speech, unsteady gait, lethargy, depressed reflexes, psychomotor retardation, tremor, general muscle weakness, blurred vision, stupor, or euphoria.

Other Substances

Prescription drugs may cause violence either by excessive doses or through side effects. Examples of this are anticholinergic medications, which can produce violence, and steroids. In addition, akathisia (restlessness) from neuroleptic medications may be interpreted as intended violence or aggression. There have been several cases where body builders using anabolic steroids have had violent rages.

Checklist 3.2

Psychiatric Diagnoses with Risk of Violence

✔ Personality Disorders
  • Antisocial personality
  • Borderline personality
  • Paranoid personality

✔ Intermittent Explosive Disorder

✔ Substance Abuse
  • Alcohol ingestion
  • Cocaine or crack
  • Amphetamines or other sympathomimetics
  • Hallucinogens
  • Inhalants
  • Some prescription drugs (e.g., anticholinergics or steroids)

✔ Schizophrenia

✔ Posttraumatic Stress Disorder

✔ Delusional (Paranoid) Disorder

✔ Mood Disorder

✔ Neurological Disorders (e.g., brain infections, head trauma, etc.)

✔ Other Medical Disorders

✔ Mental Retardation (rare)

Schizophrenia

Schizophrenia is a chronic disorder that begins usually in early adulthood and is a characterized by episodes of psychosis. Schizophrenics can be violent.(15,16) There are delusions (false beliefs), hallucinations (false perceptions), disorganized speech and thought and often withdrawal. There is generally deterioration in interpersonal and social functioning despite a diminished psychotic state as the result of antipsychotic medications, such as Haldol, Thorazine, and Clozaril. As a result, a schizophrenic person will have difficulty holding a job. If intellectual functioning remains intact, as it can especially in paranoid schizophrenia, the employee can function in positions not requiring a lot of interpersonal contact such as file clerk, computer programmer, or night watchman.

In paranoid schizophrenia, there is delusional thinking involving persecution. Schizophrenic persons may believe that people are trying to harm them, that the police or FBI is spying on them, that some unknown mechanism is controlling their minds, or that the therapist is harming them, for example, through medication. Paranoid schizophrenics may react to these persecutory delusions by retaliating against the presumed source of this persecution.

Other types of schizophrenics may attempt to kill others because of some form of psychotic identification with the victim, usually a well-known entertainer, a political figure, or, in some cases, the patient's therapist. Hallucinations associated with schizophrenia, particularly command hallucinations—the patient is commanded by God to kill someone—have been known to result in violent behavior and homicide. In addition, hallucinations in which people are cursing or insulting the patient may result in retaliation against a supposed source of these insults.

Some schizophrenics are violent because of generalized disorganization of thought and a lack of impulse control, with purposeless, excited psychomotor activity resulting in violence. Schizophrenics may be violent because of akathisia secondary to antipsychotic medication. With the agitation and restless from akathisia, they may bump into other people and start fights.

Other disease processes superimposed on the schizophrenic disorder may be responsible for the violence rather then delusions per se. These include brain damage secondary to heavy drug or alcohol use, head trauma, or any other of the numerous neurologic or systemic diseases discussed later in this chapter. Other psychiatric disorders such as mental retardation or a personality disorder may be responsible for violence by schizophrenic patients.

Finally, schizophrenics may be violent to attain what they want, to express anger or to deliberately hurt others. It is very important to determine the cause of violence by a schizophrenic person and not to assume it is due to psychosis.

Posttraumatic Stress Disorder

This disorder follows exposure to a traumatic event—such as, war, automobile accident, sexual assault, hostage-taking—which involves threatened death or serious injury.(17) The person experiences depression, anxiety, distressing dreams, intrusive thoughts about the event, hyper vigilance, avoidance of activities of persons associated with the event, detachment from other persons and difficulty concentrating. An individual may have distress when exposed to cues that symbolize or resemble an aspect of the traumatic event. In addition, he or she may act or feel that the traumatic event is recurring with flashback experiences or even hallucinations. Some have irritability and outbursts of anger and violence due to increased arousal and frustration as the result of continued incapacitation and symptomology.

Case Vignette

A 50-year-old Latino man served in the Vietnam War and was involved in a bloody firefight where his friends were killed. He developed symptoms of posttraumatic stress disorder (PTSD) and was discharged. Through years of treatment as an outpatient in the V.A. system, he was able to begin work as a repairman for the telephone company. He would periodically feel that he was almost losing control of this temper but was able to control himself. One day he was stopped for speeding by the police. A routine check of his name by computer showed that an arrest warrant for him was outstanding. He was arrested and taken to central booking. Some hours later the police realized they had arrested the wrong man. He developed symptoms of PTSD again and compared the police to the Viet Cong. One day at work he attacked a security guard as he was examining one of the trucks used for telephone repairs.

Delusional (Paranoid) Disorder

Although delusional disorder is uncommon, it can often be associated with violence. The persistent nonbizarre delusion possessed by these patients may be of the persecutory type in which people feel conspired against, cheated, spied on, poisoned, or otherwise harmed. Persons with delusional disorders may resemble those with paranoid personality except the beliefs are more severe, i.e. psychotic. On the other hand, persons with delusional disorder differ from schizophrenics in that their delusions are not as bizarre as those found in schizophrenia. In addition to resorting to legal action and appeals to government agencies, persons with this disorder often become resentful and angry and may become violent against those they believe are harming them. Delusional disorders of the jealous type involve the persistent belief that the patient's spouse or lover is unfaithful. These people attempt to restrict the activities of and follow the spouse or lover. They may resort to physical attacks on the spouse or lover or someone who is identified as the "other partner" in this "infidelity."

Case Vignette

A 32-year-old white man worked as a computer programmer in a corporation which makes televisions and other electronic equipment. For several years he believed that the FBI was monitoring his home telephone. He wrote letters to the director of the FBI, the local police, and other law enforcement agencies asking them to stop the monitoring. At work he was considered a valuable employee, although rather odd, since he confided in some of his co-workers about his beliefs regarding the FBI. One day he read an article in the newspaper describing how the FBI used electronic equipment. He wrote a letter to the chief executive officer of his company threatening him and telling about his beliefs and the FBI.

Mood Disorder (Mania and Depression)

Persons with mania may be violent as a result of their extreme agitation or as a result of irritable mood associated with angry tirades.(1–3) Most violence by manic patients is not premeditated and is purposeless.(4) Rarely, a manic may become violent as a result of delusional thinking where the person believes that he or she is being persecuted because of some special attribute. It is usually the case with the manic that all impulses are put into action. If some of these impulses are violent, then they too become violent actions.

The typical situation where manics erupt with violence is when they feel contained and not free to do what they want to do. This may be physical, as being contained in a small examining room, or interpersonal, as when someone insists that they do something they do not want to do or when their freedom is limited in some other way. Depressed patients are rarely violent. An infrequent exception is the psychotic depressed person. In this situation, extreme hopelessness, feelings that life is not worth living, or delusional feelings of profound guilt may result in violence, usually involving murder, followed by suicide. If this occurs, it most often involves a woman killing her children and then herself, or a man killing his family and then himself.

Case Vignette

A 42-year-old Latino woman worked as a secretary in a hospital. She had a history of several depressive episodes and one mania episode two years ago— characterized by going on a shopping spree where she bought three mink coats she could not afford. Her mood was stabilized with lithium; however, she did not like the "depressing" feeling while on lithium. She soon discontinued the medication.

Over a month she became increasing hyperactive and had difficulty concentrating on her work and typing. Her boss, an administrator in the hospital, told her to stay in her office and finish a document in one hour. She threw a book at him and fled the office.

Neurological Disorders

A number of primary diseases of the brain can be associated with violent behavior.(18) Following generalized seizures, violence has been found with encephalopathy. Violence has occurred with infections of the brain, including viral encephalitis, acquired immune deficiency syndrome (AIDS), tuberculosis and fungal meningitis, syphilis, and herpes simplex. Other primary diseases of the brain associated with violence include head trauma, normal pressure hydrocephalus, cerebrovascular diseases, tumors, Huntington's chorea, multiple sclerosis, Alzheimer's disease, Pick's disease, multi-infarct dementia, Parkinson's disease, Wilson's disease, and post anoxic or post hypoglycemic states with brain damage

Other Medical Disorders

There are a number of systemic disorders associated with violence.(19,20) Unlike the primary diseases of the brain, many of these are treatable and reversible. Thus, recognition is important, and appropriate medical care is necessary. These disorders include hypoxia, electrolyte imbalances, hepatic disease, renal disease, vitamin deficiencies such as B12 folate or thiamin, systemic infections, hypoglycemia, Cushing's disease, hyperthyroidism, hypothyroidism, systemic lupus erythematosus, poisoning by heavy metals, insecticides, and other substances, and porphyria.

Mental Retardation

Although most persons with mental retardation are not violent, when violence does occur it is often difficult to treat. Violence due to poor intellectual ability is associated with anger and frustration at not being able to obtain what is desired or at not being able to verbalize concerns and feelings. This is accompanied by poor impulse control and then violence toward others or the self.

History of Noncompliance with Treatment

Finally, when assessing the potential for violence, one should consider the person's compliance or noncompliance with treatment. Whether a person keeps clinic appointments, returns after hospital passes, and/or takes medication regularly goes into the formula on the risk of violence in the future. On the latter point, for schizophrenics or other psychotic persons with a history of violence, acceptance of long-acting intramuscular antipsychotic medication is very reassuring.

Demographic Characteristics

Demographic characteristics of persons should be considered—with increased risk of violence among the young males and persons coming from environments of poverty, disruption of families, and decreased social control, where violence is a more acceptable means of attaining a goal than in other segments of society. I have not found race to be a factor associated with increased risk of assault among psychiatric patients when socioeconomic variables and education are taken into consideration. Rather, the environment from which the person comes must be considered in the determination of violence potential. Is it one that views violence as an accepted means of obtaining what one wants in the face of poverty or lack of other legitimate means, education, work, and verbal skills?

Summary of Prediction of Violence

The assessment of violence potential for the short-term—i.e., in days or a week—is analogous to the assessment for suicide potential. The clinician must consider the following:

✧ Subtle questioning of the person if violence is not mentioned

✧ Appearance of the person how well planned is the threat of violence is

✧ Available means of inflicting injury

✧ Past history of violence and impulsive behavior with attention to frequency, degree of past injuries to others and self, toward whom, and under what circumstances

✧ Alcohol and drug use

✧ Presence of other organic mental disorders

✧ Presence of schizophrenia, mania or other psychosis

✧ Presence of certain personality and impulse control disorders

✧ Noncompliance with treatment in the past

All of these factors are weighed in the final assessment of whether the person poses a significant risk to others so that some action is necessary on the part of the evaluator. Action may include suspending the employee, hospitalizing the person, or warning the intended victim and/or the police. All of the data influencing the decision about whether the person is or is not a risk for violence must be documented in writing. The thinking process through which the decision was made should be evident in the written documentation. Reassessment of violence potential should be made at short intervals—e.g., from visit to visit or every few days—if the person is to continue to be treated outside of the hospital or other institution.

Checklist 3.3

Information Sources for Violence Assessment

✔ Interview employee

✔ Interview other employees about this and any other episodes

✔ Interview police about prior episodes of violence

✔ Interview any others with information about this or past episodes

✔ Review old charts

✔ Review arrest records

✔ Review judicial proceeding records

Threats of Violence

Employees can threaten in a number of ways: the impulsive, emotional outburst; the calm, serious statement; a joking, flippant manner; or through vague innuendoes. Threats can be made face-to-face, on an answering machine, or by letter. All threats of violence must be taken seriously. The employer should not deny the existence or seriousness of a threat. Often the manager can confront the patient and clarify the meaning of the threat. If it is resolved, then therapy can proceed. If there is uncertainty or the clinician feels the threat may be serious, it should be discussed with one's supervisor, colleagues, and family so as to assess the risk of harm and to develop a plan to deal with the threat. Whether the setting is a health care setting or a company, I suggest a meeting consisting of representatives of various parts of the organization such as security, legal affairs, administration, human resources, director of clinical services, or employee health and a psychiatric consultant familiar with violence. This group will benefit from the various perspectives in terms of evaluating different options, from the legal to the therapeutic, in responding to the threat.

In evaluating the risk of violence, information along the lines I have discussed earlier in this paper must be obtained. This may involve meeting with the employee in a safe setting or obtaining information from other employees, records, or other means. This is particularly problematic where threats by telephone or mail are anonymous. Use of telephone technology and other means of determining the identity, and then the mental state, of the threatener are often creative.

Plan of Action

If the risk of violence is significant, a plan of action must be in place. This includes security measures, restraining orders, and other means of preventing access to the intended victim. The mental state of the threatener must be assessed so as to determine whether there exists grounds for involuntary hospitalization. It is helpful to use the institution as a buffer between the threatening employee and the victim—for example, "it is the policy of the company to not tolerate threats of violence to other employees, therefore the business intends

---

Checklist 3.4

Action Plans: Options

✔ Suspension from work

✔ Hospitalization

✔ Warning the intended victim

✔ Warning the police

✔ Security measures to limit access

✔ Restraining orders

✔ Protecting the intended victim

to...etc." This hopefully will deflect or at least not intensify the wrath of the threatener as the plan is implemented

Anonymous threats are difficult to respond to and frightening. Correspondence should be kept, preferably in a plastic bag, for further investigation. Telephone threats should be documented in terms of exactly what was said, whether the threatener had an accent or other speech characteristic, whether there were background noises and so on. If possible I suggest that the clinician attempt to engage the threatener in a nonconfrontational manner in order to obtain further information as to the identity of the threatener and further details of the threat so as to determine the risk of violence.

Conclusion

What we know about the prediction of violence and prevention of violence comes from studies of the frequency of violence among different types of patients and from clinical experience. Future research on the prediction of violence should involve prospective methodologies and a model that is as close to clinical decisionmaking as is possible. It should not depend on complex rating instruments.

References

1. Tardiff, K., Sweillam, A. "Assault, suicide and mental illness." *Arch Gen Psychiatry*. 1980;37:164-169.

2. Craig, T.J. "An epidemiological study of problems associated with violence among psychiatric inpatients." *Am J Psychiatry*. 1982;139:1262-1266.

3. Tardiff, K. "Characteristics of assaultive patients in private hospitals." *Am J Psychiatry*. 1984;141:1232-1235.

4. Tardiff, K. "The current state of psychiatry in the treatment of violent patients." *Arch Gen Psychiatry*. 1992;49:493-499.

5. Addad, M., Benezech, M., Bourgeois, M., et al. "Criminal acts among schizophrenics in French mental hospitals." *J Nerv Ment Dis* 1981;169:289-293.

6. Yesavage, J.A. "Inpatient violence and the schizophrenic patient." *Acta Psychiat Scand*. 1983;67:353-357.

7. Hare, R., Mc Pherson, L. "Violent and aggressive behavior by criminal psychopaths." *Int J Law Psychiatry*. 1984;7:35-50.

8. Tardiff, K., Koenigsberg, H.W. "Assaultive behavior among outpatients." *Am J Psychiatry*. 1985;142:960-963.

9. Holcomb, W.R., Anderson, W.P. "Alcohol and multiple drug use in accused murderers." *Psychol Reports*. 1983;52:159-164.

10. Swanson, J.W., Holzer, C.E., Ganju, V.K., et al. "Violence and psychiatric disorder in the community: Evidence from the Epidemiologic Catchment Area surveys." *Hosp Comm Psychiatry*. 1990;41:761-770.

11. Lowenstein, D.H., Massa, S.M., Rowbotham, M.C., et al. "Acute neurologic and psychiatric complications associated with cocaine abuse." *Am J Med*. 1987;83:841-846.

12. Honer, W.E., Gewirtz, E., Turey, M. "Psychosis and violence in cocaine smokers." *Lancet*. 1987;i:451.

13. Budd, R.D., Lindstrom, D.M. "Characteristics of victims of PCP-related deaths in Los Angeles Country." *J Toxicol Clin Toxicol*. 1982;19:997-1004.

14. Brecher, M., Wang, W.B., Wong, H., et al. "Phencyclidine and violence: Clinical and legal issues." *J Clin Psychopharm*. 1988;8:397-401.

15. Lindquist, P., Allebeck, P. "Schizophrenia and crime: A longitudinal follow-up of 644 schizophrenics in Stockholm." *Brit J Psychiatry*. 1990;157:345-350.

16. Tardiff, K., Sweillam, A. "Assaultive behavior among chronic inpatients." *Am J Psychiatry*. 1982;139:212-215.

17. American Psychiatric Association: *Diagnostic and Statistical Manual of Mental Disorders*; Fourth Edition. Washington, D.C., American Psychiatric Association, 1994.

18. Weiger, B., Bear, D. "An approach to the neurology of aggression." *J Psychiatr Res*. 1988;22:85-98.

19. Petrie, W.M., Lawson, E.C., Hollender, M.H. "Violence in geriatric patients." *JAMA*. 1982;248:443-444.20.

20. Deutsch, L.H., Bylsma, F.W., Rovner, B.W., et al. "Psychosis and physical aggression in probable Alzheimer's disease." *Am J Psychiatry*. 1991;148:1159-1163.

Chapter Four

❑ Components of a violence prevention system

❑ Elements of pre-incident planning

❑ Role of the Incident Management Team in the process of threat management

❑ How to better assess the violence risk of threats

Implementing a Workplace Violence Prevention and Threat Management System

Kenneth L. Wolf, PhD

Case Study

Joe Walker, a ten-year employee, threatened Tom Madden in the hall, saying, "If I catch you messing with my work, I will get you so you won't be able to work again." The conversation was reported to Joe's supervisor by a co-worker who was standing next to Tom at the time. Joe, a good worker, has had poor work relationships for as long as anyone can remember and his co-workers have learned to leave him alone. In the past there has been more than one parking lot fight after work involving Joe. Joe is an avid hunter and gun collector. What should Joe's supervisor do? How should he assess the threat? The personnel manager has been discussing whether they need a violence prevention policy.

Introduction

The fear and impact of workplace violence has been attracting significant responses from companies, employees, and regulatory agencies. Newspaper headlines often feature graphic accounts of workplace shootings by "disgruntled" employees. Incidents of workplace violence have even altered perceptions of major organizations—especially, the United States Postal Service—in the minds of the public and have added a new idiom to the American language, i.e., "going postal."

Certainly, there has been an increase in the awareness of the phenomena of "workplace violence." Initial attempts at quantification suggest that violent incidents are on the increase. However, the lack of standardized definitions of "violent acts" and the unavailability of a valid and large database of incidents, limits the inferences that can be scientifically made. In addition, the probable under-reporting of violent incidents by employers—because they do not want to frighten customers or current and potential employees—also serves to deny the field an accurate portrayal of the real picture. This reluctance to publish or share statistics on data, moreover, also serves to prevent a business from understanding its own risk factors for violence and to initiate corresponding protective responses based upon its own vulnerabilities. This chapter will provide guidelines on developing a comprehensive workplace violence system. First, it will look at the definition of violence and a brief review of the problem.

Definition of Workplace Violence

What is first needed is a definition of workplace violence. A **general definition** of workplace violence may be *any intentional workplace confrontation which may increase in intensity and threaten the safety of any employee, have an impact on any employee's physical and/or psychological well-being, or cause physical damage to personnel or company property*. Violence, per se, is defined by Webster as the "abusive or unjust exercise of power." Workplace violence may consist of threats; work-related conflict wherein a disgruntled employee damages company property or injures other employees; personal conflict wherein upset relatives of an employee can damage company property or injure company employees; the taking of hostages by former or current employees; or injurious attacks by clients, outsiders or nonemployees.

The Occupational Safety and Health Administration (OSHA) has developed a different perspective of workplace violence by defining three different types of perpetrators who commit violence in the workplace.

✧ In Type I events, the perpetrator has no legitimate relationship to the workplace and usually enters the work environment to commit a robbery or other criminal act.

✧ In Type II events, the perpetrator is either the recipient or the object of a service provided by the affected workplace or the victim.

✧ In Type III events, the perpetrator is an individual who currently has, or has had, some employment-related involvement with the workplace, either as an employee or a relative or friend of an employee.

This topology covers many sources of violence in the workplace.

Perhaps a **general working definition** of workplace violence would be *any act that occurs in the workplace and results in threatened or actual psychological or physical harm to persons or property.* This would include acts that are physically assaultive, behaviors which indicate a potential for violence (throwing objects, intimidating gestures), threats to harm another or endangering the safety of employees.

Review of the Problem of Workplace Violence

Lack of Data

Workplace violence is considered a relatively new problem. As such, data accurately describing this phenomenon is considered to be insufficient by most workplace violence experts. Other than homicide data, there has been almost no systematic reporting requirement for nonfatal physical assaults, intentional intimidating nonphysical behaviors, or verbal threats. Reports produced at federal, state, and local levels tend to concentrate on certain aspects of homicide such as job categories, regions of the country, or demographic information. As a result, there is no comprehensive national data base nor a standard classification or topology for violent events which adequately tracks or reflects the incidence of workplace violence. States are currently using up to twenty-five different data sources to identify and to code the circumstances of work-related deaths. Some of the major sources include death certificates; workers' compensation reports and claims; Occupational Safety and Health Administration, police, coroner, and medical examiner reports; and newspaper articles. (See Chapters 1 and 2 by Lynn Jenkins for a more detailed description of what we know about workplace violence.)

In spite of the lack of comprehensive state or national data, some meaningful statistics are surfacing from reputable sources. According to an analysis of the National Traumatic Occupational Fatality (NTOF) data for the United States from 1980 to 1985, homicide was the third leading cause of occupational injury deaths. Twelve (12) percent of all occupational injury deaths in the period were homicides. Only motor vehicle (23%) and machine-related incidents (13%) accounted for more deaths.

Increase in Workplace Violence

Data from the 1993 National Census of Fatal Occupational Injuries suggests that the problem of workplace violence has only worsened. Homicide is now the second leading cause of job-related fatalities; it accounts for 17% of all fatal injuries to workers. Robbery and opportunistic crime was the main motive for homicide at work, with about one out of seven victims of workplace homicide being killed by a co-worker or work associate. There were 1,063 job-related homicides during 1993, with half of all homicide victims working in retail establishments. About four-fifths of homicide victims were men, yet homicide was the most frequent type of fatal injury for women, accounting for 41% of their 481 deaths. Most homicide victims were shot (82%), 9% were stabbed, and the others were beaten, strangled, purposely run over by a vehicle, or killed by fire. The sales workers occupational group experienced nearly 10% of all fatal work injuries in 1993. This group, which accounted for one-third of all workplace homicides, includes supervisors and proprietors of retail establishments, salesclerks, and cashiers.

Extent of the Problem

Data from company surveys provide more definition to the problem of workplace violence. According to a *Wall Street Journal* article, almost 25% of 311 companies surveyed by the American Management Association in 1994, indicated that at least one of their workers had been attacked or killed on the job since 1990. Another 31% reported threats against workers. A review of the 1987–92 National Crime Victimization Survey by Ronet Bachman, Ph.D., a statistician for the U.S.

Bureau of Justice Statistics, indicated that nearly one million individuals become victims of violent crime every year while they are working. These violent acts represent about 15% of the over six million acts of violence in the United States annually. According to Dr. Bachman, workplace crime victimizations cost about half a million employees over 1.75 million days of work each year or an average of 3.5 days per crime. Surprisingly, she discovered that victims who were working were as likely to face armed offenders as those victimized while not working. Workers injured on the job from violent crime lost an estimated 877,000 days of work annually, costing these employees over $16 million in wages, not including days covered by sick pay. Her analysis revealed that six out of every ten incidents of workplace violence occurred in private companies, but that 30% of the victims of such violence were federal, state, or local government employees, even though the latter represent only about 18% of the U.S. workforce.

✦ The U.S. is the most violent nation in the western world. In 1993 there were 110,000 reported incidents of violence in U.S. workplaces, resulting in 1,063 deaths and costing employers over $4 billion.

✦ Homicide in the workplace is the fastest growing form of murder. This rate has doubled since 1983.

✦ Eighty percent of all workplace homicide victims are male.

✦ Of those who commit workplace murders, 40 percent then commit suicide.

✦ Nearly 42 percent of women who die in the workplace are murdered.

✦ Most U.S. companies do not have a plan to manage crises of workplace violence.

Table 4.1: Facts about workplace violence

Violence includes more than homicide, however. Threats, assaults, robberies, intimidation, sabotage, and vandalism are other examples that can cause emotional and physical injury on the job. When this violence occurs, the workplace suffers in terms of lost production, worker's compensation claims, and litigation.

Importance of Training

A recent study (Johnson and Kinney 1994) of "employer directed violence," with significant implications for prevention, suggested that in approximately 85% of workplace violent incidents where people were physically injured or killed, there were prior clues/information/ warning signs given in the form of verbal threats or other early behavioral indicators. This study suggests that efforts to train personnel managers, security departments, supervisors, and employees to recognize such early behavioral indicators of potential violence, and to intervene with methods to defuse or to deflect such anger, may be effective in reducing those incidents of workplace violence where there is "foreseeability."

Legal Consequences

Incidents of workplace violence not only affect employee morale and public perception, but there are significant legal consequences as well. Violent acts may result in litigation exposures from three sources. These include regulatory authorities, third parties, and the potentially violent employee himself or herself. Regulatory agencies include the U.S. Department of Labor, OSHA, and the state authority responsible for regulating health and safety practices in the particular state where the business is located. These issues are usually related to violations stemming from OSHA's General Duty Clause.

Other sources of liability may emanate from third parties—i.e., customers, contractors, family members and estates of individuals injured or killed by employees—and may include exposures from negligent hiring, negligent retention, negligent training, negligent supervision and negligent security.

A final source of litigation exposure for the employer may be the potentially violent employee himself in the form of claims of defamation, slander, invasion of privacy, Americans with Disabilities Act issues, and violation of First Amendment freedoms.

Other Consequences

Low morale and litigation are not the only consequences of violent incidents. Another facet of workplace violence receiving attention pertains to procedures to reduce the post-incident traumatic impact of violent incidents both to minimize human suffering and disability consequences. Certainly, reduced productivity, physical injury, psychological posttraumatic reactions, lost time, resignations, and anger are other consequences that must be addressed.

Developing a Comprehensive Workplace Violence System

Employers are now viewing workplace violence as a business problem that can be managed. Effective violence prevention systems are now being implemented in the workplace as the phenomenon of workplace violence becomes more familiar and data and response requirements become available.

There are a variety of essential tasks that are core components of a comprehensive workplace violence prevention system. A well-designed system should address the policies, training activities, systems, structures, and procedures, that are outlined in Table 4.2.

⋄ Developing a Violence Prevention Policy and the consequences of violating this policy

⋄ Defining "unacceptable" workplace behaviors

⋄ Procedures describing how, and to whom, employees and supervisors can report threats, intimidating and violent incidents

⋄ Procedures describing how, and by whom, threats and violent acts will be investigated

⋄ Implementing strategies to protect threatened employees and assets

⋄ Establishing an Incident Management Team to take "ownership" of the Violence Prevention Program and to respond to threats when they arise

⋄ Post-incident activities to reduce the impact of trauma in employees and the organization after a violent act has occurred

⋄ Defining audiences for violence prevention awareness training

⋄ Identifying internal and external resources to assist in the management of threatening situations

---

Table 4.2: Components of a workplace violence prevention system

These tasks comprise a violence prevention system that may be envisioned as activities focusing on prevention, threat management and response. A diagram of this model is seen in Figure 4.1.

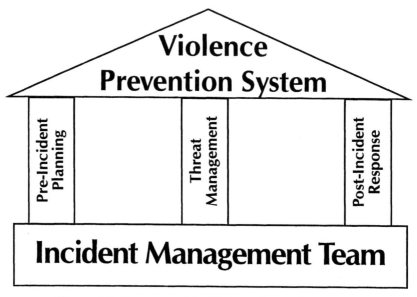

Figure 4.1: Structure of the Violence Prevention System

Pre-Incident Planning

Pre-Incident Planning includes the development of policies, structures, and training needed to prepare an early warning system that reduces the possibility of a violent situation and to manage program operations. The first component is to develop a policy statement that informs all employees about acceptable and unacceptable forms of workplace behavior.

Components of a Policy Statement

Some of the elements of a workplace violence prevention policy are a clear statement that there will be a "zero tolerance" for threats, intimidating behaviors, and violent acts, the consequences for violating the policy, and information regarding employee responsibility for reporting violations of the policy and to whom. Other parts of the policy statement should indicate that an articulated threat will be presumed to constitute a statement of the employees intent to do harm and that once an employee violates the policy, he loses his expectation of privacy in those areas that need to be investigated in order to assure the safety of the workplace. These elements serve to give employees notice as to what is expected of them, and provide the employer with certain courses of action to investigate threatening behaviors and defenses against litigation when employees cross the line.

Incident Management Team

The policy statement may also identify that the establishment of an Incident Management Team (IMT) as the central group which will take "ownership" of the workplace violence prevention program, receive reports of threats, and have the responsibility for investigating them. Membership of the Incident Management Team (IMT) may include representatives from human resources, security, legal, health and safety, EAP, occupational health, operations, and the union. In smaller companies, the IMT may include the coordinator of the health and safety program, a superintendent, the occupational nurse, or other designated individuals. In essence, the IMT implements and operates the systems, procedures, and training to enable supervisors and employees to know organization policies, to report problematic behavior to appropriate personnel, and to manage incidents once they occur.

Once a policy statement is developed and approved by senior management, it becomes the foundation on which other program components are built. The Incident Management Team (IMT) must now develop a dissemination strategy to communicate the existence of the violence prevention policy statement and to define which various audiences which should be trained in order to allow for an effective program roll-out.

It should be noted that there are sometimes barriers or reluctance to report threatening or intimidating behaviors by co-workers. Often, supervisors and employees do not report threats out of fear that the alleged perpetrator may turn their anger at them or at their family members. Other barriers to prompt reporting of threats is the lack of knowledge as to what organizational resources exist to report a threat, whether such resources are trained to manage threats, and whether the company would do anything at all, if called about such a concern. Moreover, lack of training as to what are early warning signs of the potentially violent individual denies to both supervisors and employees knowledge of the at-risk behaviors which they should report. The training content of the following audiences would therefore reflect a significant organizational commitment of resources and expertise to manage threats and assure workplace safety.

Violence Prevention Training

This section provides an overview of training needs for different groups of employees. More detail about setting up a training program is covered in Chapter 5 by Pater and Russell. Audiences for workplace violence prevention training usually include the following groups:

✧ Senior managers/union leadership/facility directors

✧ Incident Management Team members

✧ Supervisors and union representatives

✧ Employees

Senior Leadership, Union Leadership, Facility Director Training

The executive overview for senior leadership focuses on several different issues. Leaders must understand that threats and intimidation are contrary to the organization's mission and to those corporate "cultural values" which advocate respect in the workplace for all employees. Violence is not only incompatible with such respect, but violent acts will also leave an aftermath that will interfere with productivity, morale, and employee well-being. Content for the executive briefings should include the phenomena, definitions, and data on workplace violence, litigation exposures associated with violent acts, the response requirements to implement a violence prevention system, and the need for endorsing and allocating resources to the Incident Management Team and empowering it to launch and operate the program.

Incident Management Team Training

If the Incident Management Team is to assume responsibility for receiving and assessing threats against employees and the organization and implementing protective strategies, the training its members receive must be comprehensive and professional. As opposed to attending just "another stress management class," the IMT is being asked to learn how to assess the risk of potentially dangerous individuals and to develop protective options when threats are made against employees and the organization. These skills are ones rarely ever taught in MBA programs, in night schools, during union apprenticeships, or during staff in-service training programs. Consequently, such training should occur periodically and be coupled with simulated exercises on how to recognize different types of high-risk situations and how to initiate risk mitigation responses.

The content of the Incident Management Team training should include the following topics:

✧ How to recognize early warning signs of potential violence

✧ How to investigate and verify reported threats

✧ How to assess the context in which the threat occurred

✧ How to communicate strategies with persons threatened, the subject making the threat, and other key company personnel (e.g., supervisors, legal, risk management, local law enforcement, threat assessment experts)

✧ How to develop appropriate response options given the level of risk

✧ How to document their activities to demonstrate that the IMT acted reasonably given the level of risk it was able to verify.

Since the IMT will usually interview the at-risk subject, it is important that they be trained in interviewing techniques, verbal diffusion skills, and awareness of their own safety during this process.

Supervisory and Union Representative Training

The training of supervisors and union representatives should include the following topics:

✧ Information about the policy statement

✧ Responsibilities of the Incident Management Team

✧ How to report threats

✧ Recognition of behavioral indicators of potentially violent individuals

✧ Verbal diffusion skills

For supervisors, it is important to point out their general responsibilities for directing and motivating employees, and for holding them accountable for their behavior and conduct. Supervisors are also accountable for maintaining the general health and safety of the work environment and therefore must report any behaviors that violate the policy and may escalate into intimidating or violent acts.

While union representatives have a duty to represent employees, they too, are also concerned about preventing potential violence. It should be pointed out that the violence prevention awareness training and response system is a means to help union representatives enhance their own ability to recognize potential problem behaviors and to assist their members who exhibit these behaviors before they are subject to discipline or worse and before they may commit acts which could harm co-workers, supervisors, or themselves.

Employee Orientation

The employee training is a communication session which creates awareness about the problem of workplace violence, the content of the policy statement, and the employees affirmative responsibility to ensure safe work practices by reporting violations of the policy. Employees should be briefed on how to report threats and how the Incident Management Teams operates to manage threats in order to maintain the safety of the workplace.

Threat Management

It is perhaps a sad commentary on contemporary society that organizations are both considering and implementing Threat Management Programs. Such programs used to be the exclusive domains of intelligence agencies or the Secret Service. Now, they are becoming part of corporate America.

The process of threat management is composed of activities to define the risks an organization faces from employees, customers, or outsiders. In order to assess risks from employees, the IMT usually has access to a vast repertoire of past and current behaviors or the "subject" and sources of information (co-workers, supervisors, sometimes customers) to validate alleged threatening, intimidating, or violent behaviors. When asked to assess risk, the IMT must first ask itself several questions including those shown in Checklist 4.1.

Checklist 4.1

Threat Management Process Questions

✔ What kind of opinion is being sought?

✔ Is this a doable request?

✔ What sources of information are needed to confirm alleged behavior?

✔ What are the consequences of making an incorrect assessment?

✔ What other resources should be consulted for the assessment?

IMT Responsibilities

A core issue in threat assessment is how to differentiate between the difficult employee as opposed to the employee who poses a threat to co-workers or the organization. When a threat is reported, the IMT will begin to evaluate the nature, content, and situational context of the incident. The IMT must determine whether the alleged threat reflects either a misunderstanding of the behavior or the subject, or whether there was a misunderstanding on the part of the observer. The Incident Management Team (IMT) becomes the internal corporate resource to coordinate and direct the receipt and investigation of threats against employees. The IMT's general responsibilities include the collecting and investigation of threats, developing systems to communicate with affected individuals, including the person reporting the threat, the recipient of the threat, the person making the threat and the supervisors of the affected employees.

Checklist 4.2

Incident Management Team Responsibilities

✔ Collection and investigation of threats

✔ Develop communication system to manage threat

✔ Identify expert resources to assist in threat management

✔ Develop workplace response options

✔ Develop protective strategies for credible threats

✔ Establish and maintain database for recording and monitoring threats and incidents

✔ Maintain relationships with law enforcement resources

✔ Develop mental health resources including for assessment, management and treatment

---

Other functions of the IMT include identifying expert resources to assist in threat management and developing workplace response options and protective strategies when threats are deemed to be credible. The IMT should establish and maintain a database for recording and monitoring threats and incidents at the workplace. The IMT will also develop relationships with law enforcement and mental health resources. The law enforcement linkage includes relationships with local police, ATF, FBI, and prosecutors who specialize in domestic abuse and stalking situations. Mental health resources include counseling centers that can be used as referral resources for distressed employees, and forensic psychologists and social workers with specific expertise in the assessment, evaluation, and management of the dangerous individual.

A particularly valuable function of the IMT is trying to determine risk potential to the organization once an employee makes a threat. The IMT will seek to assess the accuracy, credibility, and imminence of risk. The process to accomplish these objectives includes having the IMT interview witnesses of the alleged behavior, co-workers, supervisors, and knowledgeable others who can validate the threat or other behaviors suggestive of risk.

IMT Information Sources

The IMT may review a variety of information sources to determine the employees potential for harm. Public sources of information include background checks for criminal convictions, legal gun registration, driving history, and previous employment reference checks. Internal company sources of information may include work/ disciplinary history, grievances/worker compensation claims filed, complaints from customers, co-workers or contractors, transfers, accidents or interpersonal problems. Other employee behaviors to assess are previous threats, destruction of property, job performance problems, the making of veiled or conditional threats, references to other acts of workplace violence, or to other perpetrators who have committed violent acts. Other indicators of potential violence by an employee may include whether the person is a "loner," inappropriate references to weapons, bizarre statements, impulsivity, paranoia, stalking, apparent feelings of futility, or statements about getting a "raw deal" from the company.

Assessing the Context

It is important to realize that correlation is not causation. Individuals can display some or many of these behaviors, and yet, never reach the threshold where they resort to violent behavior. What is also critical is to assess the situational context in which the behavior is occurring. To assess the context, attempts should be made to try to define other factors that may be generating stressors for the subject. Such information may include workplace and organizational changes, job loss, loss of a promotion or arbitration, downsizing, financial problems, family conflicts, changes in physical and/or emotional health, recent "losses" (e.g., divorce, death), or other events perceived by the subject to be "traumatic."

When trying to assess the context, it is most important to identify situations which are "coming to a head," which if not resolved in a manner acceptable to the subject, may ignite the subject into destructive activities which otherwise might not occur. Precipitants that can push the person over the edge are important to determine. Since people often make threats when they themselves feel threatened, it is important to try to determine what stressors—which if increased or decreased in the person's life—might raise or lower the threat of violence. It is also important to identify support systems or "inhibitors" which can be mobilized positively to help the subject stay below that threshold which would result in violence.

Post-Incident Response

The last part of a comprehensive violence prevention system includes developing a crisis management plan and identifying resources to be deployed if an incident occurs. The post- incident crisis plan includes helping supervisors and employees understand the psychological impact of a violent event, conducting individual and group criti-cal-incident debriefing sessions to facilitate recovery, identifying particularly distressed employees and referring them to counseling resources, and assisting with restabilization of the organization.

Checklist 4.3

Information Sources for Threat Assessment

✔ Background check for criminal convictions

✔ Gun registration

✔ Driving history, accidents, summons, DWI

✔ Employment reference checks

✔ Work/disciplinary history

✔ Grievances, if any

✔ Accidents or workers compensation claims

✔ Complaints from customers, co-workers or contractors

✔ Interpersonal problems

✔ Any prior threats, veiled or conditional

✔ Any destruction of property

✔ Any job performance problems

✔ References to other acts of violence

✔ References to other perpetrators acts

✔ Any inappropriate reference to weapons

✔ Bizarre statements

✔ Evidence of impulsivity

✔ Evidence of paranoia, stalking

✔ Suggestions of "getting a raw deal"

✔ Potential stressors which may be precipitants

✔ Indentification of support systems, inhibitors

The crisis response resources may be either internal to the organization, or available on a contract basis through either the EAP or community resources. Regardless of whether the crisis responders are internal or external, they should be adequately trained in types of traumatic events, onsite logistics and crisis intervention techniques, how to assess trauma in employees, rumor control and media management, and follow-up strategies to assist employees experiencing posttraumatic stress reactions.

Conclusion: Current Status of Workplace Violence Programs

Workplace violence has become a "new frontier" for American employers. Like the former frontiers of the Old West and voyages to the moon, we knew where we wanted to go, but getting there was fraught with risk and danger. The dangers involved with workplace violence include physical harm, litigation, psychological trauma, and human pain and suffering.

The awareness of the problem, the new OSHA Violence Prevention Guidelines, increasing commitments to workplace safety, respect in the workplace, and concern to employee well-being, have all motivated employers to initiate proactive violence prevention efforts. While the name of the program is "workplace violence prevention," the real message to employees and to stakeholders is "we value human life."

References

Baron, Anthony. *Violence in the Workplace: A Prevention and Management Guide for Business*. Pathfinder Publishing of California. 1993

De Becker. *The Gift of Fear*. Boston: Little Brown and Company, 1997.

Feeder, R., and Victor, B. *Getting Away with Murder*. New York: Simon and Schuster, 1996.

Jenkins, L. *Violence in the Workplace: Risk Factors and Prevention Strategies*. NIOSH Bulletin 57, June 1996. Cincinnati, Ohio.

Labig, Charles. *Preventing Violence in the Workplace*. New York: RHR International/ American Management Association 1995.

Mantell, Michael. *Ticking Bombs: Defusing Violence in the Workplace*. Albrecht Publishing Company 1994.

Minor, Marianne. *Preventing Workplace Violence: Providing a Safe Work Environment*. Crisp Publications, Inc., Menlo Park, California, 1995.

Timm, H. And Chandler, C. *Combating Workplace Violence*. International Association of Chiefs of Police / Bureau of Justice Assistance Grant N. 95-DD-BX-0166. IACP, Alexandria, VA. 1995.

Chapter Five

❑ Training as a linchpin to other violence prevention strategies

❑ Steps for setting up a violence prevention training program

❑ Overcoming typical barriers and getting buy-in for violence prevention training

❑ Suggested topics for training

❑ Hints for developing the content of violence prevention training

❑ Strategies for maximizing training effectiveness

Training Employees and Managers in Violence Prevention

Rob Russell, BS, and Robert Pater, MA

Case Study

At a seminar for supervisors and managers on workplace violence, one of the supervisors commented that he thought some forklift truck drivers in the distribution warehouse were using the trucks as tools of intimidation. They would brush people back as they drove by, and occasionally they would pin people with the load they were carrying. Others in the group agreed this was a problem which they could not let continue. Much of the time remaining in the session was devoted to how they were going to address this issue on the warehouse floor and how they planned to observe, confront, and coach the drivers.

Introduction

When push comes to shove in the realm of workplace violence, people are the problem, and ultimately, people can be the solution. Physical safeguards and practices designed to prevent violence in the workplace, such as fencing, security checkpoints, adequate applicant screening, grievance procedures, and others are important. But, as a variation of one of Murphy's laws says, any system designed to eliminate human error won't.

The success or failure of violence prevention hinges on suitable actions taken by people in the organization. Training employees and managers is a cornerstone for any effective violence prevention program. Those who are well trained respond more appropriately in crucial moments than those who are left to their default reactions. Besides providing staff with greater internal security—which can be applied on and off the job—training can reduce panic-driven decisions. In addition, training can help people best use other important security measures intended to prevent violence.

We know one teller whose entire holdup training consisted of a curt "just don't do anything stupid" admonition from her supervisor. Such minimal "training" makes the unsafe assumption that common sense will guide people into proper actions if violence threatens or strikes. Training anticipates situations and helps people rehearse intelligent and safe action. With everyone operating from a clear and intelligent strategy, many acts of violence can be prevented or minimized.

This chapter provides an overview of how to develop and administer a violence prevention training program. Of course, every organization has unique needs based on location, nature of the business, staff makeup, whether staff are working in the field or only internally, etc. But the focus here is on planning in order to develop an effective, systematic program.

Development of Violence Prevention Training—First Steps

Training is a linchpin to all violence prevention strategies. The concern about violence in the workplace is often kept in the shadows because the topic is viewed as unpleasant and alarming. Some organizations activate safeguards to prevent violence but remain strangely silent on the subject. Training is a positive way to address issues of violence and to link the organization's total violence prevention program to individuals and their actions. Training helps to protect people where security measures cannot, is needed for improved customer relations, and is necessary to help staff utilize antiviolence procedures. Training also helps people to understand and make the best use of administrative or mechanical means of handling conflict and violence prevention.

There are a number of effective violence prevention strategies which can be heightened through effective communications and training. These strategies are shown in Checklist 5.1.

Checklist 5.1

Violence Prevention Strategies for Business

✔ A management style which treats employees equitably

✔ Open communication at all levels of the organization

✔ Clear policies about workplace violence

✔ A strong harassment policy*

✔ A clear drug testing policies and practices

✔ "Difficult customer" policies and procedures

✔ Surveys to identify concerns

✔ Hotlines to make it easy for people to be heard

✔ Humane discipline, termination, and downsizing procedures

✔ Means of handling grievances and problems

✔ Employee assistance programs

✔ Screening to avoid hiring high-risk applicants

✔ Safe facilities which discourage acts of violence

✔ Alarm systems for warning others or requesting assistance

---

* **Sample Harassment Policy Statement**

We believe it is the right and expectation of all staff to feel safe at work. Therefore, we will not tolerate any indications or suggestions of violence, even when made in jest.

Linking some of these strategies with a strong training program builds a solid line of defense against violent acts. It is tempting for an organization to focus on tactics that require little human interaction. Understandably, writing a policy, putting up a fence, or hiring a security service is easier than getting involved with the emotional issues surrounding violence when people talk about it through training.

Initial Proposal

An initial recommendation has two primary functions:

1. It provides a broad overall plan to work from.
2. It develops just enough detail to gain the approval of individuals or groups who must bless the program.

To develop a plan, first identify in your organization the key areas of highest exposure to violence. Any history of violent acts will provide obvious targets. Areas of concern that training could address might include those shown in Checklist 5.2.

Next, using these key areas of concern as a starting place, develop a broad plan for what training should be done and how it might be accomplished. You can now think about your detailed plan, but it is may not be desirable to flesh out a plan that doesn't have firm approval yet. Senior managers are seldom interested in details. The key is to present just enough of a plan for management to understand, be comfortable with, and approve. Chances are that if your initial plan cannot be summarized in one page or less, it is too complicated. On the other hand, management will withhold support if a vague recommendation raises too many uncertainties.

Your recommendation should include these elements:

✧ Why violence prevention is critical for your company

✧ Why training is an effective means for violence prevention in your company

✧ The main training topics and how they might be delivered

✧ The importance of the topics you desire to cover

✧ Estimates of the time, money and coordination requirements

Secure Management Support

Never take management support for granted. Even if you have tacit agreement to go ahead with "needed training," don't skip this step of securing management's

---

Checklist 5.2

Areas of Concern for a Violence Prevention Policy

✔ Baseline issues for everyone in the organization (harassment, etc.)

✔ Security measures already in force which training could augment

✔ Money handling

✔ Securing robbery/theft prone materials or products

✔ Solo workers in late night or early morning shifts

✔ Individuals traveling alone

✔ Workers in high crime areas

✔ Public safety employees

✔ Coping with highly stressed or angry people

✔ Customer complaint handling

✔ Chronic discrimination or harassment behavior

✔ Conflict-prone jobs or departments in the organization

✔ Adverse relations between groups or individuals

✔ Resistance to unpopular policies and decisions

✔ Adverse relations between groups or individuals

✔ Resistance to unpopular policies and decisions

✔ Dispute and complaint management within the company

✔ Handling terminations and layoffs

✔ Operations scrutinized by protest groups

✔ Facilities particularly vulnerable to sabotage or foul play

✔ Hiring from a high-risk labor pool

✔ Employees facing unusual stress in their personal lives

---

support. Clarifying your desires and the support you need helps you to avoid disappointment.

A violence-prevention training program will be successful only to the extent that it receives genuine, ongoing management support. Without support, the program will quickly and quietly fade away. Many organizations prefer to spend money on the mechanics of prevention and downplay communications and training. Understanding some of the reasons upper management might resist violence prevention training helps form strategies to overcome barriers and get approval.

When selling the program to upper level management keep these things in mind:

✧ They must see the specific benefit to the organization.

✧ They will want some ideas as to cost and scheduling demands.

✧ You will need to overcome two basic objections to the program, which are 1) lack of time and money and 2) emotional resistance.

Checklist 5.3

Seven Steps in Developing a Violence Prevention Training Program

1. Develop an overall recommendation for violence prevention training.

2. Secure commitment from management for training.

3. Develop a detailed training plan to fit organizational needs.

4. Promote the program.

5. Implement the program.

6. Monitor progress and make adjustment.

7. Reinforce and follow up.

Barriers to Management Support

The first barrier to management support is one of competing priorities and time constraints. Top management faces many demands for time and money. And, like you, everyone feels their demand should be the A-1 priority. The need to provide training in machine operation, or hazardous waste disposal, or back injury protection is obvious. The chance of an extremely violent act seems relatively small in comparison. The attitude may be "we'll take our chances that nothing like that will never happen." But ineffective responses to intimidation and threats can handicap productivity and customer service. Upper management must see the very high financial and public relations exposure consequences that may occur when worst-case violent acts strike. They will discover that they can ensure a greater peace of mind for themselves and their staff with a relatively small expenditure of resources. You might also appeal to their general concern for human welfare.

The second barrier to management support is emotional resistance. Most people feel uncomfortable talking about violence for several reasons. Delving into the dark side of humanity makes many of us squeamish. It may suggest that management suspects everyone of harboring latent intent. Or managers may fear that others may take it personally as an implication that the morale of their unit is suspect. Some executives may feel that offering violence prevention training is an admission that the company is a dangerous, unsafe place. Denial—"it couldn't happen here"—is also a natural response. Because upper level managers are generally less susceptible to violence in the organization, they may generalize their security to the rest of the organization. Some basic statistics on the prevalence and cost of violence may be necessary for persuasion.

Don't be surprised by management resistance. Be ready for it by making a strong case for how violence prevention training can benefit the organization. The next section describes key benefits of violence prevention training that you can emphasize to management.

Benefits of Violence Prevention Programs

The key to gaining commitment is selling the program. This is best done by knowing and appealing to the concerns and interests of the person or the group who must approve the program.

Reduced Exposure

If violence does strike an organization there is often a high cost in terms of morale, reputation, time, and money. Productive time is diverted by violent episodes. While violent acts may not be eliminated, they can be minimized. Situations that might escalate into violence can be predicted and controlled. Recognizing inappropriate actions by an employee or a manager, especially those that can lead to violence, can help us deal with them in time. The issue of organizational liability for not properly addressing violence and its potential is always a high concern. The National Institute for Occupational Health and Safety (NIOSH) estimates that violence at work cost American business $4.2 billion in 1992. Think of that statistic when you emphasize the prevalence and cost of workplace violence.

Improved Productivity and Teamwork

Many of the topics covered in violence prevention training will help people generally communicate and coordinate work better. Supervisors learn skills to more effectively coach and guide people. Good violence prevention training will complement and supplement good basic supervisory training and will improve the communication and comfort in the general working environment.

Positive Impact on Morale

Training provides skills and information to those threatened by the prospect of hostile actions from co-workers, customers, or other people. The anxiety caused by a feeling of helplessness and foreboding wastes both the energy and spirit of people in the organization. Training can remove much of this anxiety by giving people tools for taking more control of negative situations. People appreciate a sincere effort to address problems rather than seeing them swept under the rug.

Checklist 5.4

Training Topics for Managers

✔ Need to model nonviolent relationships

✔ Building trust and respect

✔ Balancing daily demands with violence concerns

✔ Screening out potentially violent job applicants

✔ Intervening in employee disputes

✔ Defusing anger

✔ Proper disciplinary actions against violent behavior

✔ Informal coaching to help improve behavior

✔ Humane termination

✔ Setting up detectors to catch problems at early stages

✔ Responding to employee complaints

✔ Counseling individuals with specific concerns

✔ Discussing violence problems at staff meetings

✔ How to break up a fight without getting hurt

✔ When and how to step into customer relations problems

✔ Working with Human Resource Specialists

✔ How to refer employees for EAP (Employee Assistance Program) help

✔ Listening to, and evaluating employee problems

✔ Spotting early warning signs of violence

✔ Legalities of trespassing and antistalking laws

✔ Keeping helpful documentation

Improved Performance in High Risk Situations

Training points toward sensible behavior before a violent event. During a stressful event people often panic. One of the authors worked in a retail operation where a store manager jumped an armed robber and was shot in the stomach. He survived and when asked why he did such a crazy thing, he just shook his head and said, "Now that I think about it, that wasn't real smart, was it?" Training helps people rehearse and plan to take intelligent action in a low-risk environment.

Important Issues for Management Training

Attitude control is a critical topic to address in violence prevention training. This is especially true for supervisors and managers because attitude drives action. Our experiences have shown that unless those in authority have a proactive attitude they will do little to fulfill an important role in violence prevention. Generally, managers are in a position to spot and constructively deal with potential violent behavior at an early stage. It's important to discuss with supervisors and managers that violent behavior is not the realm of a few "wicked" people. While it may be tempting to categorize people either into "violent" and "nonviolent" categories, this is unrealistic. Like most other expressions of human behavior, violence is better represented by a continuum as in Figure 5.1 below.

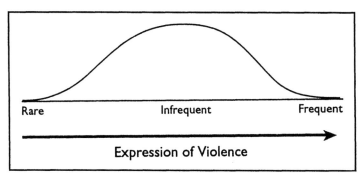

Figure 5.1: Expressions of violence

Responsibility of Supervisors

Supervisors who worry only about the aberrant of the world may overlook basic strategies for reducing the potential for violent acts of "ordinary" people who might suddenly move toward more overt expressions of anger or revenge.

Events in an individual's life will move him or her up or down the violence scale. It is important for supervisors and managers to realize that various pressures move people to violence. We have all seen a normally mild mannered and easygoing person express low levels of violence by slamming doors or throwing things when frustrated or stressed. An event or series of events moved that person up the violence scale. Similarly, other "friendlier" events might move a person down the scale away from violence. (See Figure 5.2.)

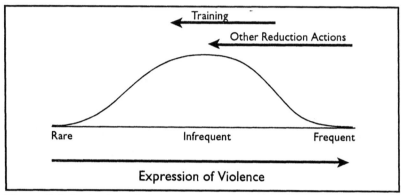

Figure 5.2: Reduction of violence

It is the responsibility of the supervisor to supply positive events, while avoiding or counteracting the negative events as much as possible. When a supervisor assumes an attitude of personal responsibility and influence, the likelihood of positive action is enhanced.

The intent of training—and all other violence prevention strategies——is to reduce events and actions that build towards violent action. This is the power of "negative thinking" at work; by reducing or eliminating those forces that drive toward conflict, violence can be diminished. Perhaps as important, teamwork and morale are simultaneously increased.

It is easier to prevent violence and anger before it builds than to tone it down once present. Many people fervently hope that anger, negative feelings, and the potential for violence will go away by themselves. Wishing alone can create victimization. Supervisors can learn to see the early warning signs of violence. Some of these signs are listed here:

✧ Sudden changes in normal behavior

✧ People who stop communicating directly

✧ Occurrences of horseplay and "practical jokes"

✧ Increasing complaints or grievances

✧ Withdrawal

✧ Absenteeism and tardiness

The presence of these warning signs may not necessarily indicate potential violence, but they are a warning of problems that should be addressed. Avoiding and combating workplace violence is the responsibility of all supervisors. When supervisors ignore danger in the workplace, they are increasingly vulnerable to the resulting lawsuits. For example, a supervisor should be aware that hiring a person with a history of violence could lead to a negligent hiring lawsuit if that person harms another employee or a customer. Supervisors cannot afford to look the other way when violence or hints of potential violence appear. (See Chapter 9.)

Negligent Hiring and Retention

Supervisors should be aware of liability if legal action is brought by employees or customers who are 1) harmed by staff who have a record of violent behavior that was ignored or not revealed due to carelessness in the hiring process, or 2) harmed after a potentially violent situation has not been dealt with aggressively on the job.

Those who interview job candidates should learn to ask questions that uncover potentially violent attitudes and past behaviors. Interview questions should be directed toward relations with past supervisors and co-workers in order to provide helpful clues as to attitudes and behavioral patterns. Reference checking should also explore such attitudes and actions.

It is important to screen and interview job candidates in a manner that itself does not give rise to violence. More than one rejected job candidate has come back to deliver threats because they felt poorly treated in the job interview process.

Failure to Confront Instances of Harassment

If signs of harassment are seen or an employee indicates he or she has received threats or harassment, it is the obligation of management to explore and resolve the problem. Looking the other way may lead to lawsuits. It may also provide implied approval for aggressive behaviors. Harassment should be seen to include not only with sexual harassment, but any form of illegal harassment on the job. It is important to note many organizations have supervisors and managers who themselves treat others abusively—and have been allowed to operate in this manner. As part of an overall violence prevention plan, organizations should set the tone by curbing this kind of behavior—including behavior by people in positions of authority. Experience has shown that telling an employee simply to "stop doing that" has little possibility of creating needed changes. Attending a one-time training class will also probably not effect the full range of desired changes. Chronically abusive supervisors may require ongoing individual guidance so they can learn the new attitudes and skills of handling people in a more humane manner.

Topics for Employee Training

Like supervisors, employees should receive coaching on personal control. Too often the expectation is that the company is responsible for every employee's personal security. While the organization certainly has an obligation to take appropriate measures, staff must also see that they can do a great deal to take personal responsibility for their own safety and well being.

Topics for training all employees in violence prevention training should include:

✧ The organization's approach to human relations

✧ The importance of taking personal control in difficult situations

✧ Harassment policy and how to handle problems

✧ Channels for handling personal problems and complaints

✧ EAP availability

✧ Hot lines and their use

✧ How to handle abuse and threats from co-workers

✧ How to handle abuse and threats from customers

✧ Physical security systems including escape routes and hiding places

✧ Using signal systems to alert others to problems or call for help

✧ Using a team approach to problems

✧ Alerting and keeping supervisors informed about problems

✧ Helping co-workers deal with the aftermath of threats or physical attacks

Of course, organizational and individual needs and resources will help determine which of these specific topics to include, in what order to include them, and how much time to spend on each issue.

Topics for training at-risk employees in violence prevention training include:

✧ Armed robbery procedures

✧ Handling physical threats and attacks

✧ Setting up a safer more secure environment

✧ How to provide police with helpful information

✧ Cash handling to reduce exposure

✧ Protective tips for frequent travelers

At-risk employees should annually review procedures and refresh their ability to avoid and handle violence. It is important to include domestic concerns in the program. Research shows that many workplace assaults stem from a domestic conflict spilling over into the workplace. Therefore, it is important that violence prevention training also address domestic violence issues. This can be planned to do double duty. Many of the same procedures and methods used to detach oneself from a ranting customer can also apply to separate from unsuccessful personal relationships.

Checklist 5.5

Five Questions for a Violence Prevention Training Plan

✔ What topics should be covered?

✔ How the training will be scheduled and delivered?

✔ What methods will be used in during the training?

✔ Who will do the training?

✔ How will the plan be implemented?

Issues to Consider

Moral and Ethical Issues

We understand that many employees feel their employer has no business getting involved in what they do on their own time. However, a company and its managers should address behavior which could adversely affect the workplace environment. For example, if two employees are carrying on an affair, management must decide how to address the situation. In this case, an in-the-know management that ignores the relationship could be liable for negligence if a jealous spouse comes to the plant and does harm.

Designing Training May Reveal Security Needs

In many ways, training becomes a vehicle for laying a more complete foundation for overall violence prevention. The trainer is often a catalyst for unifying overall tactics and strategies. Quite often a training topic will uncover a deficiency in the organization. For example, it is important to train supervisors in how to intercede in an employee dispute. However, it is not unusual to find that there are no standard agreements on how supervisors are expected to handle such situations, nor what to expect in the way of help from contract security staff. Therefore, it is important to train all linkages in a unified approach to violence prevention.

Resources for Training Content

While providing a list of general training topics is easy, the challenge is to expand these topics into high-impact training designs. Start with some basic research to find what information and activities to include in the training, who should receive the training, and who could deliver the training.

The sources listed below can provide valuable ideas for program content. For example, if you are training cash-handling employees in what to do during an armed robbery, a local police authority will probably be able to supply lots of guidance concerning procedures and what to do and not to do. This authority may even be willing to provide some of the direct training.

Training Sources

Your Competitors

Competitors in your field may provide a great source of useful information. Safety training does not generally face the competitive boundaries between organizations. Companies who don't normally talk to one another are willing to exchange information and ideas about how to make the workplace safer. Ask local professional associations which organizations have in-house violence prevention training. Also check on the strengths and limitations of outside sources they have used.

Law Enforcement Agencies

Municipal and State Police Agencies often have an in-house specialist who focuses on workplace violence. The FBI has developed much expertise in this area. Government AgenciesState Occupational Safety and Health organizations are often a prime source for consultation and written material.

Books and Articles

As the subject of violence has gained notoriety, the number of books and articles has proliferated in the past few years.

Checklist 5.6

Topics for Training

✔ Specific issues violence prevention training should address will depend on an organization's needs.

✔ The dynamics of conflict and violence

✔ Attitudinal techniques: How to take control of yourself as early as possible

✔ Internal vs. external sources of violence

✔ Steps individuals can take to reduce and prevent violence

✔ Options for responding to violent actions

✔ Internal relationships

✔ Harassment

✔ Securing facilities, cash, and products

✔ Handling threats

✔ Interceding with other parties

✔ Physical assault

✔ Robbery prevention and response

✔ Bomb threats

✔ Hostage situations

Internet

A search of Internet sites may uncover helpful information. If you are not an adept "surfer" find someone in your organization who knows how to access common search engines such as Alta Vista, Lycos, or Yahoo.

Insurance Companies

Insurance carriers are very concerned with violence issues. (See Chapter 7.) Some, such as State Farm, have produced helpful booklets on domestic violence prevention. Such publications could be helpful for content ideas as well as to be used as an employee handout.

Outside Consultants and Counselors

Because of the rise of violence in the workplace, consulting firms have sprung up to provide assistance. Many firms specialize in physical security and providing security personnel. Unfortunately, such specialists can only offer limited training assistance (mostly slanted towards standard security procedures). Screen "security" firms carefully to ensure that they have the broad view and expertise needed to help you in training design.

How Should the Training Be Scheduled and Delivered?

There are a number of options as to how one can deliver training to employees. The decision will depend at least in part on the business, its needs, and how it is organized.

General Orientation

Because the formal company orientation includes much procedural information, violence issues are usually touched on briefly at best. Many managers are cautious no to start an employee off on an apparently negative footing. But orientation is an appropriate time to reassure new hires with your commitment to protecting their physical well-being and peace of mind. Explain your company's zero tolerance policy, including general guidelines for what an employee should do if confronted with verbal assault or physical violence. If the orientation group is composed entirely of at-risk employees, you might include greater detail material. We suggest every company have a section of their employee manual devoted to violence prevention and control.

Departmental Orientation

Following the general orientation, most departments or teams conduct a more informal orientation for new hires that is more germane to their actual jobs. Part of this briefing should include specific violence prevention training that addresses unique concerns of that group. Most often this orientation is given by people within the work unit. The violence prevention training coordinator should provide guidance and materials to those doing the actual training to ensure that appropriate topics are covered in an effective manner.

Specific Classes

Some violence prevention topics should be addressed in classes designed to give more indepth strategies and techniques. These classes should allow time for answering individual questions, demonstration, and trial of techniques. There should be opportunities for hands-on practice and discussion. Two challenges in any training are to make sure there is careful instructor preparation and to schedule people to actually attend.

Supervisors who manage volatile groups might benefit from a training that provides specific skills and practice on how to confront behavioral problems in a defusing manner, how to intercede in disputes, how to break up fights, and how to appropriately discipline acts of aggression.

It is critical that all violence prevention training trainers are themselves skillful in handling conflicts and confrontations that might arise during a class.

Regular Class on a Different Topic

If the organization is conducting training on customer relations, part of the session could easily be devoted to handling customer anger and confrontational behavior. When supervisors and managers are taught hiring interviewing skills, part of that session might include what questions to ask and clues to look for which help screen out candidates with violence potential. The one major advantage to weaving in violence prevention training into other seminars is that you can save time and integrate this topic into daily issues (which may make it appear less threatening, as well as provide a broader perspective). The disadvantage to this approach is that the violence prevention training message may be lost in a sea of other information.

Group Meetings

The violence prevention trainer can be available to do brief presentations at departmental staff meetings. Many managers are happy to invite visitors to their meetings if for no other reason than offering a change of pace. Being a guest speaker may provide good opportunities for quick hits on key violence prevention issues.

Informal Coaching

Much training takes place informally with one-on-one exchanges or in small groups. The trainer can take advantage of such opportunities to quickly share ideas with specific individuals or groups.

Another benefit of this method is that informal coaching seems personal and focused. It is easier therefore to address individual needs with this approach. The drawback is that training staff individually may not be time efficient—and there is no guarantee staff in need will receive the necessary training.

Printed Training Materials

Although not training in itself, disseminating written materials on violence prevention can support training efforts. Printed materials are easy to distribute and provide a consistent message. Readers also have the opportunity to refer to the information at their convenience as often as they like. Handouts also may provide internal marketing for your live training. The drawback of relying on printed materials is that people may choose not read them. These materials also offer no chance for feedback, discussion, questions, and clarification.

The following are some ways in which printing materials can supplement violence prevention training:

✧ For people who travel alone, you can offer a list of "do's and don'ts" for protecting themselves on the road.

✧ During orientation a few remarks regarding violence in the workplace may be supplemented with some expanded information for wishing more detail.

✧ The company policy of zero tolerance to violence should be posted prominently in appropriate places.

✧ Mailers to employees can be an effective way to offer information on improving domestic conflicts, home security, and personal safety. Many employees and their families will appreciate this expression of concern for their welfare and safety. To avoid appearing to be overly intrusive, it might be best to have employees sign up to receive these materials.

What Methods Will Be Used in the Training?

After selecting the content, the next step is to develop the best training delivery methods. Too often, lecture is used in violence prevention training. While lecturing can be a time efficient way to deliver information, some overriding weaknesses: it doesn't allow for trial of a range of techniques for conflict management and it precludes participants' actively examining the strengths and limitations of their default conflict responses.

Learning Principles

Here are key learning principles as applied to violence prevention training:

Physical and Mental Readiness

Training should be scheduled when people are alert and not under so much stress that they are distracted from calmly getting perspective on their current behaviors. Immediately after a violent incident, it is preferable to support affected individuals, rather than rush them into a training session (to "correct" their inadequate responses).

The facilities should be as conducive to learning as possible. Adequate notice should be given to people so they are able to arrange their work schedules properly. The objectives of the training should be clear and positive.

Value

People learn what they think is beneficial to them. Training should begin with a clear statement of personal benefits (e.g., to boost confidence in handling difficult situations, to improve personal control, to help one become more persuasive, is applicable in home as well as work situations, etc.).

Active Involvement

People learn more by doing than by listening. Training should design in as much involvement as possible. Here are some methods for involving people:

- ✧ Discussions
- ✧ Poll for opinions and experiences

✧ Case situations with discussion

✧ Question and answer periods

✧ Role play situations

✧ Divide into teams to work on a problem or make recommendations

One thing to remember about involvement—it should never put people on the spot or cause embarrassment. Therefore, it's always better to ask for volunteers and invite participation than to call on someone by name and demand a response.

Multiple Exposures

People often don't get the impact of an idea until they have heard it more than once. A key to aid retention is to enlist the power of repetition by introducing ideas, then expanding on them, and then summarizing them at the end of the training. Referring back to previous ideas is another way to fortify information and skills. Our experience has been that issues of violence are often emotionally wrenching to most people and their ability to concentrate may be diminished because of that. When this dynamic occurs, reiteration helps get ideas across.

Practical

All training should boil down to helping people make realistic behavioral and attitudinal changes—at work and at home. It is critical in violence prevention training to illustrate all theories or philosophies with practical suggestions for implementation, anecdotes, and methods.

Reinforcement

Information begins to fade immediately after people leave a training session. It is important that training be reinforced through follow up of some kind. This may be through individual contact or with written reminders, handouts, company newsletter articles, postings on bulletin boards, follow up training, etc.

Supported

What is said in training must be consistent with organizational policies and procedures for violence prevention. If you instruct employees to carry their concerns to their immediate supervisor, it is critical these supervisors have the training, availability, and receptivity to receive violence-related concerns.

Who Presents the Training?

There are three options here, each with advantages and shortcomings: trainers, service agency representatives, and nontraining personnel.

Trainer

If your organization already has available training professionals, they may be a natural choice. They are comfortable with training and hopefully proficient at conveying information and skills. However, they may have many training demands to compete for their time and energy. They may also lack credibility regarding specific violence topics. It is possible for staff to develop specific content proficiency during a 5-day violence prevention training train the trainer program.

Service Agency Representative

As mentioned above, a representative from the local police department or a governmental agency may be available to provide all or part of the violence prevention training. These professionals have developed areas of specific expertise and using them may save you of time and money. Be sure to work closely with outside trainers to ensure they provide training relevant to your organization's needs. Check the individual's references as a trainer. Some subject matter experts are deadly presenters. It's important that poor outside speakers not trample the reputation of your program.

Nontraining Personnel

The great value of using internal line workers or supervisors as trainers is their credibility with peers. They know the work and can help make the training practical. The downside is that you will have to provide strong guidance and coaching to ensure that they train well. Often a line employee can be used to assist the regular trainer by presenting sections of the training.

Once the detail of training content, delivery method, and teaching assignments has been made, the final step is to implement the plan. Following are a few suggestions for doing so effectively.

Documentation

All training plans should be well documented. Documentation ensures consistency and provides a baseline for future development. Documents become important sources to others who work on the violence prevention training. Here is a suggested format for individual seminar lesson plans using a section of supervisory training as an example:

Time: 9:00 to 9:45

Topic: Breaking Up a Fight

Objective: Teach supervisors a safe and effective way to stop a physical fight.

Sample Content:
1. Disperse any observers. This helps relieve ego tensions.
2. Don't get physically involved. It may be seen as taking sides.
3. Protect yourself.
4. Assess the level of violence (just beginning, explosive, etc.).
5. Get the fighters' attention.
6. Consider using distractions (voice, drawing their visual attention, etc.).
7. Don't reason, deal with the "energetic." Focus on lowering their energy level.

Methods:
✧ Present the steps using an overhead.
✧ Role play an example for the group.
✧ Break into teams of three and have them role play a situation with one person using the steps with the two "employees."

Implementing the Violence Prevention Training Plan

Promote the violence prevention training in a positive manner. Much safety oriented training assumes a "let me straighten you out" tone. People naturally resent and resist such an approach. Make sure violence prevention training and follow up written materials are convey a positive, helpful, nonaccusatory tone.

Get Supervisors on Your Side

As mentioned above, first line supervisors provide a critical defense against workplace violence. Ways to gain supervisory support for the training include the following:

✧ Asking their advice and input when designing the various parts of the program

✧ Asking and incorporating their ideas for how best to schedule the training

✧ Including some of them as instructors for sections of the training

✧ Checking with them to see how the training is going for their people

✧ Being available as much as possible to provide coaching or advice on violence issues

✧ Never criticizing supervisors or managers in your remarks, whether they are present on not

✧ Scheduling the program realistically. Most organizations are operating under increasingly demanding time restraints. Therefore, schedule the violence prevention training to be compatible with other demands. Reduce the time that employees are away from high-demand jobs. Consider scheduling training in shorter blocks, rather than in one longer session. Convey violence prevention training during slower work periods.

Make It a Company Project

Make sure the program presents a united front. It is critical that violence prevention training is seen as a company endorsed activity with management backing, not as the pet project of only one person. To boost program impact:

✧ Have a top manager introduce the program.

✧ Include an executive name and signature on written material.

✧ Weave other security efforts into your presentations.

✧ Make sure the organization supports what you present.

✧ Don't allow training participants to make light of violent behavior. Sometimes people try to lighten a heavy subject with inappropriate humor.

❖ Keep training groups small. For increased interaction and trial of techniques, ideal training group size is below fifteen, where participants will be able to surface underlying concerns.

❖ Check your progress. Solicit a range of feedback on the effectiveness of the training. Some organizations conduct regular written surveys to inquire about employee opinions. Some questions could be directed toward the violence prevention training program and violence prevention measures in general.

Conclusion

It seems that many organizations have seen an increase in abusive behavior. To maintain control of business focus and to reduce organizational and employee exposure, it is important to reduce violent behavior. Well designed Violence Prevention Training is an critical element in any initiative for protecting your company and your people.

References

Barker, T. "How to prevent violence in the workplace." *Safety & Health*, July 1994.

Cawood, J. "On the edge: Assessing the violent employee." *Security Management*, Sept 1991.

Glass, L. *Toxic People*, Simon & Schuster, 1995.

Kinney, J. *Violence at Work*, Prentice Hall, 1995.

Kroehnert, G. *Basic Training for Trainers*, McGraw-Hill, 1995 (2nd edition).

Laird, D. *Approaches to Training and Development*, Addison Wesley, 1991 (3rd edition).

Labig, C. *Preventing Violence in the Workplace*, Amacom, 1995.

Oregon OSHA Department of Consumer and Business Services, *Guidelines for Preventing Violence in the Workplace*, 1996.

Pater, R. and Russell, R. *Quality Assurance for Training*, an unpublished paper by Strategic Safety Associates.

Chapter Six

- ❑ Role of security in responding to potentially violent situations
- ❑ Responsibilities of private security personnel
- ❑ Components of workplace security assessment
- ❑ Factors in hiring and training qualified security officers
- ❑ Problems with using surveillance

The Role of Security in Preventing Violence at Work

John T. Horn, MS

Case Study

An employee who has been put on notice and sent home for a pattern of repeatedly threatening a coworker drives up to the front of the building the next day. He walks into the lobby carrying a gun and tells the receptionist he is looking for his manager to settle things.

Introduction

For a number of years now, it has been widely reported that private security is the primary means, when measured by numbers of employees and expenditures, for securing personnel, facilities, and other corporate assets in the United States. Because of how security services are provided, it should be clear that private security is not intended to be an extension or mirror image of law enforcement.

Private security and law enforcement personnel, for the most part, are uniformed and in the private sector, may or may not be armed. Although they have similar objectives, there are differences in purpose, methods, and focus.

In the case of law enforcement, statute requires that the public interest in the community at large, as promulgated by codified ordinances, laws, and various rules and regulations, be served. In the case of the private sector, codification is to be found in organizational policies and procedures and, of course, the public interest is reinterpreted as being the maintenance of access control and security within a specified organization. In this environment, access by the general public may be denied, except for local authorities.

Objectives for Private Security Personnel

The primary objectives for private security personnel can be identified as follows:

✧ To establish and control security at the perimeter of a facility or at entrance locations to prevent access by unauthorized individuals or vehicles

✧ To conduct periodic watch tours or patrol of facilities for the purpose of identifying hazardous conditions, unusual situations, or suspicious activities and observing specific events

✧ To respond and assist in the event of emergencies

✧ To be otherwise helpful to the organization, as directed

In either of the latter two objectives, security personnel may come into contact with situations of potential workplace violence.

The role of security officers in dealing with situations of potential workplace violence depends on a variety of considerations. Those considerations include the nature and character of the workplace environment, the culture and values of the

organization, the level of professionalism of the security force, as well as their training, staffing, and resources. A little later in this chapter, in reviewing a number of hypothetical situations, we will explore alternatives that will suggest the appropriate role of workplace security officers.

Qualifications of Private Security Personnel

In order to establish basic qualifications for involvement or participation in this type of crisis management, let's address several scenarios. For discussion's sake, we have identified three levels of workplace violence:

Level A

"Suspicions," hearing indirect statements by an employee, reports of aggravated domestic, recreational, or social incidents, out-of-character behavior

Level B

Threats, intimidating conduct, acts of harassment and/or hostility, displays of anger, aggression, obvious frustration, "tantrums," stalking

Level C

Violent events or incidents on company property, such as serious confrontations with co-workers or members of supervision or management, assaults, displays of firearms.

The company objective should be to resolve each situation safely. If, by inserting unqualified personnel—whether security officers, supervision, or professionals—we make the situation worse or perhaps put people at risk, we have failed. Failure most certainly affects the people immediately involved, but it also dramatically increases liability for other individuals and the organization and causes damage to the company's reputation.

Essential qualifications for all security officers should be maturity and judgment based on training and experience or education. Clearly, a security officer

hired at near the minimum wage with limited training and whose usual duties and responsibilities are to serve as a receptionist or to log trucks in and out—in effect a watchman—should not be expected to personally deal with emotionally charged situations.

On the other hand, if the organization has on staff a corporate security director, one who has achieved the position based on standard professional qualifications, i.e., a Certified Protection Professional (CPP) or an individual with significant education, training and experience, there should be every expectation that the person has the maturity, judgment, and leadership skills to react appropriately to almost every situation.

While there are no clearly set distinctions regarding the use of security personnel, certain characteristics become obvious. Large corporations engaged in production operations with significant investments in plant and personnel will usually have the more professional security operation. Security becomes a less critical issue in smaller organizations, especially in urban environments with higher percentages of professional or administrative employees where there may be a reliance on response by law enforcement personnel.

What to Expect from Security

In developing a plan to deal with workplace violence, management has to first candidly assess the mission and capabilities of their security organization, the nature and purpose of their function, their personnel, and their capacity to take on additional responsibility or respond appropriately in prospective emergency situations involving workplace violence.

In some instances, because of the limited capabilities and restricted role of security personnel at a particular site, company management would be better served by notifying local police when any of the three previously mentioned levels of violence occur. An alternative might be to establish a relationship with a workplace violence or crisis management consulting group that has capabilities to assist in areas of policy, strategy, and response.

Where there are significant capabilities among security personnel and they have a broad mandate to provide security protection, it is incumbent on the employer to make the security function part of the crisis management team and depend on it to play a significant role in working toward resolution of threatening situations.

Normally, the security organization would be the unit to establish and maintain the incident history record within an organization. This record would provide data on past incidents, events and activities that have taken place on company property,

the identities of those involved, details of precipitating activity, and/or follow-up events, related actions including interviews, evidence collection, medical treatment and ultimate disposition, if any, regarding the reported event. In a historical context, during the incipient stages of a current event, especially a serious event, these records take on a much greater value especially as a predictor of future individual behavior, than their initial collection and maintenance for statistical purposes would suggest.

Special benefits of the involvement of professional security personnel include extensive knowledge of the property facilities and operations, familiarity with the workforce as a whole and, most likely, many individual employees, and perhaps most important, a familiarity with the culture and values of the organization. Additional intangible benefits accrue to crisis managers if security personnel have earned the respect of employees, maintain good relationships and are recognized as being part of an effective security operation.

Let's reexamine the role of a fully functioning security organization in the context of the three levels of violence mentioned earlier.

Level A Scenario

Co-workers reported "suspicious" hearsay or indirect statements by an employee, reports of incidents away from the workplace, or out of character behavior. The "empowered" security organization could be expected to review security files for records of previous incidents involving the subject employee(s). Records might reflect a history of previous, similar types of incidents. In that case, frequency, degree of seriousness, and target or focus of the behavior might reveal a pattern. If a pattern exists, does the current behavior fit within the boundaries of that pattern or is it outside the boundaries? All of the above data is important and useful information that should be able to be obtained from the incident reporting system of the security organization.

If appropriate, a senior security organization member could be tasked to act as liaison with local law enforcement, access public records, and generally delve into the background of the subject.

As a participant in the crisis evaluation team, the senior security person would be expected to comment and offer opinions as other company records are reviewed. These opinions might address the context of the reported issues, the reliability of the individual reporting the events or incidents and, perhaps, relationships of various parties, if known. This person, by virtue of experience and training, should be able to suggest strategies for addressing the instant situation. Strategies, typically based on the concept of progressive discipline, might range from continued observation without immediate action to focused interview and referral to an Employee Assistance Program (EAP).

Level B Scenario

Level B, of workplace violence might be characterized by threats, intimidating behavior, and/or displays of anger or hostility. At this stage, a determination needs to be made as to whether company rules have been broken and, if so, what sort of response the organization wishes to make. The security officer, as in Scenario A, assists in data collection outside the company and may become involved internally by interviewing witnesses and other knowledgeable individuals. Again, the security officer helps evaluate findings and develops strategy. Disciplinary strategies, again based on organizational precedent, may range from employee counseling, closer supervision, written or verbal warnings, and paid or unpaid suspensions— with or without Employee Assistance Program treatment requirements. On the other hand, if the incident appears to be caused by a medical illness (prescription drugs, etc.), psychological or physical problem (stress, overwork, alcoholism, etc.), a nondisciplinary solution may be more appropriate. Strategies may include referral for evaluation by medical professionals, appropriate treatment on either an inpatient or outpatient basis, or a leave of absence.

Level C Scenario

In contrast to the previous scenarios, at this level of workplace violence, there may be a violation of statute, ordinance, or breaking of law. The security force may have responded to the incident in progress and taken immediate action as necessary, including escorting the instigator off company property, if a suspension is ordered, or summoning police authorities to take appropriate action. The role of the security force in this instance may include first aid for the victim, assistance in making a complaint to law enforcement authorities, and perhaps some sort of arrangement for protection or special attention for others involved when they leave company property.

The situations described are intended to be realistic, fairly common scenarios. The limited data provided is intended only to assist in establishing perspective or degrees of reaction and response. In no way are they complete or comprehensive, but instead intended to illustrate some of the duties that may be ascribed to the security officer.

Workplace Security Assessment

It is important to briefly review the issue of physical security when discussing the role of security officers in providing a safe place at work. The fact that there have been instances when even the most secure of workplaces have been the scene for violence supports the truism that "there can be no guarantees." As a practical matter, workplace violence is most frequently perpetrated by a person familiar with the environment of the workplace, such as a co-worker, former employee, spouse or "significant other," service contractor, supplier, etc.

The concept of an appropriate level of security can be illusory. Except in regulated environments, such as Department of Defense, Nuclear Regulatory Commission and certain Aviation facilities the determination of an acceptable level of security can be very subjective. Factors that go into establishing a security profile include the attitudes of management, values and culture of the organization, local environment, size of the organization, types of facility, number of employees and nature of the business.

Checklist 6.1

Workplace Security Assessment

Organization Features

✔ Attitude of management

✔ Values and culture of organization

✔ Local environment

✔ Organization Size

✔ Types of Facilities

✔ Nature of business

Physical Security

✔ Electronic security equipment

✔ Clearly designated property lines

✔ Use of gate arms, speed bumps, signs

✔ Designation of interior areas as public, common, proprietary

✔ Control of exterior and interior space

Policies, Practices, and Procedures

✔ Limit access to areas by time of day

✔ Define access of contractors, vendors and other service personnel

✔ Develop guidelines for visitors and other nonemployees

✔ Outline unacceptable behaviors

Security Officers

✔ Qualifications

✔ Training

✔ Presence

A preliminary assessment of security at the workplace must consider three components: 1) physical and electronic security equipment, systems, and devices, 2) policies, practices, and procedures and 3) the presence of security officers. To briefly elaborate, physical security equipment refers to fences, gates, locks, lighting, and temporary or permanent barricades set either manually or automatically. Electronic security systems would include alarms, sensors, readers, intercoms, badge accessing systems, and CCTV/video recording. Policies, practices, and procedures refer to documents that control or limit access of individuals/employees, vendors/service personnel, and visitors, to various areas by time of day and/or day of week. These written documents, often part of an employee handbook, also define prohibited actions, behavior, and conduct. The term "security officers" can apply to contract or proprietary security personnel or off-duty law enforcement officers.

Contemporary security theory seeks to provide security through environment design. At the property's perimeter, this concept refers to clearly designated property lines, gate arms, speed bumps, and signage. Interior to buildings, it means designations such as tenant space (private), semiprivate areas, and public areas. Typically, as one passes from public areas to private space, more controls are encountered. The controls may be systems and equipment, policies, practices and procedures, security officers, or a combination of these controls.

In the context of employee concerns about workplace violence, the presence of these controls for access can be very comforting. If they don't exist, start-up capital costs for systems and equipment can be very expensive. The same can be said for manpower. A contract security officer, at a rate of $10.00 an hour, assigned to a 24-hour, seven-day-a-week post will cost $20,800. The cost for a proprietary security officer will be higher. Company policies and procedures, which codify conduct and behavior, are the least costly of the security components. However, in a realistic world, policies and procedures are for the purpose of communicating workplace rules. They are a deterrent to those with whom some leverage exists. In and of themselves, they do not constitute a level of physical protection.

Security Officers: Qualifications and Training

In addition to the discussion in the previous section, two major considerations, both involving security officers, come to mind. The first is the recruitment, selection, and employment of qualified security officers. The second consideration is training.

Before addressing these considerations, let's examine the range of roles or duties and responsibilities of security officers. Depending on the attitude of the organization, security can be perceived as a necessary nuisance or an important contributor to the mission of organizations. Security officers may watch hub caps in the company parking lot, do watch tours and monitor production systems and plant utilities, control access, perform receptionist duties, carry out emergency response and/or other routine functions, or they may be proactive individuals actively participating in or initiating problem solving.

In nearly every case, the presence of a security officer can be a deterrent. If security officers are properly selected, trained, and supervised and if they have reasonable communications skills, experience, and judgment, they should perform properly. However, as mentioned, cost is sometimes an inhibiting factor to the employment of well-qualified security officers. In other cases, it is the failure of the retaining organization to stipulate in the contract with a security agency the qualifications of individuals being sought. Many organizations leave it to the agency to provide the number of weekly security officer hours with little regard for stipulating qualifications and stating performance expectation.

Qualifications

It is the responsibility of the organization to specify the qualifications of the personnel to whom they will entrust the safety and welfare of their employees and the security of their property. It is not unreasonable to ask for a minimum of actual or related experience (five years), education (high school or GED) and training (40 hours classroom plus reasonable on-the-job training at the

Checklist 6.2
Qualifications of Security Personnel
✔ Minimum experience (five years)
✔ Education (high school or GED)
✔ Training
✔ Physically active
✔ Good judgment
✔ Common sense
✔ Courtesy
✔ Ability to act with restraint
✔ Good attitude
✔ Sense of Fairness

work site), and that the person be physically fit and active and possess good judgment and common sense. Also, someone in the organization should individually review each candidate's application or resume and conduct a personal interview with those who would be working on company property. In this way, facility management can be an active part of the process. The personal evaluation should assess attitude, courtesy, fairness, and the candidate's capacity to act with restraint. (This can be evaluated by asking "what if" questions to which the candidate has to respond with a description of how they would handle a given situation).

Training

The second major consideration is training. Readily available are a wide variety of seminars, programs (written, audio, and video), consultants, and trainers. Numerous publications, studies, and articles in professional journals appear each year adding to a rapidly growing collection of material on the subject of private security. There is something in the training marketplace for any organization.

However, some of the most useful types of programs are crisis exercises or gaming programs. The theory behind gaming is that it makes more sense to practice and make mistakes in an exercise than in real time when the consequences could be fatal and/or result in damaged reputation, litigation, employee morale problems or business interruption. In terms of value for money spent, these three considerations—selection, training, and exercises—will give the greatest return on investment.

Role of Local Law Enforcement

Depending on the community where the organization is located, local law enforcement can be a significant resource or a slow responder to an emergency. While these two characterizations are at opposite extremes, it is reasonable to expect law enforcement reaction/response. Capabilities will vary depending on the community.

The role of local law enforcement is to enforce statutes and laws governing that jurisdiction. When infractions occur, the authorities are empowered to take action. Depending on the seriousness of the infraction, the officer can make an arrest at the scene or take a complaint and make a written report for later presentation to an officer of the court, who may or may not authorize an arrest.

Generally speaking, if an offense occurs in an officer's presence, he is obliged to take some sort of action. The action the officer takes may or may not be the action desired by the company (warning, citation, arrest).

Frequently, the presence of an officer subsequent to an incident, or follow-up by an investigating officer, affects a change in an offending individual's conduct or behavior. In some instances, this may be the only intervention needed.

There is no rule of thumb for when to call local law enforcement. Certainly, the organization must call authorities when a serious incident, especially injury or death, has occurred. In that scenario, they have primary jurisdiction. The role of the security officer in such an instance is to assist and support police, as necessary.

In less serious but chronic situations, it may be very beneficial to notify law enforcement authorities. Their training and experience with the law can crystallize issues so that informed judgments and decisions can more easily be made. Intervention by police can also have the salutary benefit of transferring to authorities responsibility for addressing, in the short term, the unacceptable behavior or conduct of the hostile person on company property.

Generally, police are summoned to handle the most serious incidents like those in Level C Scenario. They are usually capable of responding quickly, in numbers, with necessary resources. They are highly trained and well qualified to deal with such events.

On the other hand, to present them with a routine Level A Scenario may not provide the desired results and may, in fact, aggravate the situation.

Use of Surveillance

Surveillance has many downsides and few upsides. Let's look at the downsides first. Clandestine surveillance can go on for extended periods of time with no remarkable observations or conclusions. If it involves direct interaction with a suspect or undercover surveillance, it will take time to develop a relationship where a certain level of mutual trust and sharing or confidence can occur. When surveillance is at a distance, you are always in a position of having to try to anticipate movement, or, once on the move, losing the subject in transit. Surveillance, because of the duration and possibly the numbers of members of a surveillance team involved, can become very expensive, very quickly. Surveillance is not without risks. One is that the existence of a surveillance may be compromised and lead to serious employee morale problems. Also, if the subject is alerted, it may put those performing the surveillance in jeopardy and the organization at significant liability.

If the surveillance is electronic in nature, there are limitations. First, electronic surveillance may not be conducted in locations where there is a reasonable expectation of privacy (i.e., rest rooms and locker rooms). Secondly, total surveillance of an area usually requires a significant investment in equipment, maintenance, and monitoring. Thirdly, depending on the environment, employees may develop a perception that the surveillance is not in place to protect them but to spy on them, that a performance or production monitoring technique has been installed.

Coordination with Other Parts of the Organization

Issues related to the conduct and behavior of employees are normally the responsibilities of company human resources personnel or employee relations departments. On a day-to-day basis, these responsibilities are to some extent delegated to staff or line supervision. When an unusual situation occurs, like one of the previously described scenarios, a team approach is an appropriate way to respond. The bringing together of various disciplines to support the personnel function—security, legal, administrative or production supervision, and possibly medical or an EAP representative—can greatly expand access to important information as well as assist in determination of reasonable or alternative strategies for dealing with any and all situations. Each of the mentioned resources brings to the table a different perspective and set of experiences. All can contribute to the situational "field of knowledge" as well as take responsibility for completion of relevant tasks, as determined by the group, in a timely fashion. With moderation, the more resources available to problem-solving group, the better the outcome.

Conclusion

The qualified security organization has a key role to play and direct, but shared, responsibility for the outcome of potential workplace violence situations.

From the discussions in this chapter, as well as in the other chapters of this book, one can clearly see there are no simple or standard solutions that might be invoked to deal with these situations. Because of individual human personalities, the degree of emotional content of any given situation, the extent or absence of self control or effective organizational controls, and many other factors, these situations can be highly unpredictable and potentially very risky.

Many security initiatives can be taken but all must be measured against a candid appraisal of the quality, capabilities, and resources of the security staff.

References

Cunningham, W., Strachs, J., VanMeter, C. *Hallcrest Report II*, Butterworth and Heinemann, 1990.

Fay, J.J. *Encyclopedia of Security Management*, Butterworth & Heinemann. 1993 edition.

Post, R.S., Schactsiek, D.A. *Security Managers Desk Reference*, Butterworth and Heinemann, 1986 edition.

Purpura, P.P. *Security and Loss Prevention*, Butterworth & Heinemann, 2nd edition, 1991.

Sennenwald, C. *Effective Security Management*, Butterworth & Heinemann, 1985 edition.

Walsh, T. (Editor). *Protection of Assets Manual*, Merritt, 1977.

Chapter Seven

❏ Risk Assessment as the first step in protecting employees, property, and customers

❏ Establishing and enforcing policies and procedures concerning threats and intimidation

❏ Access control and perimeter design as a means to ensure building security

❏ Emergency response system designed to handle to a variety of risk and threat scenarios

❏ Specific training for employees who travel

❏ Actions that can reduce one's risk of general liability or security liability

Risk Management

Warren F. Miller, ARM, ALCM

Case Study

A computer repair technician showed up at lunchtime and spoke to the relief receptionist. He showed her his work order and explained that he was there to remove and repair the computers. She asked, "Which ones?" "All of them," he explained. The regular receptionist returned early from lunch and called the police who found almost every computer from the office—even their server unit that contained all their files and records—loaded in a van. Sheer luck prevented a huge loss.

Introduction

Workplace violence can have many different impacts on your risk management program. If you have a significant incident, some of your traditional insurance programs will be affected as well as areas of your risk management program that rely on risk retention. As an example, robberies not only create the loss of cash or goods, but may result in injury or death of one or more employees. In addition to the physical and emotional harm and tragic loss of life, such violent incidents will also cause problems with your workers' compensation insurance program. Repeated robberies may impact the company's ability to hire qualified employees, and the quality of service or products may diminish. Your company's reputation in the marketplace may suffer, thus putting you at a competitive disadvantage, leading to loss of income and cash flow problems. Eventually you may be out of business. Dramatic, yes, but it is a realistic possibility.

Another more common example might be a simple case of harassment and intimidation that leads to a fist fight resulting in an injury. If management takes no action with these participants, there could be a perception by other employees that lack of management action led to this fight and injury, and as a result they would not feel secure from this kind of harassment. Turnover or a significant decline in employee morale could result. Supervisors may also be frustrated by their inability to deal effectively with the harassment. This is a small risk management problem that could grow larger. Continued intimidation by a group of employees might lead to a lawsuit by those who are being harassed. If another employee is assaulted it might lead to a suit based on negligent retention. Or again, the company may have difficulty in attracting and keeping qualified employees. And so on.

There are a number of actions a business can take to minimize the risk of a violent episode, such as developing, communicating, and enforcing policies and procedures, ensuring building security, good facility maintenance, and specific training for employees at risk. Risk management reduces the frequency of problems and ensures you are prepared if problems occur.

Violence Prevention and Risk Management

Attention to prevention of workplace violence should be incorporated into your regular risk management activities. Loss control activities can reduce the chance of an incident occurring and also the severity of an incident if one does happen. As with loss control activities to control other exposures, the most effective actions are a combination of policies, procedures, work practices, and the physical condition of the premises. Management, supervisors, and employees need to work together if the program is going to be effective. For example, if you have taken action to increase exterior door security, but the employees prop open a rear door for a smoke break near their work area, this diminishes the effectiveness of the door security. Good training and enforcement of policies can overcome this.

In addition to the prevention efforts, your program should include post-incident activities to reduce the impact on your organization. Critical Incident Stress Debriefing (see Chapter 5) can reduce the impact on both the people and finances in the organization. You should also do a post-incident investigation, similar to an accident investigation, to determine how this can be prevented from happening again. Evaluation of policies, procedures, work practices currently in place, and other necessary actions are a part of an effective program.

Another consideration is OSHA. At the time of this writing, there have not been any standards issued by OSHA regarding workplace violence, although there have been guidelines issued for the Health Care Industry. Labor Secretary Robert Reich has been quoted as saying that OSHA would pursue any actions against companies for workplace violence under the "general duty clause" of the OSHA standards. Part of the delay in issuing a standard is the lack of consensus among industry groups, labor, and safety professionals about how this issue should be addressed. There are many different approaches to the issue of workplace violence. Lack of standards doesn't mean that companies can let this reside on the back burner. A serious incident involving workplace deaths will most likely result in an investigation and action by OSHA against your company.

As with other worker safety issues, you will want to be able to document the effective actions that were taken to prevent an incident from happening. While fines may still result, you may be able to get significant reductions of the dollars as a result of demonstrating your good-faith efforts. A review of the Health Care Industry guidelines that were issued by OSHA is a good way to begin to understand the integrated approach that can be taken in a workplace violence prevention program.

Risk Assessment

One of the first steps in risk management is to determine where the violence is most likely to come from at your company. The violence generally comes from one of three areas: robbery and random violence, internal workplace violence from co-workers or former employees, and domestic violence that spills over into the workplace. Evaluate each of these three areas for exposures and the subsequent plans or actions that can be taken to reduce or eliminate opportunities for violence. Another way to assess exposures is to determine which employees are most at risk. Those employees most frequently subject to violence are employees with public contact, employees working in isolation, and employees handling money or perceived to be handling money. Which jobs meet these criteria? Those people are most at risk. Then consider program activities that can reduce their exposure. For example, the receptionist is probably the first point of contact for someone entering your business. The receptionist may be separated from the rest of the office in the entrance area or simply be distant from co-worker desks. Visitors may notice that the receptionist handles petty cash or has personal money nearby. This job meets all three criteria as someone at a higher risk.

There are some things that can be done to reduce this person's risk level. Install some type of physical separation from visitors such as a wall with a window and a door release buzzer to prevent those who don't belong inside from progressing past the lobby area. Also, install a system to discreetly call for assistance. While these actions would not eliminate all risks for the receptionist, they would significantly improve safety and security. While many businesses feel the need to appear open, friendly and ready to do business, in today's environment both employees and customers expect and accept a higher level of security. They will both cooperate and understand if policies are clear and apply to everyone equally.

Robberies and random violence prevention should be a top priority. Depending on your type of business this is probably the area of greatest risk. Robbery is the major exposure to violence for any retail trade business, especially so for food and gas station/mini-marts. However, any business has robberies and random violence exposures that need to be addressed. Every business needs to be concerned about building security, parking lots, service or installation workers, and traveling employees. (See Chapter 13, "Service Occupations and Workplace Violence.")

To reduce internal workplace violence, policies and procedures addressing threats, harassment, and intimidation are probably the number one action a company can take. Of course, strict enforcement of these policies should take place.

Domestic violence spillover is discussed in Chapter 11. This is a real exposure that companies often fail to recognize and incorporate into their overall program. Don't ignore this threat source; every company of every kind can experience this. You can do a lot to convince your employees that you are serious about workplace violence prevention by including domestic violence prevention in a well-rounded program. A risk management program not addressing this issue leaves open a big gap in their risk assessment.

Building Security

Business Premises

Controlling access to your facility and what goes on around your building and property has a significant impact on many different components of your risk management plan. The concept of combining access control with surveillance is put forth in a book by Timothy D. Crowe titled *Crime Prevention Through Environmental Design*. This concept works very well when designing new buildings or renovating space. It also has practical application for existing buildings and businesses. Controlling access and improving visibility in and around the facility can improve safety and security. Mr. Crowe provides excellent examples for application in a variety of situations. The use of locks, access cards, and lighting is best described by documents devoted to those types of items. An excellent reference source is the *Handbook of Loss Prevention and Crime Prevention* by Lawrence Fennelly.

Building security should separate those who belong on the premises from those who don't. People having business in the workplace are those who belong; others should be limited to reception areas. This is sometimes difficult to observe in actual practice. Let's look at several examples.

Office Environment

The first example is an office operation with no direct retail, that is service oriented, and has phone operations. The general public and visitors would be limited to the reception area. Former employees, family, and friends also are limited to the reception area. This helps reduce risk in all areas of exposure but is especially helpful in reducing domestic violence and that from disgruntled former employees. Vendors, such as the printer/copier repairer and vending machine service people, can go into the work area, but only after they check in and receive approval each time. Locked doors, badges, and clearly written and posted policies are the best method for controlling access.

Manufacturing Plant

Much the same criteria would apply at a manufacturing plant. Here, there are also delivery drivers to consider. Drivers should be restricted to a specific area, preferably a separate room designated for their use. Conflicts frequently arise between outside drivers and loading dock employees. A room with phones available works very well in keeping drivers satisfied. This access restriction complements another aspect of your risk management program—because of the liability you don't want nonemployee drivers using equipment like dock plates or machines such as forklift trucks. Customers or suppliers may have business both on the shop floor and in the office area. Again, a sign-in system at the front desk and the issuance of visitor badges can work well for these important people.

Retail Location

The third example is a supermarket. On the retail floor you want lots of customers. Access here is more than open; it's inviting. A higher level of security is maintained for the storeroom; you don't want customers there. A big sign on the swinging doors stating "Employees Only" will keep most everyone out. Then you need to train employees to watch for customers who don't belong and help them back to the retail floor. Vendors should have access to the back room but only when they have been identified and authorized. The highest level of security is for the money handling room. This door is locked! Only a restricted number of employees should have access here. This area is often raised up from the main floor, with windows so that employees can see what is going on around them.

These varying levels of security provide the appropriate level of access to the facility based on the different needs of employees, vendors, delivery and service personnel, customers, and family members.

Parking Lot

In parking lot security the phrase to remember is "clean and well lighted." Good lighting, without any places of concealment, works to deter crime. While landscaping is nice, it often provides a place for criminals to hide. The space from two feet off the ground through seven feet above ground level should be kept clear. Generally this provides a good line of sight so that potential trouble can be avoided. Bright lighting contributes to good visibility and discourages vandals or others who might rob or assault employees or customers. Fencing, security cameras, and guard patrols can increase safety even more.

Parking garages are a special problem. Lighting can be difficult and there are often places for criminals to hide, such as stairwells, behind pillars and between vehicles. Restricted access to the garage at ground level helps, as do security patrols and video surveillance cameras.

For parking security, one reasonably low-cost idea that your company may be able to implement is to have employees who will be working into the evening go out to their cars in late afternoon (4:00 PM) and move their vehicles to a designated area closer to the building. Choose an area that has better lighting and better visibility from the building. Also, with the vehicles concentrated in one area, the employees who are leaving in the evening may be able to support one another. Make it company policy, not an option, that vehicles must be moved. This removes the pressure from people who may be reluctant to ask for help, or who get pressure from their managers to keep working. All employees and managers follow the policy. This process is low cost and sends a strong message about the company's concern for safety. Look for other ways to increase security for parking areas.

Building Security Lapses

Control of building access has other benefits that go beyond direct-assault prevention. Lack of building access control is often cited as a factor that leads to loss of personal property or company property. One manager explained her outrage at her co-workers for allowing someone posing as a maintenance person to enter her office, rifle through her purse and personal items, steal what he wanted, and then just walk out. Her office was located beyond all the other work spaces. In another example, in a multistory, multitenanted building, a person dressed in maintenance clothes and pushing a large, gray plastic trash container loaded with light bulbs went to many offices in the building apparently checking the fluorescent light bulbs and fixtures. Standing on a short step ladder he checked out the areas around him, then stole purses, petty cash, and small valuable items using the trash can to conceal his loot. He got away clean. These are only two examples of many building security lapses. Both employees and customers appreciate good security.

Employees: Training and Response

Employee training needs to be a part of any effective plan. Train people so that they know what their roles are during an emergency. Employees need to know how they can help and what their responsibilities are in preventing a crisis. This is similar to a community watch concept in the workplace. Employees are often aware of things that are happening and can alert management so that a disaster can be avoided. For example, when a gun is brought into the workplace in violation of a company policy, other employees often know about it. If they could inform management knowing the matter would be handled discreetly, safety for all employees would be improved. Good, fair enforcement of policies and procedures (such as the threats and intimidation policy) and training for employees regarding these policies and the employees' role will increase the likelihood that information will be passed along. When their personal safety is threatened and employees are confident in how management will handle the situation you are much more likely to get information. This attitude also applies when dealing with the threats and intimidation policy. Will the concerned employee be taken seriously? Will the situation be addressed appropriately?

Incident Response Plan Alternatives

When an incident of some kind does occur, how do you set in motion emergency notification to employees and customers. Of course, you have an evacuation plan in place and an evacuation alarm. However, maybe that's not the best response in every situation. A former disgruntled employee of a plant shot his doctor and told the staff he was going to the plant and get the human resources manager and his former supervisor. The doctor's staff first called 911 and then they called the plant. They said, "You better be ready because he already shot the doctor and he's coming there...." The plant did the only thing they were prepared to do. They evacuated the building. Timing is everything in life. As all the employees poured out of the building and into the parking lot, in drove the gunman. The situation was very confusing, and he did not get out of the car. The police resolved the situation.

This turned out well for the plant, but it could have been much worse. However, the employees did the only thing they were prepared to do; they evacuated. What they needed were alternatives. What about moving to safe areas of refuge inside the building and securing the outer doors. This wasn't an option for them. There was no plan. How about at your facilities? Do you have other options? How do you notify employees? In the Midwest a company could use their tornado alert with the addition of securing doors. Prepare some options so that you are ready if a crisis ever does start.

Traveling Employees

Local Travel

With regard to traveling employees think back again to the criteria for high risk exposure: public contact, isolation, and access to cash. Route delivery drivers, elevator repair technicians, telephone/cable installers, sales/marketing people, insurance adjusters and real estate agents are some examples of those at increased risk. They may have equipment that can be stolen. There may not really be any money available, only the perception of money, such as in the case of a claims adjuster. The vehicle itself may attract a violent assault. Recently, in the Illinois area, a telephone technician was killed in his service van. He was sitting in the vehicle, parked at the curb, completing his paperwork from a service call. He was unaware that he was parked outside a crack house. The occupants thought he was doing surveillance and killed him.

> *Check List 7.1*
> ## High Risk Exposures for Employees Who Travel
> ✔ Public contact
> ✔ Isolation
> ✔ Access to cash
> ✔ Valuable equipment
> ✔ Perception of money
> ✔ Vehicle as a target

Train your people to complete paperwork inside buildings or to move to a different location such as a fast food restaurant parking lot. There are still risks in these parking lots, but probably less than on the street. You also reduce the risk of the vehicle being struck by a moving vehicle while parked on the curb. A comprehensive vehicle maintenance program and regular inspection reduces the risk of breakdown on the road with the resulting exposure to random violence. Equip your vehicles with hazard triangles and signs asking passing motorists to call police. Generally, it is felt that the safest place for the driver to be is with the vehicle, locked inside.

There are video tapes and other types of training programs available to help employees understand the risks and make good decisions for their safety. Local police departments often have a community service unit which will address personal safety and security. Private companies also provide this service. You will want to prescreen their presentations since the focus of their presentations is often to sell personal security products such as pepper spray or body alarms. Be sure you're comfortable with the methods they advocate.

Out-of-Town Travel

Those employees who travel overnight on company business are also at risk. Oftentimes we think of those who travel most frequently as being most at risk. But while the more frequent traveler learns from his mistakes, those who travel infrequently often don't learn how to travel safely. The regular traveler has a higher frequency of exposure, but the occasional traveler probably has a greater risk each time. Training for traveling employees, including those who travel only once a year, can reduce their risk. Good, written company policies and training for both of these groups of people can help them avoid high-risk behaviors. For example, expect them to stay in hotels that have secured exterior entrances, rekeyable room locks and chains, or bolts on room doors. These hotels may cost a few more dollars per night but significantly increase security. Also, when at conferences or meetings one should remove badges when traveling outside the hotel or conference center. These badges are a marker for criminals who target out-of-towners. Travel in groups when walking out in the evening and during the day whenever possible. If employees don't have travel experience, they probably haven't even thought of some of the situations they can get into. Training can help them think about how to travel smarter and will help them avoid mistakes.

Checklist 7.2

Precautions for Traveling Employees

✔ Complete paperwork in building

✔ Avoid sitting in car on street

✔ Use parking lot in public areas if you must work in car

✔ Ensure comprehensive vehicle maintenance

✔ Equip vehicle with hazard triangles

✔ Equip vehicle with signs asking motorists to call police

Security Liability

Our focus is almost always on the workers' compensation issues and employees when we think about workplace violence. Media attention is certainly focused on this aspect. Security liability is a relatively new area of risk management concern. It is a serious and growing concern mostly because the courts are setting new precedents with judgments against companies, often with six-figure-damages awards. This potential financial impact, of course, gets our attention.

Security liability addresses the issue of the responsibility your company has to provide some level of safety and security for customers, visitors, tenants, and employees. There is still some uncertainty about a company's responsibility. This relatively new area being expanded and more clearly defined by the courts. The lawsuit awards and settlements have been increasing steadily in recent years. Many of the same risk management techniques you use to control exposures for employee safety will also reduce the exposures for liability.

Usually you don't think of liability as an issue regarding employees. However, some employees are trying to circumvent the workers compensation system to take advantage of the potential for huge awards available from a civil liability suit. Suits for negligent hiring and retention are becoming more common. Contract, temporary agency employees and vendors are another exposure in this area. They are having some success.

Basically, the courts have held that companies have a responsibility to provide a level of security and to follow through on any stated or implied offer of security. For example, if you have an apartment complex or office park and you advertise "24-hour security" that's what should be provided, and that security should be consistent and effective. Security devices should work. Cameras, alarm systems, and locks should be in good working order. It is generally felt now that cameras should record and tapes should be held for thirty days or more. Locks should work and be changed as needed. For tenanted properties, door locks should be changed between old and new tenants and at other times when personal security is an issue. One company failed to respond to repeated requests for nine days from a tenant to change the apartment door locks. An assault occurred and the property managers were held liable. Of course, alarm equipment should be in good working order. One company lost a lawsuit because, among other reasons, the interior motion detectors of its alarm system were not maintained in working condition. Even contracting companies can be involved. In one case, two employees of a contractor were working at a retail site. The two workers noticed suspicious activity but failed to report it to local management. After an assault occurred, the company was held partially liable in the resulting lawsuit. Do your employees work at the premises of others? Are they trained to report any unusual or suspicious activities they observe?

No matter what type of facility you operate security responsibilities are a major concern. You could be a health care facility providing protection for newborn babies against kidnapping, a shopping mall protecting customers in the parking lot against assault or car jacking, or a manufacturing plant protecting buyers or suppliers against assaults or robbery. The situations are varied, but the concerns for security liability are shared by all.

Conclusions

While workplace violence prevention is often held to be a human resources function, it is really a part of an overall risk management program. For a prevention program to be effective it needs to include operations, facility maintenance, security, construction and planning, and finance/accounting—basically, all the phases of operating a business. Risk management can pull together these functions. As with other business operations, this program will only be effective with the support and commitment from top company management. Many parts of the program come together to support one another. Evaluating incidents that have happened in the surrounding area can be used to determine security needs that affect both customers and employees. Good lighting, fencing, strict money handling procedures, tight rear-door security, and following well-established closing procedures can make you a tough target and send criminals elsewhere to look for an easier target. Management often makes the difference. While interviewing a manager of a fast food restaurant in a tough city neighborhood, I asked her why the places around her had been robbed, but not her store. She said that one of the reasons might be her store's strict following of closing procedures and attention to good money handling. She said, "They know that following proper procedures is a condition of continued employment. I train them and then expect them to follow strict procedures. I make clear the consequences, both in terms of termination and increased potential to be robbed. People will almost always do what's expected if they clearly understand." This is a management attitude that can make a difference. The opposite would be lax security, unlocked rear entrance doors, and taking out garbage to dumpsters late at night.

You can spend money on great systems and work with human resources to establish policies and procedures, but an effective program will always come down to good implementation by managers, supervisors, and employees. Does a good program and effective implementation mean you'll never have a problem? No, but you do give yourself the best chance. That's effective risk management.

References

Capozzoli and McVey. *Managing Violence in the Workplace*. DelRay Beach, FL: St. Lucie Press. 1996.

Crowe, Timothy D. *Crime Prevention Through Environmental Design*. Boston, MA: National Crime Prevention Institute/Butterworth-Heinemann Publishing. 1991.

Fennelly, Lawrence J. *Handbook of Loss Prevention and Crime Prevention* 2nd Edition. Boston, MA: Butterworth-Heinemann. 1989.

Harpley, Thomas D, Ph.D. *Defusing Workplace Violence*. National Trauma Services, 3544 Front Street, San Diego, CA 92103, (619)298-2811.

National Crime Prevention Institute. *Understanding Crime Prevention*. Stoneham, MA: National Crime Prevention Institute/Butterworth Publishers. 1986.

Chapter Eight

❏ Relationship of the Americans with Disabilities Act (ADA) to workplace violence

❏ How to address a threatening employee who is suffering from an emotional disability

❏ Key concepts for dealing with workplace violence arising from emotional disability

❏ Legal rationale for development of a violence prevention program

❏ Emergence of a common law duty to warn

The

Legal Implications of Workplace Violence

Role of the ADA and Other Legislation in Violence Prevention Program Development

John W. Kyle, JD, and Benjamin W. Hahn, JD

Case Study

An employee with a psychiatric condition marked by periodic episodes of uncontrollable assaultive behavior was discharged because of an incident in which he became violent in a supervisor's office and began to destroy property, throw equipment, and make threatening comments. Following his discharge, the employee sued, contending that his outburst was stress related. The employee contended that his supervisor had singled him out for harassment and that his disability could have been accommodated by his reassignment to another area of the workplace where the risk of harm would be lessened. The court was asked to decide whether this employee was protected under the Americans with Disabilities Act (ADA).

Introduction

The American workplace has evolved significantly over the last century, as has the law relevant to employers and employees. The once-insurmountable rule that the employment relationship existed "at-will" and could be summarily terminated by an employer, at any time, for any reason, has given way to an array of statutory and judicial limitations on the employer's freedom to discharge. On-the-job protections for employees have grown as well, with government-enforced safety, health, and welfare regulations having become an accepted fact of daily life for virtually all workplaces. Accidental industrial injuries, once unevenly dealt with in the law, are now routinely compensated by the states under an administrative scheme that has all but done away with concepts of individual negligence and fault. Contractual and implied contractual rights abound, many of which provide strong protections to employee interests. Other, purely voluntary safeguards and entitlements may be found, many of which have been adopted by well-intentioned employers seeking to enhance employee moral and productivity through progressive personnel policies and handbooks.

When dealing with the issue of workplace violence an employer must balance competing, and oftentimes contradictory, interests. On the one hand, it must take reasonable steps to minimize the potential for physical harm and the legal liability that flows from that harm. On the other, it must avoid undue infringement of the liberty and privacy interests of employees and third parties such that substantial legal risk is created by that invasive behavior.

Given this tension, employers are frequently required to take the middle ground—choosing an approach that is "cautiously" aggressive. Even those employers who have a policy of "zero tolerance" when it comes to workplace violence must exercise care in dealing with less clear-cut legal questions. Issues arising out of the Americans with Disabilities Act, state tort and criminal law, workers' compensation legislation, and third-party actions or injuries may present complicated and difficult questions of potential liability. The good news for employers is that most of these questions may be answered in a way that furthers an antiviolence objective. By creating and implementing a practical workplace violence plan that carefully manages the flexibility available in the law, employers can take much of the uncertainty out of this endeavor.

In this and the following two chapters, we shall explore many of the more prominent legal challenges faced by employers who wish to implement a workplace violence program. We also present our practical recommendations to responding to workplace violence in a manner that, to the maximum extent feasible, incorporates the law in a constructive and useful way. It is hoped that the information presented may offer encouragement to those employers who now see the law more as an impediment to action than as a tool for accomplishment.

ADA and Workplace Violence

Principles of Law under the ADA

Under Title I of the ADA, an employer covered by the Act may not discriminate in terms and conditions of employment against a "qualified individual with a disability because of the disability." The ADA's antidiscrimination provisions also require than an employer make reasonable accommodations for the known physical or mental limitations of an otherwise qualified employee, unless the employer can demonstrate that such accommodation would cause the employer undue hardship.

Psychological disorders may be considered disabilities under the ADA. The relevant test in this regard is whether the impairment "substantially limits" one or more "major life activities," such as caring for oneself, performing manual tasks, walking, seeing, hearing, speaking, breathing, learning, working, and participating in community activities. Individuals may also qualify for protection under the ADA if they have a record of mental impairment or if they are classified (even erroneously) as mentally impaired by the employer. Where such perception of impairment exists, the law will not permit an employer that discriminates to escape liability on the ground that the employee or applicant was not, in fact, disabled.

The ADA also prohibits employers from requiring medical examinations prior to offering employment, with the exception of examinations for illegal drug usage. However, offers of employment may be conditioned on the results of a medical examination prior to the commencement of duties. All prospective employees must undergo the same examination, regardless of disability, except that the employer may limit examinations to designated job classifications based on legitimate business reasons. Psychiatric or psychological testing is permissible under the ADA to the same extent as other medical examinations, although such tests may raise considerations of privacy or test validity subject to regulation under state law.

The implications of these legal requirements under the ADA are both "obvious" and "subtle." "Obviously," an employee who has epilepsy may frighten other employees unfamiliar with his disability if he has a seizure at work. However, epileptics do not pose a danger of violence to other employees. Epileptics may, however, pose a danger where the job duties would create an unsafe situation in the event of a seizure, such as a school bus driver. "Less obviously" an employee suffering from panic attack disorder may perceive an aggressive managerial style as being highly threatening, even dangerous, where the employees' co-workers would not. Both of these medical conditions raise ADA protection and accommodation issues.

Workplace Violence and Mental Disabilities

The substantial majority of workplace violence appears to be the result of purposeful behavior, unconnected to mental illness. Sources of violence commonly include the following:

✧ Strangers who enter an employer's premises to commit robberies or other crimes

✧ Patrons or customers of establishments who have unresolved issues with the employer or one or more of its employees

✧ Current employees or others known to them, such as an estranged spouse or lover, who may enter a workplace to confront a former mate or a suspected rival

Each of these sources implicates a wide variety of legal issues related to the role of security, the use of the criminal and civil justice systems, and the potential for liability to employees and third parties. Although at times complicated, these issues generally may be resolved without fear that the law will protect a perpetrator, or alleged perpetrator of violence, who complains of reasonable conduct by an employer intended to ensure the safety of employees and others on its premises.

In a small percentage of violent, or potentially violent episodes, the source of violence may be an employee or patron who suffers from a mental or emotional illness that produces aggressive behavior. Many of these individuals may have a history of hospitalization and treatment for their illnesses and many may be under doctor's care at the time of the incident. Recalling that violent behavior takes many forms and that even modern psychiatry lacks the ability to predict such behavior with any reliability, the question arises: what are an employer's rights and obligations under the ADA when an employee engages in threatening or aggressive conduct that may be the product of a covered mental or emotional disability? To answer this question, we have to look to the ADA itself.

Analytical Framework for Discrimination Claims under the ADA

An emotionally troubled employee may claim that discipline or discharge is a form of discrimination. Under the discriminatory discipline theory, a court must first determine whether the evidence shows that the employer may have relied on an alleged disability in discharging the employee or whether the employer's asserted reasons were unconnected to an alleged disability. If the employee shows that an employer's stated justification for discharge was the employee's disability or the symptoms of the disability, the case is one of alleged direct discrimination and the employee must show that:

- ✧ (S)he has a disability.
- ✧ (S)he is qualified for the position at issue.
- ✧ The employer's action constitutes unlawful discrimination on the basis of the disability.

If the employer has offered some other, nondisability-related explanation for the discharge, such as poor work performance, the employee may use the indirect method of proof allowed in discrimination cases. The employee must offer enough evidence to show that he was a qualified employee with a disability, who was disciplined in circumstances where the disability may have motivated the action. If such a showing is made, the employer must then articulate a nondiscriminatory basis for the disciplinary action. If the employer does so, the employee then must show that the employer's asserted basis is either a false explanation, intended to mask discrimination, or that the proffered basis, although valid in the abstract, did not really motivate the employer in the particular case before the court. If the employee can discover enough evidence to raise a question about the employer's motivation in the mind of a reasonable person, the case can proceed to trial by the jury. A verdict in favor of the employee will be sustained on appeal if the question of the employer's motivation exists and the jury finds that disability discrimination was a motivating factor in the employer's decision.

Treatment of Employees Who Pose a "Direct Threat" under the ADA

In the context of workplace violence, one of the principal tools available to an employer who is concerned with potentially violent, disabled employees is the so-called "direct threat" provision of the ADA. The statute permits an employer to institute a general qualification standard requiring that an employee not pose a direct threat in the workplace. The Equal Employment Opportunity Commission (EEOC) has defined the term "direct threat" in this way: "a significant risk of substantial harm to the health or safety of the individual or others that cannot be eliminated or reduced by reasonable accommodation." 29 C.F.R. Section 1630.2(r). Thus, an employer able to show that a given individual's disability carries with it an inherent and realistic potential for serious harm by the employee, may exclude the individual from the workplace. Of course, the flip side of this coin is that an employer may not reject an individual whose disability poses a lesser risk, falling short of the "direct threat" standard. Fortunately, the case law has tended to be fairly solicitous of good-faith concerns offered by employers in the area of potential workplace harm by employees who pose a realistic threat.

Failure to Accommodate and the "Undue Hardship" Standard

Even so, where an employee's disability is of questionable risk to himself or others, it is likely that a "failure-to-accommodate claim" will be raised. Such a claim would generally seek to show that an employee with a known disability was inappropriately subjected to discharge for presumed inability to fulfill position requirements. To make his case, the employee would need to show that the employer was able, but failed, to make a reasonable change in the job or the work environment that would have allowed the disabled employee to meet the essential requirements of the position. Such accommodations are determined on a case-by-case basis and take into account the employer's resources, the employee's abilities, the functional requirements of the job and the employee's functional limitations. In assessing the accommodation obligation, the law does not require that an employer undergo undue hardship. Thus, where a proposed accommodation would be unduly costly or imposing, or would work a fundamental change in the business operation, it need not be made available. Again, the inquiry is made on a case-by-case basis, looking at the employer and position involved.

The EEOC's Broad Interpretation of "Reasonable Accommodation"

In addition, employers should keep in mind that there is a tension between the expansive interpretations of the "reasonable accommodation" obligation made by the EEOC and the more conservative interpretations of that obligation rendered by a majority of the federal courts. The EEOC has defined the concept of reasonable accommodation very broadly to include "any modification or adjustment to... the work environment that makes it possible for an individual with a disability to enjoy an equal employment opportunity." In the case of an emotionally-troubled employee, for example, the EEOC regulations raise the prospect that an employer may be required to change an employee's work schedule to permit psychiatric treatment or may need to transfer a distressed employee to a less stressful or disruptive position or location in the organization. EEOC TECHNICAL ASSISTANCE MANUAL FOR TITLE I OF THE ADA, SECTION 3.10 (JAN. 26, 1992). It is a very short jump from this position to one, for example, that seeks a "modification" to an employer's automatic discharge policy for workplace aggression, where a single incident of minor aggression is attributed to a disabling mental or emotional condition. That is particularly true, where the condition may be triggered or exacerbated by stress caused by the employee's supervisor or work location. Employers faced with administrative charges before the EEOC generally should expect that agency to question the need for adherence to a zero-tolerance policy in all circumstances.

The courts, on the other hand, seem far less solicitous of a disruptive employee, particularly where there is the potential threat of serious harm. In one case, for example, an employee was diagnosed as having Intermittent Explosive Disorder, a condition marked by periodic episodes of uncontrollable assaultive behavior or destruction of property. The employee, who was otherwise qualified to perform the work of the employer was discharged because of an incident in which he became violent in a supervisor's office and began to destroy property, throw equipment, and make threatening comments. Following his discharge, the employee sued, contending that his outburst was stress related. Among other causes of stress, the employee contended that his supervisor had singled him out for harassment and that his disability could have been accommodated by his reassignment to another area of the workplace where the risk of harm would be lessened. The court disagreed, finding that the risk of serious harm would not be eliminated by the transfer of the employee and that the employee was not, therefore, qualified to do the job.

Even in circumstances of less serious violence, the courts have been willing to err on the side of protecting against disruptive behavior. For example, where an employee who suffered from feelings of inferiority had lost his temper and was verbally abusive to a supervisor, the court found that the employee was properly discharged. Another employer was found to have lawfully terminated an employee with posttraumatic stress disorder where, despite the employer's attempts to work with the employee, the latter could not handle constructive criticism without reacting explosively (passive-aggressive personality, aggressive type).

It is in connection with these less dramatic incidents of threatening conduct that an employer may need to exercise greater care in an analysis of the situation. Where disability-related behavior rises to the level of conduct capable of inflicting bodily harm, it is likely that both the EEOC and the courts will find the conduct unprotected as a "direct threat" to the health and safety of the workplace. Where behavior involves "mere" oral threats or simple verbal abuse, a suggestion that the employee is "unqualified" to hold any position by virtue of the conduct may be rejected. In the latter cases, discharge may be effected pursuant to the employer's ordinary code of conduct.

Recommendations for Dealing with Workplace Violence That Arises from Disabilities

There are three key concepts in dealing with the employee who poses a potential for violent or dangerous behavior in the workplace:

✧ Employers should, at all times, keep the focus on actual employee behavior for purposes of evaluating performance and disciplining employees rather than focusing on the psychological condition of the employee.

✧ Preventative workplace violence programs should identify and deal with individuals who may have a propensity for violence, rather than trying to "predict" violent behavior.

✧ While ensuring "safety first," enforce the policy in a way that maintains the integrity of the individual employee to the maximum extent feasible.

Focusing on Actual Behavior

As with many other forms of disruptive conduct, threatening and assaultive behavior—whatever its origin—is a legitimate basis for discipline. Just as the courts have tended not to forgive rank insubordination or abusive conduct by employees on the grounds that a psychological disorder "caused" the behavior, so too should employers be able to take resolute action against employee conduct that is violent. The legal concept, again, is that nonaggression is a standard, essential qualification for the performance of any position in the workplace. An employee whose behavior is violent is not "otherwise qualified" within the meaning of the ADA, even if the violence is associated with a mental or psychological disability.

Identifying Propensity for Violence

The second, key concept in dealing with violence in the workplace is to be alert for early warning signals of potential violence and to assess the degree of danger posed by the individual based on the facts. In the context of the ADA, it is also important that the employer have an understanding of the relationship between various forms of mental illness and a propensity for violent conduct. Frequently, the latter will require that an employer have access to a psychiatrist or psychologist who may assist with supervisory training and, in appropriate circumstances, analyze the potential for violence. Often, this assistance may be rendered to an employer through the auspices of an Employee Assistance Plan (EAP).

Employers must appreciate the role of the therapist in the treatment of employees, when considering issues of workplace violence. Many employees have direct access to the EAPs that are provided for them. It is not unusual for an employer of a treated employee to be informed only that the employee has been taken under doctor's care and that the employer will be notified when the employee is released to return to work. In these circumstances, an employer may not receive information about the violent propensities of an employee unless the employee's behavior is sufficiently threatening to induce the therapist to give the warnings as described in *Tarasoff vs. Regents of the University of California* (Sup. 131, *Cal. Rptr.* 14, 1976). Assuming that the employee-patient does not otherwise consent to disclosure, an employer may receive little information from this source. Accordingly, employers are well advised to establish relationships with nontreating professionals who may act as consultants with respect to information and behavior that a treating therapist is unwilling or unable to discuss with the employer.

That is particularly true, inasmuch as the law has begun to shape an anomaly in the "duty-to-warn" arena: while treating therapists have a duty to warn an intended victim only where a patient has actually threatened violence to that victim, employers may soon find themselves under a broader duty to protect employees from foreseeable workplace violence. If this potential for greater liability comes to pass, employer workplace violence policies will need to account for this independent responsibility. Importantly, an employer who has a reasonable medical basis for believing that an employee poses a threat to himself or others can insist that the employee undergo an independent medical evaluation by a medical professional of the employer's choosing.

Maintaining the Integrity of the Individual

A third and final key concept to a workplace violence program is to structure the program in a manner that protects the privacy and other rights of alleged perpetrators to the maximum extent, consistent with first ensuring the safety of the workplace. As we discuss below, this concept recognizes that a workplace violence program need not be "punitive" to be effective. Although a great deal of violent behavior is undertaken by employees who suffer from no disability recognized by the law, many others may engage in conduct over which they have little or no control. By avoiding needlessly humiliating or stressful exchanges, even if such an exchange would be legally permissible in the circumstances, employers will minimize their potential for costly litigation and for a negative or disruptive response by the alleged perpetrator of violence.

Legal Implications of Program Development

Apart from having an interest in protecting the business operations of the employer and the personal health and safety of employees, there are a number of important legal considerations that motivate and inform the development of a workplace violence program. These considerations may flow from statutory obligations, state tort or contract law principles, or criminal law. Some are well established in the jurisprudence and some only now are assuming concrete form. Together, they create a compelling reason for every employer to think about the implications of potential violence on the job and to do what is feasible to protect both the employees and the business from the sometimes devastating harm of work-related violence.

Requirements of Occupational Safety and Health Acts

These requirements of federal law in many ways parallel the former common law duties imposed upon employers under state law. The latter obligations, which generally required that employers provide safe premises and equipment, and also adequate training and staffing for safe operation of the business, are now subsumed in the state workers' compensation schemes in place throughout the nation. Nevertheless, these obligations and principles continue to have relevance to the issue of workplace violence. Questions such as whether a supervisor or corporate officer may be sued personally for death or injury occurring at the workplace, whether a co-worker may sue another for violent injury, and whether an employer is liable for the death or injury of an employee caused by a third party, are questions that are determined by primary reference to state law. Accordingly, considerations of federal and state occupational health and safety statutes must be augmented with analysis of other state laws when considering a workplace violence program.

Fed-OSHA Requirements

Workplace Violence Prevention Guidelines

Fed-OSHA has used the general duty clause cited above to encourage employers to take steps to prevent injury to employees, as in the case of workers at a psychiatric hospital who suffered serious injuries when trying to isolate and restrain a violent patient. Recently, Fed-OSHA announced that it is developing workplace violence in night retail and health care operations. Fed-OSHA is reviewing California OSHA's guidelines and seeking feedback from interested parties including law enforcement agencies. Although the guidelines are unlikely to carry enforcement authority and will not affect current compliance activities, Fed-OSHA has noted that it will continue to issue citations for workplace violence under the general provisions of Section 654(a)(1) where criminal activity endangers workers. OSHA stated that it has postponed the clarification of its record-keeping requirements for job-related violence in order to focus on completing the workplace violence prevention guidelines. Fed-OSHA stressed, however, that all work-related deaths and illnesses are recordable.

Management-Employee Committees

Fed-OSHA has debated whether employers should be required to set up management-employee committees to address issues of workplace violence. This requirement was part of labor-backed job safety legislation recently introduced in Congress. However, recent decisions by the National Labor Relations Board finding that joint committees set up by management can be considered company-dominated illegal labor organizations under the National Labor Relations Act (NLRA), have cast doubt on whether such committees would be illegal under labor law. Although the U.S. House of Representatives had passed the Teamwork for Employees and Managers Act (TEAM Act) that would amend the LMRA to permit such employee participation committees, that regulation did not obtain the approval of the President and Democratic Senators and is unlikely to be enacted into law.

Influence of California Workplace Safety Guidelines

Several state safety and health agencies either have developed, or are now developing, safety standards or guidelines, with the same goal of motivating employers to address workplace violence. This is the case in California, for example, where the California Occupational Safety and Health Act of 1973 (Cal-OSHA) also imposes a general duty upon employers, similar to that imposed by the federal law, to provide "employment and a place of employment which are safe and healthful for the employees therein." CAL. LAB CODE §6400. This general duty has now been clarified in California where the Department of Industrial Relations has issued new guidelines for workplace safety which will affect most California employers. Moreover, because these guidelines are being considered by Fed-OSHA, they may have the potential for affecting employers at a national level. We will not know, of course, the extent of the obligations imposed upon employers by Fed-OSHA until its own guidelines are issued.

Development of a Common Law Duty to Warn

Given the existence of federal and state OSHA requirements, it seems highly probable that one or more state courts will soon formulate the position that an employer who possesses knowledge that an employee is at risk must take steps to warn the employee. Indeed, prior to the development of workers' compensation statutes—which obviated the need to find "fault" on the part of an employer—state common law obligations typically required that an employer warn employees of "the existence of dangers of which the employees could not reasonably be expected to be aware." W. Page Keeton et al., Section 80 at 569 (W. Keeton ed. 1984).

The foundation of such a duty may arise from judicially created public policy such as that required under the laws of many states for therapists. As courts around the nation increasingly impose liability for negligence in hiring and retaining employees who terrorize workplaces by violent acts, courts may also use the same reasoning to impose liability on employers for negligent failure to warn known, targeted victims.

As noted above, courts could also base the duty to warn employees of work-related violence on occupational safety and health laws, especially in view of Fed-OSHA's recent announcement of its intents to extend the general duty of providing a safe workplace to issues of criminal activity that endangers workers. California corporations and managers, for example, already face criminal liability for failing to disclose concealed hazards for which there is a substantial probability of death, great bodily harm, or serious exposure. CAL. PEN. CODE §387.

Notably, the California Supreme Court has also emphasized, that the creation of a legal duty is based on whether a plaintiff's interests are entitled to protection against the defendant's conduct. Although a preexisting duty being owed by the defendant to the plaintiff is necessary in order to find liability for negligent conduct, the court, in one case, observed that the duty of care may arise by statute, contract, "the general character of the activity in which the defendant [is] engaged, the relationship between the parties or even the interdependent nature of human society." The court stressed that foreseeability is the key component for establishing liability. Even though the determination of whether one owes a duty to another must be decided on a case-by-case basis, "every case is governed by the rule of general application that all persons are required to use ordinary care to prevent others from being injured as the result of their conduct."

Conclusion

Based on these types of sweeping statements of public policy, it is highly probable that some court, presented with the issue of whether an employer has a duty to take precautionary measures to protect employees from workplace violence, will conclude that such a duty exists in some degree. However, it is also probable that those courts which examine the issue will consider the cost and feasibility of precautionary measures when determining the scope of the duty of care. It is for this reason, that an employer which has already examined the workplace violence issue and put into place a substantial program to protect employees will be in a much better position to defend itself should it be sued for an alleged breach of any common law duty that might evolve in the future. Indeed, by addressing the issues and implementing a policy to prevent workplace violence, an employer will be creating an important evidentiary record to defend against claims of negligence or reckless disregard of employee safety.

References

(See Chapter 10.)

Chapter Nine

❏ How employers can protect themselves from liability in negligent hiring or retention

❏ Risks of negligent misrepresentation of employees

❏ Employer's responsibility to prevent or remedy harassment and discrimination

❏ Potential employer liabilities if they disregard the rights or safety of others

❏ Determinants of the employer's liability to third parties

❏ When property owners may be liable for negligence

Sources of Employer Liability in Workplace Violence

John W. Kyle, JD, and Benjamin W. Hahn, JD

Case Study

In a Colorado case a truck driver engaged in a long haul delivery had assaulted a motel clerk whom, by chance, he had noticed working alone at the motel. The victim's lawyer discovered that the driver had a criminal record, including a number of felony convictions and misdemeanor citations. The clerk sued, alleging that the driver's employer had negligently failed to perform a criminal background check on the driver, who presented an unreasonable risk of harm to the general public. The court eventually sided with the employer on the basis that it had acted reasonably in conducting a check of the driver's references and in promulgating rules about proper behavior by drivers.

Introduction

The tort of negligent hiring or retention is based on the principle that an employer has a duty to protect its employees and customers from injuries caused by employees whom the employer knows, or has reason to know, pose a risk of harm to others. The duty is breached when an employer fails to exercise reasonable care to avoid the risk of harm from unfit or dangerous employees. Thus, an employer may be found to have been negligent in selecting an applicant for employment when, for example, it failed to perform a reference check that would have yielded information that the employee had a propensity toward violent behavior. Furthermore an employer may be liable for ignoring signs of a propensity for violence if it did not investigate or follow through on information obtained.

State Tort Law Governing Negligent Hiring, Supervision, and Retention of Employees

Liability of Employers for Negligent Hiring

An employer is generally not obligated to exhaust every conceivable avenue of potential inquiry in hiring employees. For example, the laws of most states do not require that employers perform criminal background checks before hiring the typical employee.* Indeed, the laws of several states regulate access to and use of this information. Even in those states that recognize an employer's obligation to be especially careful with the hiring of employees who will have regular public contact, a criminal background check is generally not required for every position. (See case example at beginning of chapter.) However, the law is clearly moving in the direction of being more demanding of employer diligence in screening out those employees whose lack of fitness may be determined by a careful examination of background information.

An employer that ignores warning signals may be held liable for its conduct. In a recent hospital case, for example, a minor candystriper who volunteered her

---

* Exceptions exist for certain sensitive positions that may expose an individual employee to highly confidential information or to vulnerable persons in need of special protection from harm.

time, alleged that she had been sexually assaulted by a 31-year-old male employee of the hospital. The record revealed that, many months before the assault, it had come to the employer's attention that the victim had reportedly been touched and kissed by the older male employee. Upon investigation, the minor confirmed that the touching had occurred. The employee denied that it had occurred. Sometime later, he applied for, and obtained, a position as a security officer with the hospital. Shortly thereafter, the alleged sexual assault occurred, in an area of the hospital accessible only to security. The court found that the employer, in retaining the assailant as a security officer, had not acted reasonably.

It should be noted that an employer that comes into knowledge of an applicant's prior bad acts will be charged with that knowledge in assessing the reasonableness of any subsequent decision to hire. As a general rule, any recent record of serious violence or criminal conduct—irrespective of the cause or explanation—should serve to establish a presumption against hiring, at least for those positions in which substantial contact with other individuals is presumed. On the other hand, disqualification need not be automatic for any conviction or violent behavior, irrespective of the circumstances. An employer is permitted to consider the more

---

Checklist 9.1

Checklist for Protection against Negligent Hiring

✔ Review all information prior to hire

✔ Question applicant about gaps in employment history

✔ Contact prior employers to verify dates of employment and positions held

✔ Obtain from prior employers information about applicant's reliability, honesty, and tendency for violence (in as much as permitted by law)

✔ Document screening efforts and information received, including where unsuccessful

✔ Hire conditionally upon successful completion of screening process

✔ Inform applicant that omissions, misrepresentation, or falsifications will result in rejection of application or termination of employment

✔ Take appropriate action (investigation, termination, or reassignment) to avoid negligent retention if and when the employer becomes aware of employee's risk of violence

recent good behavior of individuals, as well as public policies favoring the hiring of rehabilitated offenders.

Steps in Guarding against Negligent Hiring

Given the principles established in these cases, there are several steps that employers should take to protect themselves against liability for negligent hiring. First, an employer should carefully review all information on employment applications and resumes prior to hiring an applicant. The employer should also question the applicant about any gaps in the individual's employment history because such gaps could be due to the individual's serving time for violent crimes. Further, the employer should contact each prior employer to verify dates of employment and positions held. The employer should also obtain from prior employers such information as the applicant's reliability, honesty, and tendency for violence. The employer should document its investigative and screening efforts and all information it receives from prior employers and references, even if its efforts to obtain such evidence have proven unsuccessful. The employer should not offer an applicant employment until the screening process has been completed. Finally, employment applications should advise the applicant that omissions, misrepresentations, or falsification of information will result in the rejection of the applicant or termination of employment.

Negligent Retention

Where an employer does not realize an applicant's violent tendencies at the time of hiring despite following steps intended to prevent negligent hiring claims, an employer must still take steps to prevent violence in the workplace. In one case, for example, a former employee shot and killed a co-worker a few days after the violent employee resigned from work. The company had employed the violent employee for two years and re-employed him after an interim during which he was imprisoned for five years for the strangulation death of a co-worker. The company rehired him as a custodian upon release from prison and transferred him twice because of workplace confrontations. The court concluded that the current victim's trustee did not state a claim for negligent hiring but did state a claim for negligent retention.

The court determined that, when, during the course of employment, the employer becomes aware or should have become aware that an employee is unfit, and the employer fails to take further action such as investigating, discharging, or reassigning the employee, the employer may be liable for negligent retention.

Employers that wrongfully hire or retain unfit employees expose the public to the acts of these employees, so that it is not unreasonable to hold the employer accountable when the employee causes injury to another.

The employer must take remedial action to separate a violent employee from other employees and customers to avoid negligent retention suits. The employer should consider suspending the employee pending a thorough investigation of allegations of violence and should expressly prohibit the employee from returning to the workplace until the investigation is completed. The employer could enforce this by increasing security measures and by retrieving the employee's key or access card.

State Tort Liability for Negligent Misrepresentation in Recommending an Employee

California Case Record

In a case that may have dramatic consequences for employers who are aware of an employee's violent or alleged violent tendencies, a court in California has found school authorities potentially liable for physical harm caused by an employee's alleged sexual molestation of a student where the authorities had recommended the employee for hiring by the school without disclosing that he had been the subject of known or suspected complaints of alleged sexual impropriety.

The case involved a school teacher who, apparently, was highly regarded for his work. However, in the period between 1985 and 1991, the teacher had also been the subject of several complaints by parents and students over what was alleged to be inappropriate sexual contact with students. One of these complaints had apparently prompted the teacher to resign from a previous assignment.

In 1990, the teacher asked a number of school officials to provide letters of recommendation that he might use to obtain a position with prospective employers. They agreed to do so, and wrote highly flattering recommendations—none of which alluded to the allegations of improper sexual conduct by the teacher, which were apparently known to the authors.

In contending that the school authorities should be held liable for their recommendations of the teacher, the plaintiff argued that their statements were misrepresentations because they did not disclose information that was materially related to the teacher's fitness for duty. The court agreed. Relying on the long-standing principle of law that one who voluntarily agrees to speak "is bound not only to state truly what he tells but also not to suppress or conceal any facts within his knowledge which materially qualify those stated," the court found that the school authorities had made misrepresentations and that California law would protect third parties who were injured as a result. The court also found that the authorities could be held liable for negligence, for failing to report what they knew. In the latter regard, the court noted that the school authorities had a statutory duty to report any reasonable suspicions of sexual abuse that they possessed. Finding that the allegations of the complaint were sufficient to find that the authorities possessed knowledge covered by the statute, the court held that the plaintiff had adequately pleaded a negligence count.

Uncertain Status of Most Employer Recommendations

There is a striking parallel between the duty to speak honestly that was imposed on these school authorities and the potential duty of an employer to speak honestly about an alleged violent employee. Thus, like the duty to students owed by those associated with the schools, employers have a statutory duty to protect employees from workplace violence. Although that duty is generally thought to extend to the employer's employees, the underlying public policy may easily be extended to a situation in which one employer is providing a workplace reference to another.

In addition, although many employers have a policy prohibiting the giving of evaluative references on former employees, most employers provide some information to those who call. Indeed, many employers will provide informal or "off-the-record" assessments if contacted in a moment of weakness. It is not at all clear how the California court would consider, for example, a "neutral" reference on an employee that stated that the employee had worked for a given length of time, in a given position, and had resigned on a certain date. May the disclosure of a seemingly "voluntary" resignation then obligate the employer, in appropriate circumstances, to add that the employee was given the option of resigning under pain of discharge for alleged sexual assault in the workplace? Is the reference to a resignation a "half-truth," that should expose the employer to liability for its disclosure?

It is too early to tell whether the reasoning of the California court will be limited to those egregious cases in which an employer makes affirmative recommendations of fitness for duty but conceals important knowledge of prior threatening conduct by the employee. In the interim, employers may want to avoid giving references that could be misconstrued as an indication that an employee separated on satisfactory terms when, in fact, the employee was forced to resign for threatening or aggressive conduct. In the latter cases, a reference may simply give the date of the employee's separation from employment, without an indication as to whether the employee resigned or was discharged.

Other Sources of Employer Liability for Failure to Protect Employees and Third Parties from Harm

Intentional Infliction of Emotional Distress

The tort of intentional infliction of emotional distress in the employment setting typically requires that: (1) the employer intended to inflict emotional distress or recklessly disregarded whether its acts would result in the infliction of emotional distress; (2) the acts in fact caused severe emotional distress; and (3) the acts constituted an extraordinary transgression beyond the boundaries of socially tolerable conduct. An employer's reckless or intentional failure to reasonably investigate applicants and employees may thus lead to a claim for intentional infliction of emotional distress. Alternatively, where the employer owes a duty of care (i.e., the duty to maintain a safe workplace) and negligently breaches that duty, causing employees or others to suffer emotional distress, the employer may be sued for negligent infliction of emotional distress.

Equal Employment Opportunity Laws

Where an employer fails to seriously consider and address an employee's concerns about threatened violence or harm by a co-worker or other individual in the workplace based on impermissible grounds, such as sex, race, religion, national origin, pregnancy, age, marital status, workers' compensation claims, military service, sexual orientation, or disability, the employer may be held liable for violation of federal or state equal employment opportunity laws.

Preventing Harassment and Discrimination

As many incidents of workplace violence involve harassment or discrimination on the basis of sex or other protected category, employers also have to exercise caution to ensure that discrimination and harassment are not occurring or is being effectively remedied once it is discovered. In a case arising out of the Oakland, California Police Department, for example, the court found that an employer must act to remedy harassment even if the harasser voluntarily stops the harassment. In this case, a female police officer had been harassed by a male police officer after she ended a voluntary romantic relationship with him. The female employee received numerous hang-up calls and had several confrontations with the male officer. These confrontations included the male officer trying to run her car off of the road, with the female officer having to swerve to avoid a head-on collision. The court concluded that the female employee was subjected to a hostile working environment. The court emphasized that once an employer knows or should know of harassment, the employer has an obligation to remedy the harassment.

The fact that the harassment stopped does not mean that the employer does not have to act to remedy the harassment since one purpose of requiring the remedy is to deter future harassment by the named offender or others. An investigation alone does not suffice to defeat liability since the investigation is mainly a way to determine whether any remedy is needed and does not substitute for the remedy itself. An employer's offer to transfer the victim was ineffective as a remedy because harassment must be remedied through actions targeted at the harasser. As the employer in this case failed to take any appropriate remedial steps once it learned of the harassment, the city was still liable for remedying the harassment.

The obligation of the employer to remedy harassment is important because a report of workplace violence may also qualify as a report of sexual harassment requiring the employer to investigate and remedy the harassment.

Obligations Stemming from Public Policy

Protections for Workers Who Expose Unsafe Conditions

An employer has an obligation not to discriminate or retaliate against employees who express concerns regarding unsafe working conditions, such as threats of violence in the workplace. In most states, an employee who feels that he or she has been discriminated against for expressing such concerns may bring a claim against the employer for violation of state public policy. Similarly, under certain circumstances, an employee who is terminated for refusing to work under hazardous conditions may bring a claim for violation of the state labor code.

In addition to the above statutory claims, an employee who complains about unsafe working conditions or refuses to work in unsafe work environments and is terminated, may be able to state a tort claim against the employer for wrongful termination in violation of public policy. In recent years, several states have allowed terminated employees to recover tort remedies, including punitive damages, from their employer notwithstanding the at-will nature of the employment relationship or the terms of an employment agreement, where the termination violates fundamental principles of public policy.

A Maryland court ruled that a teacher at a private residential and educational facility for troubled adolescent females, terminated allegedly for notifying state authorities about the danger posed to staff and residents by "gangs" at the facility, stated a claim for wrongful discharge in violation of public policy. The policy allegedly violated stemmed from a Maryland statute and its implementing regulations requiring that suspected abuse and neglect of children be reported. The court also ruled that the plaintiff could not state a cause of action in violation of public policy based on First Amendment free speech guarantees contained in the U.S. Constitution and the Maryland Declaration of Rights because those guarantees did not apply to actions of private-sector employers. However, the question of whether a public sector employee could make such a claim was left unanswered.

Obligation to Warn of Concealed Hazards

Employers may also have some obligations stemming from specific statutory mandates and incur liability for exemplary damages when they act in conscious disregard of the rights and safety of others. The California Legislature, for example, has passed the Corporate Criminal Liability Act which was signed into law in 1990. Known as the "Be a Manager, Go to Jail Act," it subjects individual managers and corporations to criminal liability for failure to disclose concealed hazards. A corporation or manager must warn the Department of Safety and Health (DOSH) as well as the affected employees in writing immediately if there is imminent risk of great bodily harm or death or, in the absence of such risk, within 15 days after receiving actual knowledge of a serious concealed danger. A serious concealed danger is defined as a condition in which there is a substantial probability of death, great bodily harm, or serious exposure to an individual, and the danger is not readily apparent to a person who is likely to be exposed. As previously stated, the definition here could be argued to require the notification of threats to kill or threats to harm other employees when such threats are not made to the victim but a supervisor or manager either knows or should know by prior conduct or by the circumstances surrounding the situation, that the perpetrator has made the threats and will probably act upon them.

Extent of Employer Liability

The liabilities which an employer may incur as a consequence of failing to abide by some statutory duty or other legal obligation can be substantial. For example, in some states, an employer may be liable for punitive damages in a tort action for the conduct of an employee which is the result of malice, fraud, or oppression, if the employer had advance notice of the unfitness of the employee and employed him or her with a conscious disregard for the rights and safety of others, or authorized or ratified the wrongful conduct of such employee. Under state laws, the definition of malice generally covers any conduct which was intended by a defendant to cause injury to another or constitutes conduct which is carried on by the defendant with a willful and conscious disregard of the rights and safety of others. In negligent hiring or retention cases, it could be argued that, under this statute, employers have a duty to the public which could subject them to punitive damages for the malice, fraud, or oppression of their employees. This could be significant in negligent hiring cases where employers are burdened with the obligation of ascertaining an applicant's background notwithstanding that the information obtained from prior employers is sometimes minimal and unrevealing at best.

As the foregoing demonstrates, employers have broad duties and responsibilities not only to employees but also to third parties. Whether such obligations are provided by special statutory provisions, contracts, or other legal doctrines, it is clear that those duties are implicated whenever an employer is faced with workplace violence.

Special Liability Claims

Third Parties' Liability to Nonemployees for Conduct of Workers and Third Parties

In most states, an employer may be shielded from most employee claims as a consequence of injury or death on the job because the workers' compensation system provides the exclusive remedy for occupational injuries. However, companies may incur substantial liability to the survivors of employees or even to nonemployees, for actions of perpetrators whose violent conduct could have been prevented. Liability in these circumstances is premised on negligence or on breach of contractual or implied duties which inure to the benefit of the victims or, by extension, to their families. The following cases illustrate this point and demonstrate the seriousness of the problem caused by violence in the workplace, even where a company is not the victim's or the perpetrator's employer.

In January 1994, the owner of a frozen yogurt shop and the owner of a mall in Austin, Texas, where the shop is located, agreed to pay $12 million to the parents of four young girls. Two of the four victims worked in the store where they were murdered during a 1991 robbery. Although the crime was not solved, the civil suit which alleged inadequate security by the defendants was settled.

In 1992, a California jury awarded $5.5 million in damages against a temporary agency to the survivors of Christina Appleton. She was a 20-year-old woman stabbed to death on August 3, 1990, by a co-worker at the entrance of the winery where they were both employed. The suspect, who had a criminal record indicating that he was a dangerous person, had been fired because of poor work habits. The temporary agency which assigned him to the winery allegedly failed to check his work references.

In the same year, a Los Angeles State Court judge ordered a shopping center owner to pay $3.5 million to the family of a sales clerk who worked at the shopping center premises. The 26-year-old victim was abducted, raped, and murdered as she was leaving work. In 1991, an Illinois court of appeal upheld a $1 million judgment against the McDonald's chain on behalf of a slain worker. The victim was the employee of a restaurant where McDonald's oversaw security. McDonald's did not itself own the restaurant.

The remedies available under situations similar to the above examples in which millions of dollars were awarded could include damages for emotional distress occasioned by the negligently caused injuries to the victims. In California, for example, damages for emotional distress may be awarded to a plaintiff if the following conditions exist:

✧ The plaintiff is closely related to the injured victim

✧ The plaintiff is present at the scene of the injury-producing event at the time it occurs and is then aware that it is causing injury to the victim

✧ The plaintiff, as a result, suffers serious emotional distress—a reaction beyond that which would be anticipated in a disinterested witness and which is not an abnormal response to the circumstances.

Property Owner Liability for Negligence Based on Foreseeable Criminal Activity

Courts from coast to coast are wrestling with whether the owner of workplace premises can be liable for negligence based on criminal activity by a visitor to the premises against an employee who works at the premises. In general, the courts deciding these questions have emphasized that the foreseeability of the criminal activity is a key factor in determining the property owner's duty to safeguard the employees of companies located on the premises.

To establish negligence liability, the plaintiff must establish that the defendant owed the plaintiff a legal duty, that the defendant breached the duty, and that the breach was a proximate or legal cause of injury suffered by the plaintiff. Courts have long recognized a landlord's duty to take reasonable steps to secure common areas against foreseeable criminal acts of third parties that are likely to occur in the absence of precautionary measures. This duty may extend to the protection of tenants' employees as well.

In assessing a landlord's duty to protect a tenant's employee from rape, for example, the court stated that "the heart of the case" was whether the landlord "had reasonable cause to anticipate that criminal conduct such as rape would occur in the shopping center premises unless it provided security patrols in the common areas." A duty to take affirmative steps to control or prevent a third party's wrongful acts will be imposed only where the conduct can be reasonably anticipated. "[F]oreseeability is a crucial factor in determining the existence of duty," said the court. To establish foreseeability, the plaintiff does not have to establish that prior similar incidents occurred on the premises although their occurrence is helpful in determining foreseeability.

In addition to using foreseeability to establish a duty, the court noted that it would balance the foreseeability of the harm against the burden of the duty to be imposed. Where the burden of preventing future harm is great, a high degree of foreseeability may be required. Where there are strong policy reasons for preventing the harm or the harm is easily prevented, a lesser degree of foreseeability may be required.

The court noted that the hiring of security guards would rarely be viewed as a "minimal burden" because the monetary cost of security guards is "not insignificant" and because of the difficulty in determining the level of precautionary conduct that will adequately deter criminal conduct. A high degree of foreseeability is required for a court to find that the scope of the landlord's duty of care includes the hiring of security guards and the degree of foreseeability required "rarely, if ever, can be proven in the absence of prior similar incidents of violent crime on the landowner's premises."

Employers may be able to defend their failure to provide security guards in the workplace on similar rationale. However, once a prior similar incident has occurred, the analysis will change. The prior occurrence will establish the foreseeability element to impose a duty on the employer or landowner. The court also noted in a footnote that "immediate proximity to a substantially similar business establishment that has experienced violent crime on its premises could provide the requisite degree of foreseeability."

Security Company Liability

In a recent California case, a security company was found liable for negligence when a customer's employee was shot and suffered permanent partial paralysis. The jury awarded over $5,000,000. In this case, a high-tech company employed a security company to provide security services for its premises. The victim of the workplace violence was a manager who terminated an employee. The terminated employee continued to return to the company's premises. The employer's representatives informed the security company on three separate occasions that the terminated employee was on the premises without authorization within 26 hours of the employee's termination. The security company's employees continued to assure the employer's representatives that they would take care of the situation, but the security company did nothing. The court concluded that it was reasonably foreseeable at the time of the security company's negligent conduct that the terminated employee would harm the victim because the security company's employees were aware of the danger that a terminated employee might pose to the person who terminated him or her. Based on the lax security despite the security company's employees being aware that a terminated employee might be dangerous, the court concluded that there was sufficient evidence that the security company's negligence was a substantial factor in facilitating the attack on the victim.

Conclusion

These cases addressing third party liability in these varying situations signal an increasing awareness of the threat of violence in today's society and an increasing awareness that pursuing a lawsuit is an effective method of forcing companies to focus on preventing violence. Employers and other companies involved with the workplace (such as property owners and security companies) need to act to effectively prevent and deter violence before they are faced with such lawsuits.

References

(See Chapter 10.)

Chapter Ten

❑ How to investigate and deal with allegations of violent conduct by employees

❑ Importance of documenting the basis for doing an investigation

❑ Employee's right of privacy in his or her affairs

❑ Right of the alleged perpetrator to be free from defamation or emotional distress

❑ Employee's right to be free from assault, battery, and false imprisonment

Balancing Employee Security and Privacy Interests

John W. Kyle, JD, and Benjamin W. Hahn, JD

Case Study

The plaintiff alleged that he suffered severe emotional distress as a result of the negligent manner in which he was fired: his supervisor, who contemptuously asked questions of plaintiff's co-workers concerning plaintiff's expense reports, stood over him and watched while he cleaned out his desk before escorting plaintiff from the building. The court reasoned that the verbal and nonverbal conduct of the supervisor could be viewed as a false and defamatory statement that the plaintiff was a thief. Because of the direct invasion of privacy, the plaintiff was permitted to make a claim for negligent infliction of emotional distress upon a showing of distress sufficient to meet the legal test.

Introduction

An effective workplace violence program is one that takes into account the security and safety needs of the employees and the business in a way that is not unduly disruptive of other important employee rights and interests. There are a number of areas in which an employer must balance the objective of protection from violent behavior against the liberty interests of employees and third parties.

Defining Workplace Violence

One of the most basic areas of conflict involves the question "What is workplace violence?" Much of the current literature on the subject of violent employees properly cautions employers to be mindful of the statements and actions of employees who may be potential perpetrators of violence. One piece of common advice is to be observant of the employee who has a fascination with guns or who speaks admiringly of violent behavior. Another obvious area of concern is the employee who uses intemperate or hostile language on the job. As we have seen above, these actions by employees may generally be the basis for discharge, particularly where employment is "at-will."

Protected Conduct

But employers must keep in mind that certain forms of speech, certain forms of conduct at work, and certain forms of conduct away from the job may be affirmatively protected by the law. In these circumstances, what might otherwise be considered "violent" or "threatening" conduct may not form the basis for lawful discipline or discharge.

For example, a New York statute prohibits discrimination against employees for engaging in "legal recreational activities" off the job, such as sports, games, hobbies, etc. Under this statute, it may be unlawful for an employer to discharge or otherwise discriminate against an employee who is an avid gun collector, marksman, or hunter. It is also unlikely that an employer could lawfully require such an employee to avoid noncoercive speech about his gun collection while at work (when other comparable speech is permissible for other employees), even if other employees report to management a degree of insecurity about the employee's possession and seeming fascination with lawful firearms.

Similarly, federal and state law may protect employees from discrimination based upon their gathering together to take concerted action to improve their wages or conditions of employment. In circumstances where protected action is involved, employees may be given some latitude in the law to engage in conduct that is "exuberant" or "defiant." For example, an employee who loses his temper while engaged in a discussion over working conditions may shout insubordinately at a supervisor. Whether the employee may lawfully be disciplined under the National Labor Relations Act (even if no union is on the scene) will depend on whether the conduct is so flagrant that it threatens the employer's ability to maintain order and respect in the conduct of its business. If it does not, the employee may be able to "get away with" making a statement that would have caused him to be disciplined or discharged in other circumstances.

Recognizing the limitations of the law, an employer's workplace violence program must account for the possibility that some forms of disruptive behavior may not be considered actionable violence, even though they may otherwise fit within a literal description of conduct prohibited by the employer's policy.

Investigating and Dealing with Allegations of Violent Conduct by Employees

Right of the Alleged Perpetrator to Be Free from Defamation

Defamation occurs when a statement which is communicated to another individual is false, unprivileged, and the cause of injury to an individual's reputation or interests. (Prosser and Keeton, 1984) In the context of workplace violence, defamation may occur where an employer warns employees or otherwise publishes information about the violent tendencies of another employee or individual. If the information communicated by the employer (or by another employee) is false, the alleged violent employee may seek to hold the communicating individual liable for any written (libelous) or verbal (slanderous) characterization that has been made.

In certain circumstances, questions may arise as to whether a false statement made by an employer or an individual employee should nonetheless by protected. These questions generally fall into one of two categories: 1) whether the employer's communication should be considered qualifiedly privileged; and 2) whether an employee's allegation of violent conduct by another is entitled to protection under a "whistle blowing" provision of law.

Checklist 10.1

Employees' Rights

✔ Freedom from defamation

✔ Freedom from retaliation for reporting violations of law

✔ Privacy in personal affairs

✔ Freedom from infliction of emotional distress

✔ Freedom from assault, battery, and false imprisonment

Qualified Privilege Protection

Where the employer's actions or statement mistakenly tell others that the perpetrator has violent tendencies, the employer may nevertheless be protected if the warning or statement is qualifiedly privileged. A qualified privilege protects a statement made with a good faith belief in the statement's truth, where the statement serves a legitimate business interest and where dissemination of the information is limited only to those individuals who have a need to know of the risk. Thus, when the employer believes in good faith that an individual has engaged in violent or threatening conduct as to which others are entitled to be warned, a qualified privilege should apply to the employer's warning, even if the communication is later determined to have been in error.

Whistle-Blower Protection

Similarly, when an employee, in good faith, reports information that the employee reasonably believes to constitute a violation of law or of an employer's policy against workplace violence, the employee's communication may be entitled to protection, even if the information is later determined to be incorrect. Unlike the employer, a communicating employee has no recognized "qualified privilege" in the law. Instead, the employee's communication will generally be protected by a statutory provision that encourages reporting of alleged violations of law.

For example, Title VII of the Civil Rights Act of 1964 contains a provision protecting employees from retaliation by employers for opposing practices that the employees believe to be violations of law. An employee who alleged, in good faith, that another employee had committed unlawful harassment, would be protected from retaliation by the employer and may also be found protected from claims of defamation, if honestly mistaken in their report.

No Protection for Knowingly False Complaints

On the other hand, there is frequently a question of fact raised in circumstances where a co-worker has made an incorrect report about another. For example, an employee who alleges that a co-worker has engaged in unlawful harassment may be held liable for defamation, if the finder of fact believes that the employee knew his report was false. This was the situation in at least one case where a plaintiff alleged that her supervisor had sexually harassed her. The supervisor denied the allegation and sued his accuser for defamation, contending that her report was made falsely and maliciously. The matter was tried to a jury and the jury found for the plaintiff, awarding him a substantial amount in both compensatory and punitive damages. On appeal, the employee argued that her complaint was protected under Title VII and that she could not be held liable for complaining of sexual harassment. The court disagreed, saying that implicit in the jury's finding was a conclusion that her complaint was false and raised in bad faith. In those circumstances, said the court, there is no protection for the complaint.

Checklist 10.2

Employers' Responsibilities

- ✔ Investigate matters of employee and customer safety

- ✔ Protect employees from retaliation

- ✔ Investigate reports of threats promptly and fully

- ✔ Document reasons for violence investigation

- ✔ Use least intrusive method for investigation

- ✔ Exercise care in handling sensitive information

Civil/Criminal Complaints Protection

Employers should also recall that employees have the right to use the processes of law to protect and defend themselves, independent of the employer. Thus, for example, an employee who seeks to stop the alleged sexual assaults of her supervisor by filing a civil or criminal complaint against him as an individual is likely engaged in protected conduct. If the employee's complaints are false, the supervisor has the ability to protect himself with a counterclaim. If the complaints are correct or, mistaken but honest, the process of law will dictate the result. In either case, the employer is well advised to take action only on the basis of an independent investigation and only pursuant to its ordinary personnel policies. Basing action on the existence of the court litigation may embroil the employer in a needless dispute over its alleged interference with employee rights.

Importance of Verification

To ensure that an employer is able to establish a good faith belief in any report of an individual's violent tendencies, it is crucial that a prompt and adequate investigation be done before any warnings are given or other communications made. This is especially true where the matter initially arises in the form of rumors or hearsay reports that an employee has engaged in conduct that may violate a workplace violence policy. Witnesses should be asked to provide statements setting forth their information and the employer should thoroughly investigate all appropriate leads (within reason in the circumstances) before taking action that could give rise to liability. An employer abuses its qualified privilege when it fails to investigate statements that lack credibility or require additional support.

As a final note, it is important to recall that actions may, in some settings, be the equivalent of statements or assertions. Employers should consider the "message" sent by certain conduct (as, for example, escorting an employee from the building under armed guard). Having once decided to act in a given situation, the employer should act reasonably and in proportion to the urgency of the situation.

Employees' Entitlement to Privacy in Their Personal Affairs

Employers involved in the investigation of workplace violence issues may frequently find themselves delving into personal matters that have spilled over into the workplace. In addition, issues such as surveillance of alleged perpetrators of violence or victimized employees may give rise to difficult and complicated questions of potential invasion of privacy. Generally speaking, such invasions may be redressed through the filing of a state tort claim under one of three theories.

Intrusion on Seclusion

One type of privacy tort involves the so-called intrusion on seclusion or intrusion into private affairs.(Prosser and Keeton, 1984) The employee who files such a claim must establish intentional intrusion, physically or otherwise, on the employee's solitude, or into the employee's private affairs when the intrusion would be highly offensive to a reasonable person. It is irrelevant to the claim that the employer did not actually uncover any embarrassing or private information. It is sufficient that the investigation is intrusive and causes the employee distress. For example, an employer who discovers that an employee suffers from a sexual disorder having no clinical relationship to aggressive conduct may not, under the guise of a concern for workplace violence, attempt to discover the intimate details of the disorder without creating potential liability under this theory.

To minimize the risk of such a claim, an employer should carefully document allegations of violent behavior and the factual or clinical bases for a good-faith belief that further investigation is warranted in a particular subject area. Using the least intrusive method of investigation will also lessen the likelihood that the investigation would be found offensive to a reasonable person. On the other hand, greater tolerance for intrusion will exist as the urgency of the situation increases or as less intrusive methods prove ineffective in producing meaningful results.

Public Disclosure of Private Facts

A second invasion of privacy tort is the public disclosure of private facts where that disclosure is offensive and objectionable to a reasonable person and the facts are not of legitimate public concern.(Prosser and Keeton, 1984) Note that this tort may be established, even though all of the facts disclosed are true. The essence of the violation is the disclosure of sensitive information to a public that has no need to know the information. In general, an employer warning intended to provide information that would promote the safety of the work force, should qualify for exception from the tort. Here again, however, the precise nature of the information disclosed and its relationship to the legitimate workplace violence concerns of the employer may be tested. In circumstances where there is any question of the validity of the communication, the employer should take pains to limit dissemination to those who have a demonstrable need to know. Note also that disclosure of private facts may implicate both victims and perpetrators of violence. Employers who come into possession of sensitive information as to either must exercise care in handling that information.

Presentation of Employee in a False Light

A third privacy tort can be established when the employee is presented in a false light to the public and a reasonable person would find such public disclosure offensive. In general, this tort would concern itself with published comments concerning a perpetrator of violence. Where an employer has issued warnings or answered public inquiries concerning objective and verified facts, the employer should not be liable because the employer has not placed the perpetrator in a "false light."

In all cases of employee privacy, the employer has a qualified privilege to investigate and address issues that are of legitimate concern to the employer. This would include, of course, workers' and customers' safety. As long as the employer's investigation in justified by legitimate interests and is undertaken in good faith, it should not result in liability. Even so, employers who undertake investigatory efforts in the workplace violence area, including surveillance of employees, should limit the scope of their inquiries to matters that have a direct or indirect bearing on the relevant issues and should protect the confidentiality of the information developed until a careful decision may be made concerning the dissemination that is to take place.

Employees' Right to Be Free from Infliction of Emotional Distress

An employer's good-faith efforts to investigate and prevent workplace violence will generally receive the protection of the law. As long as the potential for workplace violence is not used as a pretext for the malicious treatment of a given employee or individual, it is unlikely that a case for intentional infliction of emotional distress could be made out. Such a claim requires a showing of outrageous, intentional conduct by an employee that results in severe emotional distress. Conduct believed to be responsible in nature would rarely, if ever, meet this standard.

On the other hand, many states recognize a claim for negligent infliction of emotional distress in circumstances where a plaintiff is able to show that he or she suffered severe emotional distress, with resultant physical injuries, as a result of a direct invasion of rights. For example, in one Minnesota case, the plaintiff alleged that he suffered severe emotional distress as a result of the negligent manner in which he was fired: his supervisor, who contemporaneously asked questions of plaintiff's co-workers concerning plaintiff's expense reports, stood over him and watched while he cleaned out his desk before escorting plaintiff from the building. The court reasoned that the verbal and nonverbal conduct of the supervisor could be viewed as a false and defamatory statement that the plaintiff was a thief. Because of the direct invasion of privacy, the plaintiff was permitted to make a claim for negligent infliction of emotional distress upon a showing of distress sufficient to meet the legal test.

The implications for this cause of action in the workplace violence setting are clear: employers must act with appropriate discretion in dealing with putative aggressors on the job. In nonemergency situations, the level of intervention should be reasonable in relation to the nature of the alleged or actual violence, when considered in light of the security resources available to the employer.

Employees' Right to Damages for Interference with the Employment Relationship

Where a third party to an employee's relationship with the employer, such as a customer or a co-worker, demands that the employee be discharged, the employee may be able to state a claim for intentional interference with economic interests. In circumstances of workplace violence, such a claim would most likely be combined with an allegation of defamation, as the employee argued that he was falsely accused of violent behavior and that a third party maliciously interfered with his continued employment.

A party who asserts intentional interference generally must show the existence of the following five (5) factors:

- ✧ A valid contract between the plaintiff and another
- ✧ Defendant's knowledge of the contractual relationship
- ✧ Intentional conduct aimed at disrupting the contract
- ✧ An actual breach or termination of the contract
- ✧ Resulting damages to the plaintiff

All of the foregoing factors are fairly easy to demonstrate in the case of an individual who was fired from his job based upon an adverse report of threatening conduct amounting to workplace violence. Note that in meeting the third factor, a plaintiff may show that the defendant engaged in conduct that was "substantially certain" to interfere with the contract. Thus, even where an individual reports a problem to an employer but does not ask that the offending employee be fired or disciplined, the tort may be alleged on the basis that the actions of the reporting individual were very likely to cause serious repercussions for the employee.

Interference with "Prospective" Economic Advantage Recognized

In addition, to the foregoing, many states also recognize a cause of action for interference with "prospective" economic advantage. In general, these states require that an employee show the following causes:

✦ that there was a reasonable probability that the employee would enter a contract

✦ that the defendant maliciously prevented the relationship to occur so as to damage the plaintiff

✦ that the plaintiff suffered actual harm

This tort would come into play in circumstances where a former employer or other third party disrupted an individual's attempt to obtain new employment by providing a report as to the individual's violent tendencies.

Intentional Interference Requires Three Parties

With respect to both of the foregoing claims, however, the law recognizes a qualified privilege for managers and supervisors to make good-faith attempts to deal with the workplace violence issue. In addition, in the case of intentional interference with contract, the law requires that there be three (3) parties: the employer, the employee, and the third party who interfered with the contract. Because managers and supervisors are acting in the interest of the employer when dealing with workplace violence issues, they are not "third parties" within the meaning of the law. Thus, for example, a supervisor who recommends an employee for discharge is acting as the employer's agent and may generally not be sued on a claim of intentional interference. Rather, the law will allow this claim against an individual supervisor only where the facts show that the supervisor was acting for his or her personal reasons, unconnected to the objectives of the employer. This would be the case, for example, where a supervisor fired an employee for knowingly false reasons, out of malice created by a personal dispute.

A defendant who otherwise lacks a qualified privilege commonly recognized in the law (as, for example, a nonsupervisory co-worker who reports a violent fellow employee who is then fired), may nevertheless defend against an intentional interference claim on the basis that the public policy objectives furthered by the report justified the "interference." Generally, the courts examining this question will look to two factors:

✦ whether the inducement of the breach through a lawful report protects an interest that has a greater social value than the societal interest in the stability of the contract in question

✦ whether the reporting employee acted for a proper purpose

Where a third party interferes with an employment contract in order to protect the safety of himself or another, and not with improper intent, the court is apt to conclude that the interference was justified.

Employees' Entitlement to Contractual or Implied Contractual Protections

Contractual Employees' Rights

An employee who is employed pursuant to a written contract or collective bargaining agreement may have the right to procedural or substantive protections in the contract. For example, a contractual provision limiting an employer's ability to discharge to incidents of "just cause" alters the burdens that ordinarily apply to the termination of employment. Whereas, an employer which has received a report of alleged threatening conduct by an at-will employee may be free to discharge the employee, solely as a protective measure, the same freedom will not apply to a contractual employee. Instead, the employer in any ensuing arbitration or court proceeding will bear the burden of showing that it possessed sufficient evidence to terminate—evidence rising to the level of just cause. In addition, an employer may be vulnerable to a claim that it reacted to a given case or report more harshly than it had at sometime in the past. A showing of disparate treatment will likely produce an order to reinstate the aggrieved employee, perhaps with back pay.

Egregious Conduct Exceptions

Where an employer has been ordered to retract discipline that was found to breach a "just cause" provision, it will generally have a difficult time in reversing the ruling on appeal. Because of the deference shown by appellate courts to arbitration awards and to factual findings made at the trial court level, employers should presume that such ruling will be enforced. On the other hand, there have been cases in which egregious conduct by an employee has formed the basis for an appeal to "public policy" in setting the ruling aside. Such a claim might be successfully pursued, for example, in the case of an employee who engaged in admitted and severe harassment based on race or sex. Similarly, an order to re-employ an individual who has engaged in serious physical violence toward another may be susceptible to such an attack on appeal.

Role of Employee Handbook Language

In the case of employees who are seemingly employed "at-will," many states recognize the implied-in-fact contract doctrine under which an employer may, through its employment handbook and policies, create an obligation to provide certain procedural or other rights to employees. Where such rights are recognized, employers who are faced with allegations of workplace violence by an employee must account for the possibility of a suit for contract breach in the event the employee is discharged. In those states where such a doctrine is recognized, employers should take steps that minimize both the threat of violence and the risk that a charged employee may be able to challenge the legitimacy of any employer action. Before any threat or violence occurs, the employer should review its handbook and personnel policies to ensure that they contain no statements that could suggest a limitation on the employer's right to discharge for any violent action, irrespective of its level of intensity. Even where an employer otherwise chooses to give employees some procedural or other protections from summary discharge, it should be made clear that aggressive or violent conduct is an exception to the progressive disciplinary scheme and will result in immediate termination in all instances. The presence of such language in an employee handbook, for example, was discussed in a West Virginia case. There, the court rejected a discharged violent employee's claim that he was entitled to procedural protections set forth in company personnel policies. The court noted that, whatever else the company had stated, its handbook provided for immediate discharge for fighting or engaging in any activity which may result in bodily injury to employees or guests.

Resolving Workplace Violence Threat

Whether an employer has the legal right to immediately discharge is a separate question from the mechanics that should be followed by an employer in dealing with an issue of workplace violence. Generally speaking, an employer should opt for an immediate resolution of the workplace violence threat. This may be accomplished through a variety of means including, suspension of the violent employee pending investigation, the granting of leave to the employee or the victimized employee, transfers to physically separate (and possibly protected) locations and the like. Obviously, the feasibility of a given resolution will depend upon the employer's circumstances and the severity of the allegations. In general, however, an employer is well advised to take actions that err on the side of protecting employee safety, while also avoiding unnecessary confrontation or interference with the rights and interests of an alleged perpetrator who has denied the accusation of violent behavior. To the extent that an employer is concerned that it may be violating the accused employee's contractual rights, it may honor those rights by paying the employee while on leave or by providing an opportunity to be heard in defense of the allegations. It should also assure the accused employee that the matter will be dealt with confidentially, unless and until it is determined that the employer's obligation to workplace safety requires that the matter be made public.

In cases in which the accused employee has admitted engaging in the conduct at issue, an employer may (in appropriate circumstances) consider encouraging the employee to resign, in lieu of termination. The employer may also negotiate with the employee to accept a postdischarge referral to an employee assistance program, where the source of the violence may be a treatable substance abuse or psychological problem. At all times, the employer must recall that it has the obligation to act reasonably with respect to both the alleged victim of violence and the alleged perpetrator, although the safety of the former is entitled to more weight.

Employees' Right to Be Free from Assault, Battery, False Imprisonment, and Other Torts

An employee who is accused of past workplace violence, particularly that involving less serious conduct, retains his right to be free from physical harm by an employer or its agents. In the context of an investigation of workplace violence, an investigated employee may raise a claim for a number of intentional torts including

⋄ assault and battery

⋄ false imprisonment

⋄ intentional infliction of emotional distress

These claims will generally arise out of actions by the employer's management team, security force, or medical department. Employers should ensure that those who are involved in the investigation of workplace violence claims understand the limits of the law and are trained in handling investigations so as to minimize the possibility of injury to themselves or to the interests of employees.

Assault and Battery

Assault and battery are separate torts but frequently arise out of a common set of operative facts. To successfully prove the tort of assault, a plaintiff must demonstrate the existence of these two conditions:

- ✧ that the defendant acted with the intent to cause a harmful or offensive touching of the plaintiff's person

- ✧ that the plaintiff reasonably feared that such touching would occur

In the context of an intense interrogation, for example, an investigator who raised his fist in anger as if to strike the interviewee would likely commit an actionable civil assault.

Battery is defined as the intentional, unlawful, and harmful or offensive contact by one person with another. For this purpose the term "intentional" is a term of art and does not require that the defendant actually intended to touch the plaintiff in a way that would be found offensive. Rather, conduct is intentional if the defendant intended to take the action that resulted in the offensive or harmful touching. In the example above, for instance, if the investigator swung his fist, intending that it narrowly miss the interviewee's face, the battery would be completed if he should misjudge the distance and connect. It would be no defense that he did not intend the harm to occur.

Managers, investigators, and medical practitioners should be aware that their concern for the seriousness of an incident of workplace violence, or even their concern for the well-being of the accused, will not excuse an unconsented-to assault or battery. That does not mean, of course, that such personnel are not entitled to do their jobs and to defend themselves reasonably against aggression. In the case of a medical department employee, for example, a highly agitated employee who is judged a threat to himself or others may be reasonably restrained. On the other hand, an employee who has shown no tendency toward physical violence may warrant a different response.

False Imprisonment

A recurring issue in the investigation of incidents of workplace violence is the question of the level of security that should attend interviews or other encounters with alleged violent employees. One of the claims that frequently arises from employee interviews is the tort of false imprisonment. The tort represents a violation of the liberty interest of another and generally requires a showing that there was a direct restraint of another, for some appreciable length of time, however short, compelling him to stay or go against his will.

Employment cases concerning false imprisonment generally focus on the nature of the direct restraint applied to the employee. The tort is established by proof of force, but the force applied need not be physical. As one California court described the element:

The restraint constituting false imprisonment may arise out of acts, words, gestures, or the like, which induce a reasonable apprehension that force will be used if the plaintiff does not submit, and it is sufficient if they operate upon the will of the person threatened, and result in the reasonable fear of personal difficulties or personal injuries.

Given that false imprisonment may arise from "acts, words, or gestures," employers should not require an employee to participate in an interview against his will. In circumstances where an employee declines to participate in an investigation, the employer should respond by exercising its right to terminate the employee for the underlying incident or for the employee's failure to assist in the conduct of a legitimate investigation. (This form of employer economic "coercion" is not generally regarded as a basis for a false imprisonment claim). Only in circumstances of imminent harm or apprehension by law enforcement authorities should an employee be physically restrained and, then, only by employees who are specially licensed or trained for the purpose.

Where an employee agrees to engage in an interview or other face-to-face encounter with agents of the employer, care should be taken to ensure the safety of personnel while avoiding needless conflicts with employee rights. For example, staff should be trained in how to deal with the potentially violent employee, how to prepare themselves and the meeting room so that the risk of potential harm is minimized—as, for example, by appropriate dress and removal of objects that might be used to injure.

At the same time, however, consideration should be given to the concerns of the employee. If security officers are to be present for protection, or if the interviewer is stationed next to the door (for quick exit), it should be explained to the employee that he is free to leave at any time and will not be interfered with, if he chooses to do so. If the door is closed for privacy, the employee should be informed that it is unlocked and that he may exit at any time. If the employee is not to be permitted to remain on the premises, or is restricted in the areas of the facility in which he may travel, the approved path for his voluntary exit should be explained to him in the meeting and he should be informed, if appropriate, that a representative of management or security will escort him to the exit and arrange for his discreet departure from the facility. By anticipating and removing an employee's possible claim of a direct physical restraint, the employer will further its overall interests in an effective workplace violence program.

Conclusion

The law of the American workplace traditionally has focused on "rules" and the consequences of breaking those "rules." Poor performers could be terminated. Employers that discriminated against employees paid back pay and reinstated victims of discrimination. The rise of workplace violence adds a very problematic dimension to the written and unwritten "legal code" of the workplace. Violence in the workplace involves persons who not only break the rules, it involves individuals who do not recognize that rules exist.

No longer can an employer discharge an abusive employee with impunity; that employee may return with a machine gun. It is, obviously, hardly a legal victory to terminate such an employee "lawfully." Today's employers must beware of wrongful death cases filed by co-workers' spouses when the former employee "flips out." Just as someone would not step in front of an out-of-control truck simply because the "light was green," so, too, employers must use new types of judgment in addressing the "legality" of their conduct in dealing with problem employees.

Virtually all of the key legal principles that have evolved to govern the modern American workplace have direct relevance to the workplace violence issue. Employers owe many and varied duties to employees, patrons and, perhaps, to members of the public, based upon rights and obligations arising out of these employment law concepts. Most of these concepts seek to protect the innocent individual from assaultive conduct. Some, may also be applied, however, to protect the rights of an alleged perpetrator of violence. Understanding and balancing those rights and obligations is a fluid and challenging endeavor.

References

(Chapters 8, 9, 10)

Adler, W.N., Kreeger, C., and Ziegler, P. "Patient violence in a psychiatric hospital." In J.R. Lion and W.H. Reid (Eds.). *Assaults within Psychiatric Facilities*, (pp. 81-90). Orlando, FL: Grune & Stratton, Inc. 1983.

Bell, C. "Female homicides in United States workplaces," 1980-1985. *American Journal of Public Health*, 81(6), 729-732. 1991.

Blair, T. and New, S.A. "Assaultive Behavior." *Journal of Psychosocial Nursing*, 29(11), 25-29. 1991.

Bernstein, H.A. "Survey of threats and assaults directed toward psychotherapists." *American Journal of Psychotherapy*, 35(4), 542-549. 1981.

California Department of Industrial Relations, *California Code of Regulations*, Title 8, General Industry Safety Orders, Sections 303, 6184 and 3400.

Carmel, H., and Hunter, M. "Staff injuries from inpatient violence." *Hospitals and Community Psychiatry*, 40(1), 41-46. 1989.

Carmel, H. and Hunter, M. "Compliance with training in managing assaultive behavior and injuries from in-patient violence." *Hospital and Community Psychiatry*, 41(5), 558–560. 1990.

Centers for Disease Control (CDC). "Occupational homicides among women— United States, 1980-1985." *MMWR*, 39, 543-544, 551-552. 1990.

Cohen, S., Karmarck, T. and Mermelstein, R. "A global measure of perceived stress." *Journal of Health and Social Behavior*, 24, 395-396. December 1983.

Conn, L. M., and Lion, J. R. "Assaults in a university hospital." *Assaults Within Psychiatric Facilities*, (pp. 61-69). Philadelphia, PA: W.B. Saunders and Co. 1983.

Craig, T.J. "An epidemiological study of problems associated with violence among psychiatric patients." *American Journal of Psychiatry*, 139(1), 1262-1266. 1982.

Cronin, Michael. "New law aims to reduce kidnappings." *Nurse Week*, 5 (3), 1 and 24. 1991.

Davidson, P., and Jackson, C. "The nurse as survivor: delayed posttraumatic stress reaction and cumulative trauma in nursing." *International Journal of Nursing Studies*, 22(1), 1-13. 1985.

Dillon, S. "Social Workers: Targets in a violent society," *New York Times* 11/18/ 92, pp. A1 and A18. 1992.

Edelman, S.E. "Managing the violent patient in a community mental health center." *Hospital and Community Psychiatry*, 29(7), 460-462. 1978.

Eichelman, E. "A behavioral emergency plan." *Hospital and Community Psychiatry*, 35(10), 1678. 1984.

Engle, F., and Marsh, S. "Helping the employee victim of violence in hospitals." *Hospital and Community Psychiatry*, 37(2), 159-162. 1986.

Fineberg, N.A. James, D.V. and Shah, A.K. "Agency nurses and violence in a psychitric ward." *The Lancet*, 1, 474. 1988.

Goetz, R.R., Bloom, J.D., Chenell, S.L. and Moorehead, J.C. "Weapons possessed by patients in a university emergency department." *Annuls of Emergency Medicine*, 20(1), 8-10. 1981.

Gosnold, D.K. "The violent patient in the accident and emergency department." *Royal Society of Health Journal*,98(4), 189-190. 1978.

Haffke, E.A., and Reid, W.H. "Violence against mental health personnel in Nebraska." In J.R. Lion, and W.H. Reid (Eds.), *Assaults within Psychiatric Facilities* (pp. 91-102). Orlando, FL: Grune and Stratton, Inc. 1983.

Hatti, S., Dubin, W.R., and Weiss, K.J. "A study of circumstances surrounding patient assaults on psychiatrists." *Hospital and Community Psychiatry*, 33(8), 660-661. 1982.

Hodgkinson, P., Hillis, T., and Russell, D. (1984). "Assaults on staff in psychiatric hospitals." *Nursing Times*, 80, 44-46. 1984.

Infantano, A.J., and Musingo, S. "Assaults and injuries among staff with and without training in aggression control techniques." *Hospital and Community Psychiatry*, 36, 1312-1314. 1983.

Ionno, J. A. "A prospective study of assaultive behavior in female psychiatric inpatients." In J.R. Lion and W.H. Reid (Eds.), *Assaults within Psychiatric Facilities*, (pp. 71080). Orlando, FL: Grune & Stratton, Inc. 1983.

Jones, M.K. "Patient violence report of 200 incidents." *Journal of Psychosocial Nursing and Mental Health Services*, 23(6), 12-17. 1985.

Jenkins, L.E., Layne, L., and Kesner, S. "Homicides in the workplace." *The Journal of the American Association of Occupational Health Nurses*, 40(5), 215-218. 1992.

Keep, N., and Gilbert, P., et al. "California Emergency Nurses Asssociations informal survey of violence in California emergency departments." *Journal of Emergency Nursing*, 18(5), 433-442. 1992.

Kraus, J.F. "Homicide while at work: Persons, industries and occupations at high risk." *American Journal of Public Health*, 77, 1285-1289. 1987.

Kurlowicz, L. "Violence in the emergency department." *American Journal of Nursing*, 90(9), 34-37. 1990.

Kuzmits, F.E. "When employees kill other employees: The case of Joseph T. Wesbecker." *Journal of Occupational Medicine*, 32(10), 1014-1020. 1990.

La Brash, L., Cain, J. "A near-fatal assault on a psychiatric unit." *Hospital and Community Psychiatry,* 35(2), 168-169. 1994.

Lanza, M.L. "Victim assault support team for staff." *Hospital and Community Psychiatry*, 35(5), 492-494. 1984.

Levin, P.F., Hewitt, J., Misner, S. "Female workplace homicides." *The Journal of the American Association of Occupational Health Nurses,* 40(8), 229-236. 1992.

Levy, P., and Hartocollis, P. "Nursing aides and patient violence." *American Journal of Psychiatry*, 133(4), 429-431. 1976.

Liss, G. M. "Examination of workers compensation claims among nurses in Ontario for injuries due to violence." Unpublished report, Health and Safety Studies Unit—Ministry of Labor. 1993.

Mantell, M. "The crises response team reports on Edmond, Oklahoma massacre." *Nova Newsletter 11.* 1987.

Meddis, S. V. "7 cities lead violence epidemic." *USA Today,* April 29, 1991.

Morrison, E.F., and Hertzog, E.A. "What therapeutic and protective measures, as well as legal actions, can staff take when they are attacked by patients." *Journal of Psychological Nursing*, 30(7), 41-44. 1992.

Prosser, W., Keeton, W. *Prosser and Keeton on the Law of Torts* 773-778 (5th ed.) 1984.

Scott, J. R., and Whitehead, J.J. "An administrative approach to the problem of violence." *Journal of Mental Health Administration*, 8(2), 36-40. 1981.

State of California/Internal Memorandum. "Employee lost workday injuries from client violence." 1973-1980. 1980.

Tardiff, K. and Sweillam, A. "Assault, suicide and mental illness." *Archives of General Psychiatry*, 37(2), 164-169. 1980.

U.S. Department of Labor, Bureau of Labor Statistics. *Occupational Injuries and Illnesses in the United States by Industry, 1989.* Bulletin 2379. 1991.

Wasserberger, J., Ordog, G. J., Kolodny, M., and Allen, K. "Violence in a Community Emergency Room." *Archives of Emergency Medicine*, 6, 266-29. 1989.

White, S.G., and Hatcher, C. (1988). "Violence and trauma response." Larsen, R.C., and Felton, J.. (Editor), "Psychiatric injury in the workplace." *Occupational Medicine: State of the Art Reviews*, 3(4), 677-694. Hanley & Belfus, Inc., Philadelphia.

Wilkinson, T. "Drifter judged sane in killing of mental health therapist." *Los Angeles Times*, December 11, 1990, B1-B4. 1990.

Domestic Violence— Impact on the Workplace
A Polaroid Experience

James Hardeman, MSW, MPA

Case Study

Amy Jones had worked as a secretary for two years. During that period there had been times she might call in sick at the last minute and might be out for several days. A couple of times she was noted to have discoloration under her makeup that was thought to be bruises. Over the past few months this behavior had recurred and was combined with problems when she was at work. She was getting calls several times a day from her husband, who had been laid off of work two weeks ago. She was distracted at work and the quality of her work had slipped. Her co-workers were worried about her. They had been giving her the easier jobs and had noticed her almost in tears several times. She was out last week and today came back to work with a cast on her arm and heavy makeup on her face. As her manager, you are concerned about domestic violence and decide to speak with her. What do you say and how do you do it?

Introduction

In 1992, the National Institute of Occupational Safety and Health stated that approximately 750 workplace homicides occur annually. Four percent of these acts of violence involved intimate relationships. The 750 homicides do not truly represent the actual violence that occurs in the workplace. There is an estimated one million workers who annually become victims of nonfatal workplace violence. Incidents such as intimidation, sexual harassment, stalking, assaults, battery, and rape carry no price tag. No dollar amount can balance the impact of depression, panic disorders, posttraumatic stress, eating disorders, and other addictive illnesses stemming from incidents of workplace violence. For the most part, businesses do not have the knowledge to deal with family violence incidences in the workplace and many businesses still maintain the view that what occurs in partner abuse is a "private family affair." No internal protocols are in place as a response, and furthermore, no training is provided for employee assistance program staff, human resource personnel, administrators or professionals. Victimization in the workplace can cost an estimated $55 million annually in lost wages. There is no realistic estimate of dollars lost to short-term and long-term disability.

The business community should be cognizant of the OSHA General Duty Clause:

> Each employer shall furnish to each of its employees employment
> which is free from recognized hazards that cause or are likely to
> cause death or serious physical harm to employees.

The business community has only recently begun to heighten its awareness concerning the influence domestic violence has on its employees and to maintain "zero" tolerance to violence in the business environment, but businesses are unaware how to fulfill that responsibility. I hear, from corporations and businesses across the country, the same kind of arguments that I heard in courts and from the police in the 70s when I first became involved in the battered women shelter movement: "It's a private family affair. Why should we become involved? The employees can make a choice whether to stay with the abuser or leave! Employers are victims of employees' poor decisions."

What employers need to ask themselves is "Where do we hire our employees?" The question seems quite simple enough. If the correct response is "from society," then management must realize that whatever exists in the general public also exists in the business environment. The statistics shown in the fact sheet about the impact of domestic violence on the workplace clearly indicate that these acts of violence are not private family affairs, but felonies.

Fact Sheet: Impact of Domestic Violence on Corporate America

❖ On a national level, domestic violence costs employers $3 to $5 billion annually due to worker absenteeism, increased health care costs, higher turnover, and lower productivity. (The Boston Globe, March 11, 1993)

❖ Abusive husbands and lovers harass 74% of employed battered women at work, either in person or over the telephone, causing 56% of them to be late for work at least five times a month, 28% to leave early at least five days a month, 54% to miss at least three full days of work a month (New York Victim Service Agency Report on the Costs of Domestic Violence, 1987), and 20% to lose their jobs. (Schechter and Gray, "A Framework for Understanding and Empowering Battered Women," Abuse and Victimization Across the Life Span. Ed. Martha Strauss, 1988, p. 242)

❖ In 1980 an estimated 175,000 days were lost from paid work as a result of domestic assaults. The total health-care costs of family violence were estimated at more than $44 million each year. (Richard Gelles, *Family Violence*, Newbury Park, CA: Sage Publications, 1987, p. 13.)

❖ Thirty percent of all women seeking treatment in hospital emergency rooms are victims of battering by a husband or boyfriend. (American Medical Association)

❖ Every year, domestic violence results in almost 100,000 days of hospitalizations, almost 30,000 emergency department visits, and almost 40,000 visits to a physician. (American Medical Association, 1991)

❖ Murder is a leading cause of on-the-job death among women. In 1992 approximately 20 percent of the women killed in the workplace were murdered by a husband or a male partner, current or former. (Bureau of Labor Statistics, 1993)

❖ In the United States, every year between 150 and 180 women are murdered at work. That's an average of three women a week killed on the job. Reasons cited include retaliation from disgruntled employees and domestic violence. (National Institute for Occupational Safety and Health, NIOSH, November 1993)

❖ Ninety-six percent of employed battered women experienced problems at work due to the abuse. (DV Intervention Services, Tulsa, 1992)

❖ Half of the employed battered women missed three days of work/monthly; 64% were late to work; 75% used company time to deal with the violence because they could not do so at home. (Victims Service Agency, New York, 1987)

❖ Harassment on the job by the batterer, as well as the burden of time spent waiting to appear in court, reduce battered women's ability to maintain or secure employment. (Conversations with Kristin Miccio, Director and Attorney in Charge, Sanctuary for Families, Center for Battered Women's Legal Services and Beverly Sowande, New York Womens Bar Association, Committee on Battered Women, June 12, 1990, appearing in Helen Neubornes testimony at the Biden hearings)

Domestic Violence: In Search of a Safe Place

Let's take a closer look at domestic violence from a community perspective. The family unit is viewed as the foundation of American life, and, when threatened, the seeds of future generations are affected. A major threat today is family or domestic violence. Domestic violence is the number one leading cause of injury to women(Guerino). Approximately one out of every three women who enter a hospital emergency room shows the effects of injuries suffered as a result of domestic violence. The Center for Disease Control reports that more women seek treatment in our nation's emergency rooms as a result of family violence injuries than from auto accidents, muggings, and rapes combined. Women are nine times more in danger at home than in the street. Every 18 seconds a woman is beaten in the United States.(Guerino)

The problem is called domestic violence. Domestic violence can be defined as "assaultive behavior" involving adults who are married, cohabitating, or having an ongoing or prior intimate relationship. In most instances, spousal abuse is

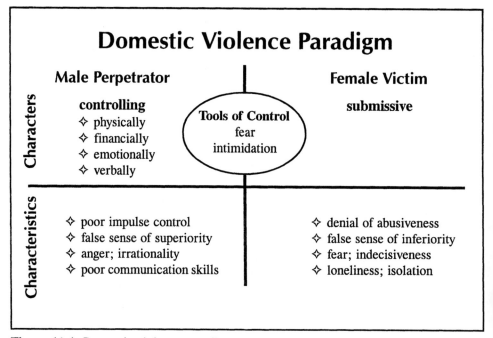

Figure 11.1: Domestic violence paradigm

perpetrated by men and often results in victims being critically injured and/or emotionally handicapped.

In October 1987, a Massachusetts Department of Public Health report stated that "every 22 days" a woman in Massachusetts is murdered by her male partner. Today the number of days has been reduced to eight (8). In 50% of domestic homicides, police had been called to the home five times or more. Local, state, and federal authorities failed to see their intervention as a viable measure toward dealing with the problem.

The effects of domestic violence can be evident over many generations. Consider the effects on children who grow up in violent homes. Sixty-three percent of males between the ages of 11 to 20 who are in prison for murder, killed their mother's batterer.

✧ These children are six times more likely to abuse alcohol or drugs

✧ These children are 50% more likely to abuse alcohol or drugs

✧ These children have a 24% greater likelihood of committing sexual assaults

✧ These children have a 74% greater chance of committing crimes against a person

Family and Workplace Violence: Common Ground

One must not forget that the two places employees spend most of their time is either at work or home. Employees who are violent and abusive at home may also be violent at work. It is ideal if both home and work are safe places, but that is not always the case. Having one "safe place" provides an individual the opportunity to obtain support, encouragement, and a sense of belonging. Candidates for acting violently in the workplace, traditionally, do not have a "safe place within the home." When the primary anchor becomes work and it no longer is a safe place, resentment, despair, anger, blame, insecurity, and victimization overwhelm employees. It is important that managers and supervisors be cognizant of employees' home situations when conducting performance evaluations. Acknowledgment of employees' privacy is critical, so the focus remains "job performance." Open-ended questions should be asked; employees will lead their supervisors into those confidential arenas without any pressure. In view of this interview training is highly suggested. (See Appendix 11C.)

Workplace violence situations will escalate when employees no longer have either home or work as safe places and they feel that their employer has victimized them through such actions as termination. Employees, in turn, feel they have the right to react violently. The profiles for those employees who are violent in the workplace are similar to those of individuals who are violent within the home. The paradigm exists in both workplace and family violence; the parallels are clear. (See Figure 11.2.)

	Workplace Violence	**Domestic Violence**
Site Of Violence:	Workplace	Home
Legal Classification:	Criminal	Civil
Victim:	co-worker/supervisor	partner

Parallels:

✧ Captive audience: family or employer

✧ Male perpetrators are usually the aggressors; see themselves as victims

✧ Power and control behavior are exhibited by the perpetrator at work and/ or home

✧ Perpetrators experience personal or environmental stressors that they can't manage

✧ Perpetrators feel insecure and threatened; impaired decision-making

✧ There is usually a history of assaultive behavior; poor communication skills

✧ Abusers are emotionally impaired (permanently or temporarily): poor impulse control skills

✧ No venue for relief from personal and environmental threats: feeling overwhelmed

✧ Violence is used as a means to re-engineer the environment to ones own liking at home and at work;

✧ Victimization could be random: warning signs of being out of control

Figure 11.2: Parallels between workplace and family violence

Figures 11.3 and 11.4 provide an interesting parallel between domestic violence from Lenore Walker's perception and the impact of domestic violence in the workplace. Figure 11.3 conveys behavior of victims and perpetrators involved in spousal abuse within the home. Figure 11.4 conveys behavior of both parties in the workplace. Ironically, the cycle theory of violence applies to both arenas.

The perspective of power and control plays a dramatic role in both the home and workplace. The concept of power and control points to the perpetrator's attempt to intimidate the victim through fear. This seduction through fear overwhelms the victim into submission. The perpetrator's desire is to capture control over the decision making process of his victim. His intent is to destroy the independent thinking of his partner. This dynamic is depicted in Figure 11.5. In the cycle of power and control, the perpetrator uses intimidation, isolation, and threats to gain control. In the process there may be emotional abuse, economic abuse, and sexual abuse as well as physical abuse. At work we can see how the cycle of violence can be played out by both the victim and perpetrator. The victim, for whom work may be a safe place, will maintain the secret of abuse even when physical and emotional evidence intrudes at the workplace. As a result, she (the victim is usually female) is increasingly isolated from her co-workers. As her job performance worsens, she may continue to deny the existence of any problems. Her co-workers are increasingly concerned. At the point where the employee is able to share the secret of abuse, the company can mobilize its resources, refer the employee to a support group, and assist in making work and home a safe place again.

The perpetrator may be intrusive at work through demanding phone calls, threats, stalking behavior, and even assault. Or, when the victim is not in the workplace, the perpetrator may bring from home the same feelings of insecurity, poor communication skills, and problems with impulse control. These may result in a series of minor incidents with supervisors and co-workers. His (the perpetrator is usually male) manipulation and threatening behavior will make both his supervisor and other employees uncomfortable and fearful. As tension builds at home or at work, there may be destruction of property and more direct threats. The company must intervene before the employee has a chance to act. The employer must ensure that work is a safe place for all employees and may need to remove the aggressive employee from the workplace.

Perpetrator	Victim
Male	Female
Phase 1: Tension Building	
Experiences increased tension	Compliant, good behavior
Increases threats	Minimizes problems
Takes more control	Denies anger
	Withdraws
	Tension intolerable
Phase 2: Acute Battering	
Unpredictable	Is helpless, feels trapped
Claims loss of control	Traumatized
Highly abusive	
Phase 3: Kindness and Loving Behavior	
Often apologetic, attentive	Mixed feelings
Manipulative	Feels guilty and responsible
Promises change	Considers reconciliation

Adapted from Lenore Walker, *Cycle of Violence*

Figure 11.3: Cycle of violence within the home

Corporate Response to Workplace Violence

Polaroid Corporation Experience

Polaroid has developed an approach to workplace violence based upon the following points:

❖ Businesses, large and small, have a responsibility to maintain a safe work environment, and the measures they take to accomplish that end are critical.

Perpetrator	Victim
Male	**Female**

Phase 1: Tension Building

Demanding phone calls	Embarrassment; face-saving
Manipulation	Denial; maintains secret of abuse
Series of minor incidents	Physical and emotional ailments
with supervisor or co-worker	appear
Absenteeism and poor job	Isolation from co-workers
performance	Poor job performance
Threats and destruction of property	Peers become anxious and fearful

Phase 2: Acute Battering

Violence in the workplace	Unveils secret of abuse
Company must take action	Company mobilizes HR
Employee may be removed from	resources
the workplace	

Phase 3: Kindness and Loving Behavior

Refer to batterers program; therapy	Refer to support group
Corporation honors court orders	Collaborate with outside
Issue of continued work	resources

Figure 11.4: Cycle of violence at the workplace

✧ Protocols, guidelines, and policies that address workplace violence are developed through a formal, well-thought-out process. Skipping a crucial step could communicate "false hopes" of safety to employees and result in serious liability concerns.

✧ Family violence has significant influence on the overall concept of a business response to the prevention of violence against women in the workplace.

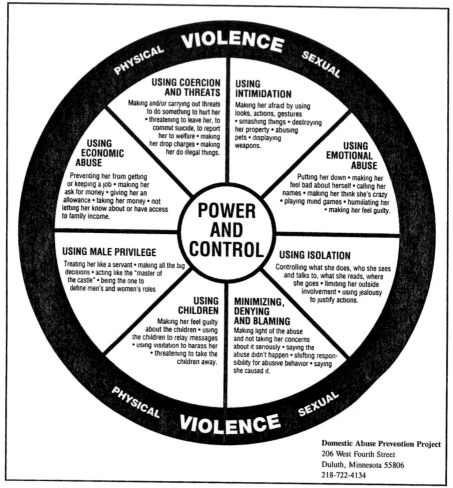

Domestic Abuse Prevention Project
206 West Fourth Street
Duluth, Minnesota 55806
218-722-4134

Figure 11.5: Cycle of power and control

❖ Issues of liability must be of considerable concern when formulating plans for implementation, including training of management and the workforce. Knowledge of company personnel policies and grievance procedures is also a must.

Management has a responsibility to maintain a safe work environment. State and federal laws exist that spell out penalties for failure to protect the workforce. False hopes of safety also exist if guidelines (policies), protocols, and training are not developed. It takes special skills and knowledge to accomplish this task. The third point above is a statement that family violence doesn't exist just in the home but

---

Checklist 11.1

Manager's Responsibilities in Case of Suspected Domestic Abuse

✔ Be aware of absence/behavior as performance concerns

✔ Be aware of bruises to face and arms

✔ Remember employee must self-disclose

✔ Consult with HR/EAP with concerns and for advice

✔ Maintain confidentiality at all times

✔ Honor civil service protection orders

✔ Contact security to review safety plan

✔ Be supportive and understanding

---

travels to the workplace as well. Management needs to accept a commitment to address various types of workplace violence and avoid issues of liability.

The case cited below is an incident that occurred at Polaroid Corporation in 1994. Guidelines for addressing the impact of domestic violence in the workplace were produced in the same year. (See Appendices 11A and 11B.) The case is one of the company's worse scenarios for management because training had not been implemented. The case is presently used in management training. The names of the Polaroid employees other than that of the author have been changed.

Case Summary: John Doe

John presents himself as a very angry man who struggles to maintain a sense of equilibrium between what is real and tangible and a world of paranoia and delusions. This fine line that separates reality and fantasy for John seems to evaporate when stress and depression engulfs him. His inability to focus and explain his feelings around the current circumstances are poor, at best, and his responses are dotted with events and facts not remotely related to the conversation.

Apparently, John was very agitated by an event that he perceived as intentional when he was pushed by a co-worker. John accused the co-worker of assault and battery. The co-worker and a witness to the event denied any form of assaultive behavior. John's response to what occurred was a threat to kill the co-worker. The threat was taken seriously and was reported to John's supervisor by the co-worker.

The supervisor, in turn, notified the employee assistance program department. John met with the Employee Assistance Program manager.

During the onset of our meeting, John presented himself in an argumentative manner. He claimed he was being set up to be terminated by his supervisor and manager. A series of meetings was scheduled with John, his advocate, and his supervisor as a means to understand what actually occurred. On each occasion John demonstrated poor impulse control and an inability to remain orientated in time and place of events. After assessing John's mental status, he was referred for an outside psychiatric evaluation. The purpose of the evaluation was to develop a risk management analysis prior to John's return to the workplace. John remained on administrative leave with pay until the psychiatric evaluation was completed and the EAP manager advised management of the risk involved in his return to the Polaroid community.

Concerns

- ✧ Series of previous events of intimidation/conflicts
- ✧ Paranoid/delusion tendencies
- ✧ Fragile impulse control
- ✧ Inappropriate demonstration of anger/resentment
- ✧ Decompensating

Chronology of Events

Let's go through the chronology of events to better understand the case.

December 5, 1994

The EAP Manager met with Jim Karl, John's supervisor who shared concerns about a threat John Doe made towards a fellow employee. The victim of the threat and Jim Karl took the verbal threat seriously and Jim sought consultation on what action could be taken. I suggested that I would meet with John Doe. The Threats of Violence guideline was reviewed and submitted to Jim Karl.

John Doe has a history of intimidating behaviors, not only to his wife, who is a company employee, but also to his peers. Many of his promotions came from supervisors efforts to get rid of John. They became part of the problem.

December 8, 1994

An intake session was conducted. John appeared agitated throughout the session and indicated his hesitancy about coming. The purpose for the session and boundaries of confidentiality were explained. John explained the circumstances behind his threat of violence and his difficulties working within the department. Upon conclusion of the session, I found John's resentment and anger, relative to being "pushed" appropriate, but not the threat to kill. My diagnosis of John's mental status was of serious concern, and I sought a second clinical opinion. My assessment was that no one was in immediate danger.

There exists a history of abuse in John's family. He has a focus on being a man and demanding respect. As John's anger escalates, his ability to think clearly diminishes. No one has the ability to manage both anger and think clearly simultaneously. Due to minimal impulse control, John seems to opt for physical intimidation to drive the victim into submission. John has a tendency to seek control. He uses denial to disqualify his behavior and proceeds to manipulate supervisors.

December 21, 1994

A joint session was scheduled with both the supervisor and John, but only the supervisor appeared. The conversation centered around my clinical diagnosis and recommendations. Jim, as John's supervisor, failed to validate John's complaints of being harassed by his peers. According to Jim, John was not one to fit in; he was always the outsider. The second meeting between John and me did occur, and Susan Day, his advocate, was also present. John had an opportunity to present his personal concerns and react to my diagnosis and recommendations. John was given 24 hours to respond to all clinical concerns and management also was informed that the Risk Management Team would be consulted if John refused to be seen for a second clinical opinion. John's abusive behavior in the workplace was the focus since John was not referred by my office for domestic violence. The cycle of violence was occurring at work. If John couldn't have his way, intimidation was soon to follow. The work environment seemed to be the enabler. John was rarely held accountable.

December 22, 1994

John notified the EAP Office that he would not seek a second clinical opinion. Telephone contact was sought with following departments: medical, legal, and security. The group collaborated in the decision to recommend to management that John be placed on "administrative leave with pay," as of December 23, 1994, and remain in this status until further notice. Management agreed to accept this recommendation and implemented it.

It was decided to assign an employee to remain in contact with John during segregation from the company. This is a preventive measure to keep John from appearing on company property until he is cleared. This assigned employee provides updates to John and assists in getting his anxiety down. Communication is extremely important in managing work situations that have the potential for violence.

March 1995

John requests that he be allowed to return to work. He is referred to a psychologist for evaluation and assessment of fitness to return to work. The psychologist recommends treatment to address mental illness and difficulties with relationships. (See Figure 11.6.)

March 29, 1995

Jim Hardeman
Polaroid Employee Assistance Program
Polaroid Corporation
750 Main Street-2E
Cambridge, MA 02139

RE: JOHN DOE

Dear Dr. Hardeman:

At your request I have conducted a fitness for duty evaluation of your employee, Mr. John Doe. As you will see from the enclosed report, I met with Mr. Doe on three occasions, conducted an MMPI-2 evaluation, and have determined that he is fit to return to work with certain conditions.

It is my primary recommendation that Mr. Doe immediately enter treatment to deal with his bipolar illness and focus on his difficulties in relationships. In my meeting with Mr. Doe today, he appeared quite willing to do so.

I hope that this evaluation is of assistance in your work with this employee. Thank you for the opportunity to conduct this interesting evaluation.

Yours very truly,

Ronald Smith, Ph.D.

Figure 11.6: Fitness for duty evaluation

April 6, 1995

The Manager sends John a letter setting conditions for return to work. These conditions include ongoing treatment and regular meeting with the Polaroid EAP manager. (See Figure 11.7.) It is recommended that employees demonstrating behavior similar to John's be kept on probation during the entire treatment period. The treatment should be monitored by a member of the internal EAP department. It should also be noted that short-term treatment is not recommended. Abusive behavior is a learned behavior and has been acquired over a lengthy period of time.

April 6, 1995

Dear John Doe:

You completed an assessment with Dr. Ronald Smith on Thursday, March 23, 1995. The assessment results require that you fulfill the following:

✧ You must sign a release of confidentiality. James Hardeman, Manager of the Employee Assistance Program at Polaroid will contact Dr. B. Thomas, your chosen therapist. Jim will review recommendations with her regarding your treatment and medication.

✧ You must initiate and maintain an appointment schedule with Dr. Thomas who will report your attendance monthly to James Hardeman at 386-8288.

✧ You must meet with James Hardeman monthly.

You are expected to comply to the above requirements. Failure to comply will result in your termination. Your employment will be probationary for one year.

    You will be contacted regarding the date and logistics of your return.

Sincerely,

Jim Karl

Figure 11.7: Return to work form

April 19, 1995

The case is reviewed in a debriefing conference with all involved parties including human resources, supervisor, security, and legal. This provides an opportunity to review the details of the case, the process, and the learning points. (See Figure 11.8 for outline of the case conference.) The conference referred to the list of risks/red flags. (See Checklist 11.2.)

A Note Of Caution

It is imperative not to lengthen the process of the employee assessment. There needs to be someone from management assigned to initiate the fact gathering of the incident. The process should not go beyond 48 hours, and the first hearing should be held within a week of the violence in the workplace incident.

It is so critical to quickly respond to an incident of violence. Incidents should be kept in the initial environment before they spread to surrounding locations. Prevention is usually accomplished in the initial environment.

Case of John Doe

1. Primary Problem
   a. Threat
   b. Clearance

2. Dr. Smith's Communication

3. Communication with Employee
   a. Personnel
   b. Medical

4. Grievance

5. Permission to meet with EAP and Personnel

6. Relationship and communication with
   a. Ombudsperson
   b. Human Resource Personnel
   c. Supervisor/Management
   d. Legal
   e. Violence Team
   f. Security

7. STD (short term disability)

8. Worker's Compensation

Figure 11.8: Outline for the case conference

Checklist 11.2

Risk Factors/Red Flags for Workplace Violence

(This information is compiled from the Federal Bureau of Investigation.)

Disgruntled Employee "Red Flags"

✔ History of violent behavior

✔ Obsession with weapons, compulsive reading/collecting of gun mags

✔ Carrying a concealed weapon

✔ Direct or veiled threats

✔ Intimidation or instilling fear in others

✔ Obsessive involvement with job

✔ Loner

✔ Unwanted romantic interest in co-worker

✔ Paranoid behavior

✔ Unaccepting of criticism

✔ Holds a grudge

Additional Red Flags

✔ Recent family, financial and/or personal problems

✔ Interest in recently publicized violent events

✔ Test limits of accepted behavior

✔ Stress in workplace such as layoffs, RIFs, and labor disputes

✔ Any extreme changes or stated beliefs

Other Profile Information Also Distributed by the FBI

✔ White male

✔ 30-50 years old

✔ Little or no criminal record

✔ Paranoid aggressive behavior blames others

✔ Troublemaker, unstable work history, substance abuse

NOTE: An employee can manifest any one, or all, of these traits and never act out violently.

As a result of the case, management realized that all parties are not collaborating and that training was a necessity. (See Appendix 11B.) Having just a guideline that was not fully operational did not satisfy our policy of zero tolerance to violence in the workplace.

Personnel Policy Development (See Appendix 11A)

When considering personnel policies in developing a guideline to the prevention of workplace violence, the following policy topics should be considered:

- ✦ Drugs, alcohol and other chemical substances

- ✦ Employees charged with crimes

- ✦ Suspension and discharge for cause without warning

- ✦ Discharge for unsatisfactory performance

- ✦ Excessive absenteeism

- ✦ Leave of absence

It is also a preference to refer to the document as a guideline instead of a policy. Supervisors and managers require as much freedom as possible to consider each case with its individual characteristics. Policies must be applied in the exact same manner by each member of management. If the document becomes a guideline, the liability is measurably limited.

Conclusion

Domestic violence impacts businesses in many ways. This chapter shows the parallels between workplace and domestic violence. The patterns seen at home can be reflected in the workplace for both the victim and the perpetrator. The chapter shares Polaroid's approach to domestic violence, including their guidelines for providing assistance and responses for employees, supervisors, human resources, and EAP or other clinicians. The case study illustrates Polaroid's early experience managing a case with the potential for violence at work.

Also, there is advice on clinical intervention strategies. Many professionals do not ask about partner abuse because they do not know how to ask and they may not be comfortable or knowledgeable about the subject. They are afraid of what they might hear and that they will not be successful, and even that they may be a target. Professionals have an opportunity to help a woman in need, to allow her to be heard without judgment, to provide support, and to let her know that she is not alone.

Such interventions may help a woman establish a feeling of control in her life and begin to solve her problems. This opportunity is one too great to let pass by. Hopefully, with more education and training we will have better resources for our employees in need. Domestic violence is not a problem that will go away, and employers who turn away from facing these issues are failing both their employees and shortchanging their businesses.

Checklist 11.3

Elements of a Safety Plan

- ✔ Review route between work and home
- ✔ Review safety of parking arrangements
- ✔ Review work schedule with manager
- ✔ Ensure safety of child care
- ✔ Provide security with picture of abuser
- ✔ Obtain contact information for employee
- ✔ Confirm emergency contact person
- ✔ Check that civil protection orders are current and available
- ✔ Ensure that health care information is provided to shelter

---

Checklist 11.4

Employee Responsibilities in Domestic Abuse

- ✔ Notify manager/supervisor of situation and of need to be absent
- ✔ Discuss options with Employee Assistance Program/counseling service
- ✔ Be clear about plans to return to work
- ✔ Maintain communication with Human Resources and manager while absent
- ✔ Provide security with photo of abuser
- ✔ Make plans to get paycheck

Checklist 11.5

Asking Questions about Domestic Abuse

✔ Indirect question: I see many women during the day with similar worries. Some of them are being hurt by someone close to them. Are you?

✔ Indirect question: I ask all my female clients if they are in a relationship with a person who is hurting or controlling them in any way. Are you in such a relationship?

✔ Direct questions:
  • Is someone hurting you?
  • You seem frightened by your partner. Has he hurt you?
  • Do you feel your partner controls your behavior too much?

✔ Do not ask: Are you a battered woman?

✔ Do not ask: Why did the violence occur? (Implies fault.)

✔ Do not ask: Why have you not left yet or why do you keep returning?

✔ Ask her to describe abuse.

✔ Listen without judgment.

✔ Empathize.

✔ Generalize. Let her know she is not alone.

✔ Educate about prevalence and effect of family abuse.

✔ Assess risk.

✔ Empower.

✔ Assist in creating safety plan and assessing options.

Checklist 11.6

Risk Assessment in Domestic Abuse

Ask about:

✔ Suicide or self-harm

✔ Availability of weapons

✔ Violent threats made toward her or the children

✔ Violent acts committed

✔ Victim's concern about risk of being killed

✔ Abuser's prior reactions to attempts to leave

References

Gelles, Richard J. *The Violent Home: A Study of Physical Aggression Between Husbands and Wives.* Sage Publications; Beverly Hills, CA. 1970.

Guerino, S. Massachusetts Department of Youth Services Study, 1985.

Langely, Robert and Levy, Richard C. *Wife Beating: The Silent Crisis.* E. P. Dutton; New York, NY, 1977.

Lobel, Kerry (Editor). *Naming the Violence: Speaking Out about Lesbian Battering.* The Seal Press, Seattle, WA, 1986.

Martin, Del. *Battered Wives.* Glide Publications, San Francisco, CA, 1976.

Nicarthy, Ginny. *Getting Free: A Handbook for Women in Abusive Relationships.* The Seal Press, Seattle, WA, 1984.

Nicarthy, Ginny; Merriam, Karen; Coffman, Sandra. *Talking It Out: A Guide to Groups for Abused Women.* The Seal Press, Seattle, WA, 1986.

Pascal, Harold. *Secret Scandal.* Alpha House, Canfield, OH, 1977.

Pizzey, Erin. *Scream Quietly or the Neighbors Will Hear.* Penguin Books, 1974.

Research in Brief. National Institute of Justice Publication, 1986.

Russell, Diana E. *Rape in Marriage.* Macmillan, New York, NY, 1982.

Schaef, Ann Wilson. *Co-Dependence: Misunderstood-Mistreated.* Winston Press, 1986.

Schecter, Susan. *Women and Male Violence.* South End Press, Boston, MA, 1983.

Straus, Murray; Gelles, Richard; Steinmetz, Suzanne. *Behind Closed Doors: Violence in the American Family.* Anchor Books, New York, NY, 1977.

Walker, Lenore. *The Battered Woman.* Harper & Row, New York, NY, 1982 and *Terrifying Love: Why Battered Women Kill and How Society Responds.* Harper & Row, New York, NY, 1989.

White, Evelyn C. *Chain, Chain, Change: For Black Women Dealing with Physical and Emotional Abuse.* The Seal Press, Seattle, WA, 1985.

Wsititz, Janet Geringer. *Struggle for Intimacy.* Health Communications, Pompano Beach, FL, 1985.

Zambrano, Myrna M. *Mejor Sola Que Mal Acompanada: For the Latina in an Abusive Relationship.* The Seal Press, Seattle, WA, 1985.

Appendix 11A

Polaroid Corporation Guidelines for Providing Assistance in Managing Family Violence

Introduction

In 1985, the United States Public Health Service and the Surgeon General brought national focus on violence as a leading public health problem in this country. This epidemic of violence has spread to the workplace, and these incidents have received intense media scrutiny.

Statistics from the National Institute of Occupational Safety and Health (NIOSH) show that murder is the third leading cause of death in the workplace and the first among female employees. Recent statistics distributed by the Massachusetts Coalition for Battered Womens Service Groups, Inc., also show that every eight days a woman is murdered by her partner and these women are employees of businesses throughout the state. While most companies have experienced threats of violence at some level, and Polaroid is no exception, the Occupational Health and Safety Act (OSHA) obligates employers to provide a safe and healthful workplace.

Purpose

For several years the company has demonstrated a corporate level concern for the plight of battered women and abused children through the involvement of the corporate EAP and the Polaroid Foundation. The company also has made every effort to become educated about the devastating effects of spousal abuse on the health of employees. We have come to believe that it makes good business sense to offer guidelines that help protect the health and safety of employees, thereby reducing abuse-related costs and ensuring continued employee well being and productivity. As such, the following guidelines, based on existing personnel policies, are offered to employees, supervisors, managers, and human resource administrators to assist employees in managing family violence situations.

When an Absence Is Necessary

At times, an employee may need to be absent from work due to family violence, and the length of time should be determined by the individual's situation. This time period shall be determined through collaboration with the employee, supervisor/manager, and the local human resources administrator.

Employees, supervisors, and managers are encouraged to first explore all corporate leave options:

Time Off Options: Paid

✧ Arrange flexible work hours so that the employee can handle legal matters, court appearances, housing and child care.

✧ Consider authorized time and family emergency as time-off options, especially if requests are for relatively short periods. Absences should be limited to three weeks.

Time Off Options: Unpaid

✧ An option for unpaid time off without taking a formal unpaid leave of absence is three weeks of authorized time without pay. This can be taken in either a three-week block of time or spread out over several weeks (totaling 15 days).

✧ If an employee cannot establish a definite return-to-work date and requires more than three weeks of time off, a specific leave of absence may be considered.

Appendix 11B

Recommended Procedures for Safety and Protection in Family Violence Situations

Definition

Family violence is any act of physical aggression that causes physical harm or any statement that could be perceived as an intent to cause physical or emotional harm. Examples would include, but are not limited to, homicide, assault and battery, rape and stalking. Statistics note that most incidents of family violence are attributed to males, but no one should ignore the fact that such abuse can also be attributed to females or occur in same-sex relationships.

How to Respond

Employee

✧ Notify your supervisor/manager of the situation and the possible need to be absent. Supervisors/managers cannot assist until an employee self-discloses.

✧ Discuss options available to you with your supervisor and Human Resources Administrator. Involve your local Employee Assistance Program (EAP) Counselor, if necessary. The EAP counselor can assist the employee in developing a safety plan.

✧ Be clear about your plan to return to work.

✧ Make arrangements for receiving your paycheck while you are absent.

✧ Submit a recent photo of the abuser to corporate security so that a possible identification can be made if the abuser appears at your Polaroid work site.

✧ Maintain communications with your human resources administrator throughout your absence.

Supervisor/Manager

✧ Be aware of unusual absences and/or behavior of employees as job performance concerns.

✧ Be aware of bruises to face, arms, etc. Remember, the employee must self-disclose.

✧ Consult with your local EAP Counselor and/or Human Resources Administrator to discuss your concerns and how to approach the employee. The EAP counselor can formally contact the employee.

✧ Maintain confidentiality at all times.

✧ Honor all civil protection orders (i.e., vacate, restraining or no-contact orders or judgments in effect). Contact the EAP counselor if there are concerns.

✧ Contact the local corporate security office and make sure that the employee has provided a photo of the abuser and other pertinent security information.

✧ Be sensitive to the seriousness of the situation.

Human Resources Administrator

✧ Be a resource to both the employee and supervisor/manager in handling the situation. Follow recommended procedures for absences and use appropriate community resources.

✧ Contact the local EAP Counselor immediately.

✧ Discuss a safety plan for the employee with the EAP Counselor.

✧ Maintain communication with the employee during his or her absence.

✧ Work with the supervisor/manager on pay and absence arrangements.

Employee Assistance Program Counselor

✧ Be a resource to the employee, the supervisor/manager and the Human Resource Administrator.

✧ Collaborate with the human resource administrator in all situations.

✧ Be available during the employee's absence, including referrals to community family violence services.

✧ Develop a safety plan with the human resource administrator. This safety plan should accompany the protection order once it is obtained.

✧ Maintain a liaison position between the local shelter staff and the corporation for the purpose of counseling needs.

Elements of a Safety Plan

✧ Review the travel route between the employees home and work.

✧ Review safety of child care arrangements.

✧ Make sure that current civil protection orders have not expired and are in hand at all times.

✧ Determine if substance abuse is involved.

✧ Make sure that security has a picture of the abuser.

✧ Have an emergency contact person if the employee cannot be reached.

✧ Consider if health care is a concern (such as, diabetes, AIDS, cancer). Shelter staff requires this information.

✧ Make sure that an address and phone number of the victim is provided to the company contact person.

✧ Review the safety of the employee's parking arrangements.

✧ Review the employee's work schedule with the supervisor/manager (in case stalking is involved).

Resources

Employees who need help in dealing with abusive relationships are encouraged to contact the Employee Assistance Program (EAP) office at their work location or the corporate EAP office at 617/386-8288.

For Massachusetts employees, the following community resources are available for your assistance:

✧ Massachusetts Coalition of Battered Women Service Groups, Inc. 617/248-0922

✧ Massachusetts Parental Stress Line 1/800-632-8188

Closing Statement

It is the company's sincere hope that Polaroid employees take violence and the threat of violence seriously. All reasonable measures within established company policies and guidelines shall be used to protect employees and to create a safe working environment for everyone.

Appendix 11C

Intervention Strategies for the Prevention of Violence

Introduction

Family violence is not a private issue. It is a crime. We, as clinicians, nurses, physicians, attorneys and personnel administrators ask intimate, personal questions all the time. Inquiries about the possibilities of family abuse need to be added to that list of questions.

The abused woman is isolated and often believes that her situation is unique. She may have feelings of embarrassment and guilt which prevent her from raising the issue in your office. In addition, an abused woman may be hesitant about raising the issue because she may have previously encountered responses that denied, minimized, or actually blamed her for the abuse.

What to Ask

Many of us do not ask about partner abuse because we do not know how to ask. The questions listed here can be asked directly or indirectly.

Direct Questions

- ✧ Is someone hurting you?

- ✧ Did someone hurt you?

- ✧ You seem frightened by your partner; has he hurt you?

- ✧ Have there been times during your relationship when you and your partner have had physical fights?

- ✧ Are you now in a relationship with a person who has hit, pushed, shoved, punched or kicked you?

- ✧ Do you feel that your partner controls your behavior too much?

Direct questions about family violence are typically asked when we either see evidence of abuse or have a strong indication that the women is being abused.

Indirect Questions

- ✧ I see many women during the day who come to me with similar worries. Some of them are being hurt by someone close to them. Are you?

- ✧ I ask all my female clients if they are in a relationship or have an association with a person who is hurting or controlling them in any way. Are you?

- ✧ Many women in our society experience violence from men in their lives; has anything like this ever happened to you now or in the past?

Indirect questions should be asked to all women regardless of any evidence of family abuse. When asking women about partner abuse, it is important to ask about present and past unresolved issues.

What Not to Ask

- ✧ Do not ask the woman if she is a "battered woman" as she will most likely deny this label because of the shamefulness and worthlessness associated with it. No one wants to be labeled.

- ✧ Do not ask the woman why the violence occurred as this presumes that she or her actions caused the violence and that she is therefore at fault.

- ✧ Do not ask the woman why she has not left her partner or why she keeps returning. Her inability to leave is part of her trauma.

Why Professionals Avoid Asking

There are a number of reasons why clinicians and those in helping professions may not ask a woman if she is being battered. These reasons may include:

- ✧ Fear that one will not be able to successfully intervene

- ✧ Fear that the woman will become depressed or suicidal

- ✧ Fear that the story will be too painful to hear

- ✧ Lack of comfort and/or knowledge of the subject

- ✧ Feeling of powerlessness in the situation

- ✧ Fear of opening "Pandora's Box"

- ✧ Fear becoming a target of the abuser because of his/her intervention

These fears are legitimate but can be eliminated with proper training and education in family violence.

Intervention Strategy

Question

Ask about the abuse and encourage the woman to discuss the abusive situations in specific, concrete terms. This helps the woman hear herself as she describes the incidents and makes the abuse a reality. This information is also important for the interviewee. As the woman describes the abuse, the interviewee can help her understand the cycle of violence and how her actions and reactions do not contribute to the violence. In the process of asking, it is important to continually offer the woman validation.

Listen without Judgment

Fear of being judged keeps the woman silent. She already feels worthless and shamed. Do not add to that.

Empathize

Communicate to the woman that you believe her, that this abuse is unacceptable, that she deserves better. Tell her how brave she is for coming forth with her story and breaking the code of silence, and that it is not her fault that this occurred.

Generalize

Let the woman know that she is not alone although she may feel that way. Educate her about the prevalence of family abuse and describe how abuse psychologically affects the battered woman.

Assess Risk

Ask about the possibility of suicide or her risk of being killed by her partner. If she says that her partner may kill her-believe her! Most victims of homicide by partners had at one time or another voiced their concerns about being killed.

In assessing risk, ask about:

✧ Weapons in the home

✧ Any violent threats made toward her or the children

✧ Any violent act made toward her or the children

✧ Her abuser's previous reactions to any attempts to leave him

And finally, help the woman create a safety plan. (Refer to the EAP)

Empower

A primary goal of intervention is to assist the woman establish a feeling of control and power in her life. These two things have been taken away from her.

Epilogue

Remember, you can make recommendations and assist the woman in regards to available services for battered woman but she must make the phone call. She must always be given the right to decide. This may be the most frustrating thing we will ever sit with, but it is essential to intervention.

With each positive encounter, the battered woman is better able to solve her own problems, feel more courageous and make changes in her life.

It is important to convey that your services will always be available no matter what she decides to do.

List

Employee Assistance Program

Medical Department

Personnel Administrators

Legal Department

Preventing Violence during Layoffs

Timothy P. Dineen, PhD, and Peter D. Olenen, MD

Case Study

You are a manager at Widget Corporation, which is planning a job reduction, and you are concerned about several of your employees. Jim Wilson often comes to work in camouflage clothing and is known to be a gun collector and combat enthusiast. Bob McCraw is an angry Vietnam veteran. He has limited skills and has always worked at your company. He is known for his chronic complaining and dissatisfaction with working conditions. Tom Mallow, one of your employees, has a history of intimidating co-workers. He has been warned previously that threats are not acceptable. On Tuesday morning, he comes into your office and tells you that if he is one of the employees to be laid off, you will be sorry. What do you do?

Introduction

Layoffs have captured the attention of the entire country as the nation's largest corporations engage in aggressive programs to reduce the size of the workforce. This effort, in recent years has focused particularly on white collar and managerial employees, the very people who in the past could be counted on to maintain the company's values and whose loyalty could be relied upon to produce the dedication and self-sacrifice necessary to enhance the company's goals. The different terms used to describe this process such as "downsizing," and "restructuring" do not obscure the fact that this particular corporate activity will have far-reaching effects on the relationship between companies and the workers in these companies for years to come.

Use of Layoffs

As a Response to Financial Pressures

Initially the layoffs were a response to financial pressures encountered as a result of changes in technology and in the marketplace. As advances in telecommunications made it possible to eliminate layers of middle management and headquarters staff, it became increasingly apparent to top management that economic survival depended on taking advantage of these changes by thinning their ranks. Management also found that it was under pressure from companies who could achieve significant cost reductions by closing down domestic operations and relocating them in other countries around the world where labor costs were a fraction of what they were in the United States. These changes began in the early 1970s, along with a slowdown in the rate of economic growth. From 1979 through 1995 the *New York Times* extrapolated from U.S. Department of Labor statistics to estimate that 43 million jobs were lost. Increasingly, it was noted the jobs that are disappearing are those of higher paid, white collar workers, many at the peak of their careers (Uchitelle and Kleinfeld, 1996.)

As a Strategic Competitive Step

While initially many companies adopted layoffs as a defensive measure when they found themselves under heavy financial pressure, once they did so, they began to perceive them in a different light. Instead of viewing layoffs as a business necessity which they were forced to carry out in order to stay viable as a business enterprise, some managers realized that technology had provided them with the opportunity to drastically reduce the number of technical and staff positions. These positions had become redundant as computers and networks made it possible to instantaneously transmit information from one corner of the globe to another.

Layoffs versus Individual Discharge

From the perspective of the individual employee facing a layoff as a result of these momentous changes, the stress and disruption can be enormous. Psychologically it makes a big difference, however, whether an individual is the only person experiencing job loss or whether the person loses the job along with many others as part of a downsizing or layoff. (Leana and Feldman, 1988) Researchers and counselors who work with people who have been fired or laid off caution about a number of physical and emotional problems which can arise for those trying to cope with the economic, psychological, and social consequences of job loss. (Levi, 1992, Fryer and Payne, 1986)

Individual Discharge

The person who is the only one losing a job is in a potentially more stressful situation than would be the case if the firing was part of a layoff involving others also. The individual is in a unique situation, and there is a greater risk of isolation and loss of self-esteem. There is less likely to be social support available for such an individual, and there are no other people in the same position with whom to identify and share feelings. Indeed, there may be pressure from others to suppress negative feelings and engage in denial of negative consequences, adding to the psychological burden and isolation.

Group Layoffs

When a group of people is laid off there is much greater opportunity for people to share their experiences and feelings with one another. The social stigma attached to the layoff is reduced because the individual isn't being singled out, and people have more of an opportunity to ventilate and express their concerns and fears.

There is also the opportunity to keep in touch with one another and to help and assist each other. Networks and support groups form, and community based organizations and churches provide assistance and resources such as rooms for groups to meet in. Classes in how to go about job hunting and how to prepare resumes can also spring up. (Kates, Grieff, and Hagan, 1993)

Advanced Notice of a Layoff

While it is stressful any time an individual is laid off, being given advanced notice, as opposed to being laid off without any warning, is much less stressful. When an employee knows that a layoff is forthcoming, it allows for some degree of control over the situation. There is a chance to plan ahead, to try to save more money, to look around and see if there are other jobs available, to cut down on expenses, to put off major purchases. Plans can be changed to meet the new reality.

On the contrary, when there is little or no advanced notice, the impact on peoples' lives can be devastating. Without any control over events, people may unwittingly find themselves caught up in debt and financial obligations which would not have been undertaken if they had known they were going to lose their incomes. Of course, that can happen even when there is advanced notice—i.e., debts can be incurred just before the notice of a layoff comes out—but at least there is time to try to make changes before the income flow from salary stops.

One negative consequence of advanced notice of a layoff is the anxiety it can generate about the uncertain future. (Kates, Grieff, and Hagan, 1993) This anxiety is experienced by everyone confronted with an upcoming loss of employment, but some individuals, particularly if they feel they have no influence whatsoever over events, ruminate and brood to the exclusion of using the time to prepare for the disruption which the layoff will bring to their lives. This can, in some instances lead to sense of hopelessness and helplessness and even to the development of a full-blown depression. We recommend that employers be strongly encouraged to address this and identify some of these more vulnerable individuals so that professional help can be made available sooner. The longer such a person goes without help the more intractable the individual's problems will be. It should not be assumed that just because people get advanced warning of a layoff that there will be no need for intensive planning and coordination in order to prevent violence.

There are usually several announcements put forth at different times prior to the layoff date. As the date of the layoff comes closer, management announcements about it become more specific, but it is not until the day of the layoffs that people find out if they are included in the layoff. Even though people react less negatively when they have advanced warning, this warning is bound to generate a period during which there is a tremendous amount of suspense and anxiety.

Violence and Layoffs

Ever since the waves of downsizing began in the late 70s, violent incidents related to the loss of jobs have been featured in the media. As a result, the public is very conscious of violence connected to layoffs in the workplace. Particularly since Patrick Sherril, a postal worker in Edmond, Oklahoma, shot and killed 14 co-workers in 1986, the public's concern has been heightened, as is indicated in an article in *Psychology Today* entitled "Workplace Violence" (January-February 1994, 20-21). A conference held by the United States Postal Service produced the information that, in the last decade, 34 postal employees have been murdered by co-workers and 26 wounded (Blow 1994). Employees who are fired or laid off and who have lashed back violently are not restricted to the Postal Service, although its problems with violent employees and its attempts to address this problem have received widespread attention. This paper represents an effort to focus on one potential source of workplace violence—violence connected with layoffs. It is our position that strategies developed to prevent violence during a layoff should be strategies which seek to preserve the self-respect and sense of personal integrity of those being laid off and to prevent the development of maladaptive responses to the trauma of the layoff on the part of survivors.

Violence in the Workplace

Several recent surveys of on-the-job violence have indicated that over the last two decades violence on the job has been increasing. (Bachman 1994) Whenever a disgruntled ex-employee returns to the work site intent on getting back at those who the attacker believes are responsible for the job loss, it invariably makes headlines and reinforces the perception that such violence is a commonplace occurrence when, in fact, it is not nearly as common as the headlines would suggest. Bureau of Labor statistics for 1993, for example, indicate that there were 1063 workplace homicides in the United States but only 10%, or 106, were classified as involving work associates. (U.S. Department of Labor, 1994) But the United States homicide rate is itself among the highest in the industrialized world. It is ten times higher than that of the United Kingdom and twenty-five times higher than that of Spain. (Simonowitz, 1996) So, while the homicide rate in the workplace is only

10% of the annual homicide rate, this is 10% of a national rate which is high to begin with.

When it comes to non-lethal violence, the figures increase enormously. Based on statistics compiled by the U. S. Department of Justice, Bachman (1994) concluded that almost a million people a year are victims of violence in the workplace.

Strategies That Lay the Groundwork for Violence Prevention

Analysis of episodes of violence involving disgruntled employees suggests that there is a relationship between such factors as confrontational labor/management relations, perceived unfairness of company practices, a rigid management approach, a harsh authoritarian management style and the incidence of job-related violence. (Johnson and Kinney, 1993; Zender, Wittrup, and Harrington, 1992; Northwestern National Life Insurance Company, 1993) Strategies designed to prevent violence during layoffs tend to avoid the appearance of being arbitrary and uncommunicative and to emphasize management approaches which are perceived by employees as fair and consistent.

Company Policy against Violence

Some companies do not address the issue of violence in their policies. In many instances this is an oversight, but in some it reflects a concern that by addressing the issue they are calling attention to it and may as a result precipitate it. There is no evidence to support such a concern, but much to suggest that an explicit policy contributes to a company atmosphere which is safer and in which there are fewer threats and acts of violence. Companies need to think through what are the limits of behaviors which are tolerated in the work environment. They need to develop a mechanism which will insure that acts which could endanger the safety of other workers will be scrutinized and evaluated and that there will be consequences and sanctions, including firing.

In most instances sanctions can stop far short of firing, but if employees understand that management will address incidents of violence which have the potential of endangering the safety of others, it serves to produce a workplace environment which makes such behavior seem more extreme than does an environment which ignores the issue.

By law, employers are required to keep the work environment free from hazards to life or physical safety. Stating explicitly that the employer intends to insure that each employee works in a safe environment is a position in keeping with legal requirements in the area of occupational safety. This requirement for safety in the workplace includes eliminating violent episodes from the workplace.

Pre-Employment Screening

The idea of setting up rigorous screening procedures to keep those with a predilection to violence out of the workplace seems to have a lot to recommend it. When it is possible to screen employees with background checks, psychological testing, and even lie detector tests, many employers will be eager to do so. However, this idea is not as simple and straightforward as it first seems. There are legal issues. Before instituting any of these procedures, employers should make sure that they have legal counsel, either through internal legal channels or external consultants. In many states and jurisdictions there are explicit legal restraints. Screening of job applicants needs to be examined by legal counsel to avoid infringing on an individual's civil rights. In addition, employment tests that attempt to identify the individual who will be violent in the workplace are seeking to focus on someone who will be committing an act that is statistically relatively rare. Such tests, if they are effective at screening out the person who will be violent, will do so by overpredicting the potential for violence and thereby produce a large percentage of false positives. This is a problem because it means that large numbers of innocent people would be denied employment because they fit the profile of the one individual who will be violent. (Fox and Levin, 1994)

Analysis of disgruntled employees who have become violent has shown that the average perpetrator is someone who is over thirty, white, male, has worked for the company for several years, and feels that he has been treated unfairly. (Barrier, 1995) Pre-employment screening under such circumstances has diminished value. Making the task more daunting is the fact that few workplace attackers have prior criminal or psychiatric records. (Fox and Levin, 1994)

Human Resource Policy as a Preventive Strategy

Company human resource policies which reflect an approach to employees marked by belief in the worth of each individual and which explicitly maintain that interactions should be characterized by mutual respect contribute significantly to a company climate which discourages violence. On the other hand rigid, authoritarian approaches to people, and policies which reflect these approaches, are associated with a higher incidence of violence in the workplace. (Cabral, 1996) In a study sponsored by Northwestern National Life Insurance Company (1993), companies which, in addition to adequate security, had effective mechanisms in place to deal with employee grievances and harassment complaints had lower rates of violence. These findings are consistent with the conclusions of researchers that stress accompanies almost all responses to layoffs (Leana and Feldman, 1988; Johnson and Kinney, 1993), and that the more open and communicative management is with respect to layoffs, the better is the response of those who survive the layoff in terms of commitment to the organization and work effort. (Brockner et al., 1990). If management communicates the reasons that layoffs have become necessary and if there is an evident effort to avoid being unfair, the reaction of both those laid off and of survivors of the layoff is less likely to be adversarial and less likely to include incidents involving violence.

Employee Support Resources Reduce Stress

Several investigators have reached the conclusion that training is one of the ways in which companies can demonstrate that employees are valued and therefore contribute to an increased sense of self-esteem. (Fox and Levin, 1994) Diversity training and training in conflict resolution fit within this paradigm. Kates, Grief, and Hagan (1993) note that providing resources, such as skills training, Employee Assistance Programs, job retraining, and out-placement packages, all serve to reduce the stress involved. Indeed, it should not be surprising to find that the more such resources are available, the less the laid off employee experiences stress.

While these studies support the idea that if people are treated with respect they respond even to bad news in ways which reflect their increased sense of self-worth and with less hostility, there is some indication that in more paternalistic companies longer-term employees develop a sense of entitlement. If that sense is shaken by an action such as a layoff, the response can be even more intense than that of employees who were hired more recently. But even in these situations, the more consistent and open the channels of communication, and the more a norm of mutual respect is in place, the less likely is it that employees will react in destructively hostile ways. Another way of stating this is that if there is a norm in place within the organization of mutual respect, this norm is likely to prevail during the layoff process. On the other hand, if management suddenly changes and disregards the norm or acts in a rigid, authoritarian manner when a layoff is involved, this inconsistency is likely to provoke a counter-reaction.

Clinically, observers have also noted that some managers, for reasons such as overcompensation, seem to view laid off employees in the worst possible light so that they won't have to deal with their own feelings of guilt.

The Layoff Process

The foregoing studies suggest how violence during a layoff can be minimized or prevented. What follows is a description of a layoff, which, however unfortunate, was conducted in a manner that was consistent with these principles and practices, and that was notable for the lack of any violent episodes. The employees and former employees involved met this event with the same values in place which had characterized their behavior prior to the layoff. This is not to say that there was not a great deal of stress in their lives. Leana and Feldman (1988) in a review of the research on people trying to cope with the loss of a job found that the one common factor in all the job-loss situations was stress. While stress was ever-present during this layoff it did not lead to violent incidents directed at others in the workplace.

For conceptual purposes the layoff process can be broken down into three phases: the period before the layoff, the actual layoff, and the period following the layoff.

Early Communication

In this layoff, which involved over a thousand people at one site, management had communicated for several months that a layoff was going to take place. The company's internal communication apparatus was backed up by articles in the local newspapers outlining the business need for the layoffs. As these articles appeared periodically they became more detailed and more focused, although the actual number of people who were to be laid off was not known until the day of the layoff. Management's statements did not just deal with the layoffs but also gave information about the steps the company was taking to position itself so that further layoffs would not be necessary, as well as outlining the austerity measures the company was taking prior to the layoffs, and the resources which would be made available to those who were laid off. This served to make it clear that the layoffs had to do with a changing market environment and not with personal shortcomings on the part of the employees who were going to be laid off.

Legal and Human Resources Involvement

A project team was set up to prepare for the layoffs. This team included staff specialists from corporate, legal, security and safety, and medical. It was coordinated by the human resources department. Legal issues such as compliance with relevant aspects of the law were involved. The issue of security was a sensitive one. If there was too much security, it could set up an adversarial relationship. If there was too little, valuable property and even the safety of other employees could be in jeopardy if someone became hostile and lost control. Some issues, such as allowing those laid off to return to their desks to retrieve their belongings and to obtain a sense of closure, had to be worked through and coordinated. While security was more in evidence on the work site, the decision was made to continue to treat employees with the same norm of respect that had prevailed in the past. The process itself was designed so that employees would have a chance to get their belongings, speak to their co-workers, and make arrangements for material that was too bulky to hand-carry all at once, but also so that they would not hang around aimlessly.

It was also recognized that how humanely this was carried out would affect the survivors as well as those being laid off. In addition to being told they were being laid off, employees would need to know what their rights were and what resources the company was making available to them. Grievance mechanisms had to be in place also. How and by whom each laid off employee was to be informed also had to be thought through and coordinated by this team.

Coordination with Security

In addition, an emergency response team involving security, medical staff, human resources, designated personal, and out-placement counselors was set up. Corporate staff worked with the project management team to insure that relevant public officials were informed on a timely basis. Security worked with local police authorities so that when the layoffs were taking place, the police were aware of it and could have their own contingency plans in place. Lastly, and perhaps most critically, a plan was set up to hold training sessions for managers who were responsible for informing those who were being laid off. Planning for this meeting included determining that employees should be told at the beginning or in the middle of the work week, not just before a weekend. In this way there would be staff on hand to deal with any crisis, and representatives of the company would be available during, and for a period of time following, the layoff. These people could provide additional support, structure, and information as employees dealt with this transition in their lives.

Layoff Process from the Perspective of the First Line Manager

Preparation for the layoff process must be undertaken well in advance of the actual notification of the employees affected. From the standpoint of the first line manager, the individual who will notify the laid-off employee, there are three components of the preparation process—management education, identification of the particularly "brittle employee," and the planning of the actual layoff process.

Management Education

It is key that the managers who will implement the layoff process receive adequate education not only about the business issues related to the layoff, but also about how they will react as individuals to the implementation of the layoff process. They must also have a clear understanding of the administrative issues surrounding the layoff. These issues include the potential avenues for administrative appeal of the layoff decision (if any), the benefits available to the former employee, and the assistance to be given to the former employees in terms of counseling and job search assistance.

Management must understand that the layoff process must be viewed as any other business problem so that it can be accomplished in a professional manner with the same high standards as any other business process and, most importantly, with the appropriate measure of sensitivity. Managers must understand that the tone that an individual manager sets in dealing with his or her employee will go a long way in determining the overall climate of the layoff process and the reaction of the individual employee affected.

Managers' Emotions

All levels of management, but especially the first line manager who will implement the layoff process and be the individual notifying an employee that he or she is among those to be laid off, will find the process to be a difficult task to say the least. They must appreciate that anxiety is a normal reaction during both the planning and implementation of the layoff. Managers will need to draw on all of their prior training and experience in management to successfully complete this task. They must have an understanding of the spectrum of the normal employee reaction to being laid off and have prepared for those instances where a severe reaction is possible or anticipated. Above all, management must follow the plans that have been set in place by the project team.

Management Goal

Management must view their task or goal as helping the employee to get beyond the initial emotional reaction to the layoff and into the process of job hunting or, in some cases, retirement. Since the individual first line manager cannot reverse single-handedly those circumstances which are the cause of the layoff, much as they might wish to, they must view their goal as helping their former employees to transition to their next job or career.

Employee Reactions

Managers must learn that there can be a wide spectrum of employee reaction to the circumstance of job loss. These reactions can include anger, shame, fear, self-pity, shock, sadness, disbelief, and in some cases, relief that the anticipated layoff is now at hand. During the first few minutes of the notification meeting in which the employee had been told that he or she was to be laid off, there may be a roller coaster effect, and several of the above-mentioned reactions may take place in a short period of time. The manager must keep clear the goal of helping the employee channel his or her emotional energy into the career transition process. It may be useful for the informing manger to think through how he or she will respond to each of these emotions if expressed by a particular employee. Groups or teams of managers might want to role play the notification scenario and begin to understand how they would themselves feel when confronted by each of the above reactions and how these can best be handled.

The emotions displayed by the laid-off employee can be likened to those seen during the grieving process. Initially there may be a sense of denial, where the former employee does not believe that this is happening. Anger can follow as the individual is uncertain why this is happening to them. A sense of bargaining can follow where the individual wishes to undo the layoff process in return for a promise to be a better worker. Later on, a sense of depression can begin as the laid-off worker begins to be concerned about what he or she will do. Finally there will be a sense of acceptance as the individual determines how to cope and begin the process of seeking new employment.

The goal of management is to implement the layoff process and help the former employee to channel energies into the search for new employment. This will promote resolution of the normal employee reactions to being laid off. Thus, disbelief and anger will not escalate into aggression, shame and sadness will be prevented from becoming depression or immobility, and fear or self-pity will be prevented from becoming a debilitating anxiety.

Checklist 12.1

Employees at Risk of Severe Reaction to Layoff

✔ Several major life-change events in a short period of time

✔ Difficulty with relationships

✔ Marital or family problems

✔ Consistently unrealistic expectations

✔ Extreme anger

✔ History of violent or bizarre behavior

✔ Financial difficulties

✔ Serious health problems

Life Change

Management will need a perspective with which to view the potential impact of job loss in order to adequately prepare itself and also to determine which employee might be at higher risk of a severe negative reaction. The Holmes and Rahe Social Readjustment Rating Scale, even though it was first published in 1967, still provides a perspective on the relative impact of life changes or life events. Several of the life events or changes and their relative rating are summarized in Table 12.1.

By utilizing this rating scale, management can see that although job loss has a significant life-change value, there are other events of even higher life-change value which the average employee has faced and successfully coped with during his or her life. This scale can also be used to identify the employee who has faced

Life Event	Life-Change Value
Death of spouse	100
Divorce	73
Marital separation	65
Death of close family member	63
Personal injury of illness	53
Marriage	50
Fired from job	47
Marital reconciliation	45
Retirement	45
Pregnancy	40
Gain of a new family member	39
Death of a close friend	37
Change to a different line of work	36
Mortgage over $10,000	31
Foreclosure of mortgage or loan	30
Outstanding personal achievement	28
Change in residence	25
Change in living conditions	25
Vacation	13
Christmas	12
Minor violations of the law	11

* Source: Holmes and Rahe (1967)

Table 12.1:   The Holmes and Rahe Social Readjustment Rating Scale

several major life changes within a relatively short period of time, perhaps during the past year, who may be at increased risk of more severe reaction to job loss.

Severe Employee Reactions

Besides individuals with several major life-change events in a relatively short period of time, there are characteristics of individuals that should alert management for the potential for a severe reaction to the layoff. Individuals who have difficulty with relationships and marital or family problems can be of concern. People who have consistently unrealistic expectations, extreme anger, or a history of violent or bizarre behavior can be at risk for a severe reaction. The individual with financial difficulties or serious health problems can have an exaggerated reaction. The employee who is seen as either extremely passive or hyperactive can be at greater risk as can those who are single parents or sole financial contributors to their families. (See Checklist 12.2.)

Checklist 12.2

Warning Signs That the Laid-Off Employee Is Not Coping

✔ Talk of suicide or "dark themes"

✔ Persistent use of hopeless language

✔ Marked change in appearance or personal habits

✔ Noticeable behavioral changes

✔ Withdrawal from group

✔ Lack of affect

✔ Lack of interest in job search

✔ Stuck in past

✔ Display constant denial

✔ Extreme sadness or anger

Conclusion

Preparation is the key to successful implementation of the layoff process. Managers must acknowledge their own feelings as they plan and eventually implement the process. A broad range of employee reaction must be anticipated. Management must become thoroughly familiar with whatever resources are available, including consultation with medical staff or employee assistance program personnel. Company policy regarding violence or threatening behavior should be reviewed and the security arrangements in place during the layoff process should be clarified.

During the implementation of the layoff with the individual employee, the manager must be specific and get to the point. The manager must also listen. Expect to allow the former employee to have some time to ventilate and express feelings. Focus on the benefits package and move the employee onto the next step in the process. Meet individually with the remaining members of your department the day of the layoff to reassure them that they were not included in the resource reduction and to begin to rebuild the morale and teamwork within the department.

References

Bachman, R. *Violence and Theft in the Workplace*. Bureau of Justice Statistics, U.S. Department of Justice. National Criminal Justice Publications, no. 148199. 1994.

Barrier, M. "The enemy within." *Nation's Business*, February, 18-21. 1995.

Blow, R. "Washington scene." *The New Republic*, 10 and 17 January, 11-12. 1994.

Brockner, J., R. L. DeWitt, S. Grover, and T. Reed. "When it is especially important to explain why: Factors affecting the relationship between managers' explanations of a layoff and survivors' reactions to the layoff." *Journal of Experimental Social Psychology* 26: 389-407. 1990.

Cabral, R. "Policies for developing workplace violence prevention strategies." In *Violence in the Workplace*, R. Harrison, M.D (ed.). Occupational Medicine: State of the Art Reviews, vol.11: 2. Philadephia: Hanley & Belfus, Inc. 1996.

Fox, J. A. and J. Levin. "Firing back: The growing threat of workplace homicide." *The Annals of the American Academy of Political and Social Science* 536 (November): 16-30. 1994.

Fryer, D. and R. L. Payne. "Being unemployed: A review of the literature on the psychological experience of unemployment." In *International Review of Industrial Organizational Psychology*, edited by G. L. Cooper and I. Robertson. London: Wiley. 1986.

Johnson, D. C. and J. A. Kinney. "Breaking point." Chicago: National Safe Workplace Institute. 1993.

Kates, N., B. S. Grieff, and D. Q. Hagen. "Job loss and unemployment uncertainty." In *Mental Health in the Workplace: A Practical Psychiatric Guide*, edited by J. P. Kahn, M.D. New York: Van Nostrand Reinhold. 1993.

Leana, C. R. and D. C. Feldman. "Individual response to job loss: Perceptions, reactions, and coping behaviors." *Journal of Management* 14 (3): 375-89. 1988.

Levi, L. "Psychological, occupational, environmental, and health concepts; research results; and applications." In *Work and Well-Being: An Agenda for the 1990s*, edited by G. P. Keita and S. L. Sauter. Washington, D.C.: American Psychological Association. 1992.

Northwestern National Life Insurance Company. "Fear and violence in the workplace." Minneapolis: Northwestern National Life Insurance Company. 1993.

Holmes, T. H. and Rahe, R. H. "The social readjustment rating scale." *Journal of Psychosomatic Research* 11 (2): 213-8. 1967.

Simonowitz, J. A. "Health care workers and workplace violence." In *Violence in the Workplace,* edited by R. Harrison, M.D. *Occupational Medicine: State of the Art Reviews*, vol. 11, no. 2. Philadelphia: Hanley and Belfus, Inc. 1996.

Uchitelle, L. and N. R. Kleinfeld. "The price of jobs lost." *New York Times*, 3 March. U. S. Department of Labor, Bureau of Labor Statistics. 1994. National census of fatal occupational injuries, 1993. Washington, D.C. 1996.

"Workplace violence: Its personnel as well as personal." *Psychology Today*, January-February, 20-21. 1994.

Zender, J. F., R. G. Wittrup, and R. B. Harrington. "Predicting and preventing workplace violence and homicides—group dynamics, stress, and labor/management relations factors." Paper presented at the second American Psychological Association and National Institute of Occupational Safety and Health Conference on Occupational Stress, Washington, D.C., November. 1992.

Chapter Thirteen

- ❏ How a safe and secure work environment is good business
- ❏ Risk factors for the service occupations
- ❏ Components of a violence assessment for the service industry
- ❏ Interventions for reducing risk in service establishments
- ❏ Value of documenting all incidents of violence including harassment, verbal threats, and physical assaults
- ❏ Taking a proactive approach to violence prevention in the service industry
- ❏ Components of a violence prevention program

Service Occupations and Workplace Violence

One Size Does Not Fit All

Kenneth R. Grover, PhD

Case Study

During a four-month period, four separate restaurants in the Nashville area had armed robberies in which employees were murdered. Citizens demanded that increased security measures be adapted by all area restaurants. The major focus of public outcry was installation of closed-circuit TV (CCTV) systems, which most experts agreed would not have prevented any of the homicides. In fact, the fourth robbery resulted in the death of two young employees at a restaurant that had a CCTV system. The suspects simply took the videotape. Though the general public often believes that security "equipment" is the solution to crime problems, it may create a false sense of security. In a situation involving multiple armed robberies and employee homicides, the only effective tool is capture of the perpetrators through the coordinated efforts of police, restaurants, employees and the community itself.

Introduction

Today's society faces an ever-growing problem of aggression. The violence that historically has been somewhat "hidden" in the privacy of the home has spilled out into every aspect of society. Violence is happening everywhere Americans spend time—a good portion of which is in the workplace. This trend has forced government at all levels to address dangers such as violent street crime, gang violence, domestic violence, drug-related violence, and violence stemming from mental dysfunction. The Centers for Disease Control (CDC) has termed violence a "public health hazard" and an "epidemic."

Now on-the-job violence is forcing American businesses to take notice and to protect its employees. Employers have always had an obligation to protect its workers. However, federal government legislation and civil litigation are geared to require employers to not only protect, but to prevent workplace violence. Violence can actually threaten a corporation's existence. In addition to the monetary loss of potential liability claims, depressive effects on employee moral and the recruitment of qualified personnel can threaten any organization. Indeed public perception of the company and shareholder confidence can be at risk. Thus in addition to the moral obligation of providing a safe work environment, it also makes "good business" sense.

Violence and Service Occupations: An Overview

When we attempt to discuss service occupations and violence in the workplace, we are faced with some unique problems. Two main issues stand out:

✧ Definition of service occupations and the hundreds of diverse job categories it includes

✧ Definition of workplace violence

Violence in the workplace has received considerable attention by the popular press. As usual, this has generated health, safety, and government scrutiny and companion proposed regulations. A specific service occupation, health care, has already been provided federal "guidelines" by the government. Other occupations such as convenience stores, restaurants, and law enforcement are also drawing federal attention.

In June of 1996, the National Institute for Occupational Safety and Health issued *Current Intelligence Bulletin 57*: *"Violence in the Workplace Risk Factors and Prevention Strategies."* (NIOSH issues Current Intelligence Bulletins, CIBs, to disseminate new scientific information about occupational hazards. The institute provides CIBs to representatives of academia, industry, organized labor, public health agencies, and public interest groups, as well as to federal agencies responsible for ensuring worker safety and health.)

This study reviewed that which is known about fatal and nonfatal violence in the workplace to determine the focus needed for prevention and research. The document also summarized issues to be addressed when dealing with workplace violence in various settings, such as offices, factories, warehouses, hospitals, convenience stores, taxicabs, and other service-related settings.

The study concluded that "Workplace violence is clustered in certain occupational settings. For example, the retail trade and service industries account for more than half of workplace homicides and 85% of nonfatal workplace assaults. Taxicabs drivers have the highest risk of workplace homicides of any occupational group. Workers in health care, community services, and retail settings are at increased risk of nonfatal assaults." Thus it appears service occupations, according to the federal study, carry a "high" risk for violence incidents.

Risk Factors for the Service Industry

An examination of the "root-causes" of workplace violence can assist in the construction of prevention strategies. According to the NIOSH study, the major risk factors for workplace violence include these situations:

✧ Dealing with the public

✧ Exchange of money

✧ Delivery of services or goods

✧ Time and location of transactions

It becomes apparent that the specific risk factors involved in any service occupation should be the driving force behind any prevention strategies. Thus each individual location must examine their individual risk factors. It becomes apparent that broad-based definitions will be of little use in designing specific business prevention tactics.

It becomes more important to study the prevention strategies available to an organization for minimizing the rise of workplace violence. These procedures include (but are not limited to):

✧ Cash handling policies

✧ Physical separation of workers from customers

✧ Good lighting

✧ Security devices

✧ Escort services

✧ Employee training

✧ Reporting and analysis

In addition, a workplace violence prevention program should include a system for documenting incidents, procedures to be taken in the event of incidents, and open communication between employees and workers. Although no definitive prevention strategy is appropriate for every service occupation all workplaces must assess the risks for violence in their specific environments and take appropriate action to reduce those risks. Clearly a broad-based service occupation definition provides little assistance in reducing workplace violence individually or collectively. Rather, a site-by-site risk analysis is the only logical approach to reducing overall workplace violence risk.

Service, Retail, Public Administration, and ...?

Before we can truly understand the extent of workplace violence problems, we must define the problem. I believe it is important to separate workplace homicide from workplace violence. Although the occasional sensational "postal- type" violence makes front-page news, it does not begin to indicate the extent of the problem. According to 1995 Bureau of Labor Statistics, there were 1,071 homicides in the United States in 1994. These included 179 supervisors or proprietors of retail sales, 105 cashiers, 865 taxicab drivers, 49 restaurant or hotel managers, 70 police officers or detectives, and 76 security guards. Although these deaths are a serious problem they are only the "tip" of the iceberg.

The American Management Association reported in April 1994, the results of a study of 589 companies on workplace violence incidents. One half of those companies had experienced threats or acts of violence in the last four years. Fifty-four percent did not look at the issue until after the violence occurred. Sixty percent had no policies or training on how to deal with violence.

Northwestern National Life Insurance Company did a study of 600 employees in 1993. One out of four full-time workers was harassed, threatened, or attacked on the job between July 1992 and July 1993. Violence cost United States companies a minimum of 4.2 billion dollars in 1992. The 1994 Northwestern study provided the following data that underscores the need for recognizing the full nature of workplace violence and not just the death toll:

✧ 16 million workers reported on-the-job harassment

✧ 6 million employees were verbally threatened

✧ 2 million Americans were physically attacked on the job;

✧ 1,004 were killed

One Size Does Not Fit All ...

It is a serious problem, but we must address it rationally. As a former police chief, I consistently evaluated each officer-related assault, injury, and death. This analysis resulted in training design, new equipment (such as a bulletproof vest), and revised safety and control procedures.

Later, as a corporate director of security for an international hotel, restaurant and hospitality organization, I was concerned about each employee injury or death. The problem was the same, but the causes and solutions were completely unique to the hospitality industry, and law enforcement solutions made no sense.

A quick review of the 1995 Bureau of Labor Statistics Report for homicides in restaurants or hotels, illustrates the problem further. It's not enough to know that restaurant or hotel managers were murdered on the job. To identify specific causes and solutions, we have to answer these questions:

✧ How many were restaurants?

✧ How many were hotels?

✧ What kind of restaurants (i.e., fast food, fine dining, etc.)?

✧ What kind of hotels (i.e., budget, business, luxury)?

✧ Where were they located?

✧ At what time of day or night did the incidents occur?

✧ How many employees/guests were present?

✧ Was robbery involved?

This analysis then must be followed up with nonfatal event identification. How many incidents of verbal threats, harassment, or assault also have taken place.

Each individual, business, company, organization and occupational group must do its own specific analysis and gather its own data to draw any meaningful conclusions. Prevention strategies are as unique as the individual business, police department, taxicab company, or convenience store. The collection of data must include all incidents of workplace violence and not just the highly visible homicide incidents.

Combining workplace violence data from general service occupational categories such as law enforcement, hospitals, social service agencies, and educational institutions results in statistics that disguise the risks that are specific and unique to each of these occupations and organizations. Without specific occupational and business location data defined by the individual company or business, no realistic solutions will be developed.

Much of the Work Has Been Done

The International Association of Chiefs of Police has examined workplace violence and officer safety for decades, and every law enforcement department in the United States assesses every officer-injury incident. Similar groups exist for every major service occupation.

The National Food Service Security Council, for instance, began dealing with the violence issue as early as 1978 and continues its work today. Security personnel of food service companies have gathered annually to review violence issues and share solutions. The National Food Service Security Council has conducted a homicide study of participating members to determine the actual incidence of homicide in the food-service environment. The preliminary findings of the study, which is to be released at the annual meeting of the membership in July 1997, suggest a homicide rate similar to that of other service and general public workplaces.

So What Is Workplace Violence?

Before collecting data, we have to define workplace violence. Certainly homicide in the work environment qualifies. So do assaults, as demonstrated by the one million cases in the 1995 Bureau of Labor report. However, workplace violence encompasses more than that. It includes any aggressive behavior that makes a worker feel uncomfortable. Technically then, workplace violence includes offensive language and sexual harassment. NIOSH and OSHA though narrowly define it as, "violent acts, including physical assaults, and threats of assault directed toward persons at work or on duty."

What about all the other "inappropriate" workplace behavior? Most studies to date have focused on physical assault and injuries, which are easier to count, report, and legislate. More work needs to be done on a more complete definition of workplace violence. Even less aggressive, offensive behavior can lead to a "violent or fatal event."

Preventing Workplace Violence

Providing a safe, secure work environment is just "good business." The success of any service related industry, from health care to restaurants, depends on the performance of its people. A well-motivated and highly trained staff is the difference between success and failure. Most service-related industries realize this and have gone to great lengths to protect the workplace from violence. In fact, recently the Clinton administration announced a significant decrease in the number of workers killed in work-related shootings. In other words, industry efforts are paying off. Strong programs already exist in most large service industries to help protect employees from workplace violence, including retailers, convenience stores, drug stores, supermarkets, restaurants, taverns, and entertainment establishments. Any attempt to address the needs of these diverse workplaces with a single program is doomed to fail.

OSHA's list of recommended elements for "appropriate" workplace violence programs deserves serious review and consideration. They include the strategies shown in Checklist 13.1. These are all good security tactics when applied to specific situations. However, "wholesale" application of them can become comical—such as a bullet-proof barrier between guest and bartender or two employees to staff a full-service restaurant with less than $50.00 in available change. Each business must select those measures that provide the most protection at the least cost. Solutions must make sense if they are to be effective.

Checklist 13.1

Risk Reduction Strategies for Service Industries

✔ Threat assessment of business

✔ Violence prevention policy

✔ Incident reporting and analysis

✔ Employee training

✔ Threat assessment team

✔ Cash handling policy

✔ Maintain less than $50.00 in cash on hand

✔ Physical separation of workers from customers

✔ Bullet-proof barriers

✔ Elevated vantage points

✔ Visible service area from outside

✔ Video surveillance equipment

✔ Closed circuit television

✔ Fences

✔ Good lighting

✔ Conservative clothing

✔ More than one employee at night

✔ Escort services at night to car or public transportation

So What Really Makes Sense for the Service Industry?

Each business and occupation needs to assess its individual workplace environment to identify specific risk factors. A number of factors have been identified in previous research (Collins and Cox, 1987; Kraus, 1987; Lynch, 1987; NIOSH, 1993; Castillo and Jenkins, 1994), including those shown in Checklist 13.2.

Checklist 13.2

Risk Factors for the Service Industry

✔ Contact with the public

✔ Exchange of money

✔ Delivery of passengers, goods, or services

✔ Having a mobile workplace, such as a taxicab or police cruiser

✔ Working with unstable or volatile persons in health care, social settings, or criminal justice/security services

✔ Working alone or in small numbers

✔ Working late at night or during early morning hours

✔ Working in high crime areas

✔ Guarding valuable property or possessions

✔ Working in community-based settings

Beyond these general risk factors, it's also important to examine the reasons for violent behavior. Five categories can be identified:

✧ Substance abuse

✧ Medical conditions

✧ Culture of violence

✧ Mental Illness

✧ Situation stress

When we review specific crime, such as armed robbery, clearly any one or all of these factors could be the motivation behind a specific armed robbery. Thus it becomes critical to consider risk factors rather then specific crime problems.

Assessment

Each business must do a thorough assessment of its specific risks before it can plan any prevention strategies. This assessment should include the following information:

✧ Crime trend analysis to determine area crime. Local law enforcement can help. It is important to determine type, frequency and times of criminal activities. Each time local police are called to handle a criminal problem, management should retain a copy of the police report for future reference.

✧ Physical security of business, which includes equipment and security procedures.

✧ Employment policies, such as interviewing, background checks for hiring, and procedures for firing and giving "bad news."

✧ Current education and training of management and other staff.

✧ Crisis response—Do you have a plan?

✧ System for reporting and tracking problems.

Prevention Strategies

Basic prevention strategies fall into two major areas: environmental and administrative. Based on the individual business assessment, solutions might encompass one or both areas.

Environmental Controls

Where cash is exchanged, a business might consider the feasibility of cashless transactions using automatic teller machines. Locked drop safes and armored car pickups are commonly implemented measures.

Visibility and lighting are also critical environmental design considerations. According to NIOSH, making high-risk areas visible to more people and installing good external lighting should decrease the risk of workplace assaults. After 30 years of crime prevention design experience, I believe this to be the single most effective crime prevention tool.

Obviously, there are numerous security devices that may also reduce assault risks in specific environments. Security barriers or enclosures, monitored access to and egress from the workplace, etc., are useful in specific applications. The use of CCTV, two-way mirrors, card-key access systems, panic-bar doors and trouble lights are all effective in reducing crime risk when properly utilized in connection with a specific problem.

The most practical use of environmental prevention is in new building design and remodeling. Security-conscious architecture and landscaping can significantly

Checklist 13.3

Violence Prevention Policies for the Service Industry

✔ General Security Policy Statement
✔ Armed Robbery Procedures
✔ Crime Incident Reporting
✔ Emergency Procedure and Plan
✔ Solicitation of Employees
✔ Back-of-the-Unit Security and Control
✔ Removal of Company and Personal Property
✔ Employee Loitering Control Procedure
✔ Arrest of Customers and the General Public
✔ Counterfeit Incidents
✔ Interview of Employees
✔ Police Response and Services
✔ Locker Searches
✔ Employees Use of Alcohol/Drug Abuse
✔ Employee Misconduct/Arrest
✔ Employee Payroll
✔ Use of Alarms
✔ Firearms and Other Weapons
✔ Customer Behavior
✔ Cash Escort Procedures
✔ Investigate Procedures
✔ Safe Combination and Door Lock Control
✔ Use of Contract and Off-Duty Officers
✔ Security of Cash Funds
✔ Armored-Car Procedures
✔ Delivery/Inventory Control Procedures
✔ Integrity Shopping
✔ Drug-Free Workplace Compliance
✔ Opening Procedures
✔ Bomb-Threat Management
✔ Closing Procedures
✔ Grounds, Perimeter, Parking Lot, and Building Security
✔ Polygraph Testing.

reduce crime risks. It is also far more effective to "build in" security devices, such as lighting, CCTV, and alarm systems at the construction stage, then to add them later.

Administrative Controls

Establish policies and procedures for work practices and staffing requirements during opening, closing, and trash runs to minimize workplace risk. Management should also set policies that deal with safe cash handling, alarms, armed robbery prevention and use. If local law enforcement resources and services. A list of potential security policies, taken from Retail Security Policy Manual, is shown as Checklist 13.3.

A written policy statement should be on file and enforced for every appropriate security area of each individual business. The policy format should include these three elements:

✧ **Policy Statement** is the specific position your company has adopted on the issue.

✧ **Objective** provides the policy manual user with a definition of what the policy is designed to accomplish.

✧ **Procedure** identifies the specific steps that must be followed to achieve the stated objective. The procedure section deals with instructions and gives specific directions on how the policy is to be used. This section is used to direct employees, therefore, it must be easy to understand and implement.

Each operation also needs a system for assessing and reporting threats so that a quick response to potentially violent situations can be provided. This information also allows employees to continuously evaluate whether existing strategies are working.

Training

Certainly, the company must provide guidelines for, and training in recognizing and managing violence in the workplace. Training should include these topics:

✧ Risk assessment

✧ Identification of violence indicators

✧ Verbal persuasion techniques

✧ Escape and de-escalate skills

Training should address how to identify, as well as de-escalate, workplace violence, and it should discuss security procedures, protective equipment, and security equipment. These efforts will only work with strong management support throughout the organization. The form of training will be dictated by the size and locations of an organization. Face-to-face training might not be practical in large organizations and will require the development of training materials and/or outside consultant delivery services.

Employee Involvement

Finally, we must involve all employees in an ongoing effort to prevent workplace violence. It takes a strong ZERO TOLERANCE policy that:

- ✧ Requires employees to report threats of violence to a specific workplace contact

- ✧ Designates who will investigate reports and how the investigations will occur

- ✧ Defines what behaviors are inappropriate

- ✧ Specifies who ensures disciplinary actions are carried out

- ✧ Describes physical securities

- ✧ Establishes a liaison with the local police department

Until every employee is charged with taking personal responsibility for preventing and reporting all prohibited behavior, workplace violence will continue to be a "government" and "management" problem.

Conclusion

No one endorses workplace violence. Violence cost United States companies 4.2 billion dollars in 1992 alone. Homicide is the number-two cause of workplace death and the number-one cause for women. The American Management Association reported in April 1994 the results of a study of 589 companies, half of which had experienced threats or acts of violence in the last four years.

No business or service occupation can ignore this problem. It just does not make good business sense. Failure to properly manage workplace violence will ultimately make it impossible to hire and keep workers and customers will not use a service that puts them at risk.

Employees in both the service and retail fields are gaining sensitivity to the effects of workplace violence and are working to create an environment that offers maximum safety and security. There is a great deal of work left to be done. The murder of an average of 20 workers each week should not be considered the cost of doing business in America.

References

California State Department of Industrial Relations. *CAL-OSHA Guidelines for Workplace Security*, Division of Occupational Safety and Health, San Francisco, CA. 1994.

Crow, W. J., R. J. Erickson and L. Scott. "Set your sights on preventing retail violence." *Security Management* 31 (9, September): 60-64. 1987.

Dyer, G.M. (Editor). "Smart and self-reliant." Foundation for Crime Prevention Education. United States of America. 1996.

Florida Crime Prevention Institute. "Homicide in convenience stores." *Trends, Risks, and Interventions in Lethal Violence: Proceedings of the 3rd Annual Spring Symposium of the Homicide Research Working Group*. 1992.

Florida Office of the Attorney General. *Study of Safety and Security Requirements for At-Risk Businesses*. 1991.

Grover, K.R. *Retail Security Policy Manual*, Butterworth-Heinemann, Stoneham, MA. 1992.

National Institute for Occupational Safety and Health (NIOSH) CDC ALERT: *Preventing Homicide in the Workplace*, United States Department of Health and Human Services, Public Health Service, Centers for Disease Control and Prevention. 1993.

Northwestern National Life Employee Benefits Division. *Fear and Violence in the Workplace*, Minneapolis: Northwestern Life Insurance Company. 1993.

U.S. Department of Justice. *Criminal Victimization in the United States*, 1992. Pub. No. NCJ-145125, Washington, DC. 1994.

Workplace Violence
and
Healthcare Workers

Tom Scaletta, MD

Case Study

At the Los Angeles County Hospital emergency department, on February 8, 1993, an armed man shot three emergency physicians, took two staff members hostage, and eventually surrendered to the police. In response to this event, twenty-five full-time security positions were added, costing about $2 million. In addition, security devices, including a metal detector, bullet-proof glass barrier, and panic buttons were installed. Simple security measures, such as a mandate for staff to wear identification badges, were strictly enforced.

Introduction

Workplace violence includes intentional use of power (e.g., threats) or physical force within the workplace against another person resulting in the possibility or reality of injury or death. Such violence in the medical setting combines internal violence seen in corporate settings such as co-worker hostility and sexual harassment with the external violence of public venues associated with intoxicated, mentally ill, or frustrated individuals. The incidence of on-the-job injury is greater for healthcare workers than for construction workers. (Lusk, 1992) The National Institute of Occupational Safety and Health (NIOSH) surveyed all occupational deaths in the United States, from 1980-1990, of individuals over 16 years old, and found that homicide was the leading cause of death for certain types of healthcare workers. It has been shown known that more assaults occur to healthcare workers than those in any other profession. (U.S. Department of Labor, Bureau of Labor Statistics, 1993)

High Risk Healthcare Settings

Emergency Department

Studies of medical workplace violence identify the emergency department (ED) as the setting for the majority of hospital assaults and the place where residents feel least safe. (*Hospitals*, Feb. 20, 1992) Sixty-two percent of residents surveyed admitted to fearing physical assault and being threatened with weapons in the ED. (Anglin, Kyraicou, Hutson) A surprising 4% of UCLA emergency medicine residency graduates admitted to carrying guns for protection while on duty. A survey of high-volume, university EDs revealed that 43% experience at least one physical assault on a staff member and 18% have weapons involved in threats every month. (Lavoie, 1988) Three of every four ED nurses admit to being assaulted at least once during their careers. (Poster, Ryan, 1994) The reasons for ED violence seem clear. There is a reliable influx of intoxicated and mentally ill patients, and urban trauma centers attract gang members either as victims or visitors. A trip to the ED usually represents an unplanned, uncomfortable disruption in the lifestyles of patients and their families and often involves long waits. This breeds frustration which in turn breeds violence. During periods of overcrowding, ED staff are particularly vulnerable since they are focused more on basic patient care than observing and defusing pre-violent behavior.

Other Hospital Areas

Violence is also prevalent in other areas of the hospital. In psychiatric wards it is common and has been shown to increase with resource shortages. (Davis, 1991) The pharmacy may become a target for money or drug theft. Measures of prevention include installation of drop safes, limiting cash on hand, and using bullet-proof glass.

Non-Hospital Locations

Checklist 14.1

Healthcare Settings with Increased Risk of Violence

✔ Emergency Department

✔ Psychiatric Wards

✔ Hospital Pharmacy

✔ Emergency Response Teams

✔ Substance Abuse Treatment Centers

✔ Occupational Health Centers

✔ Abortion Clinics

✔ Animal Research Laboratories

✔ Visiting Nurses Services

✔ Child Protective Service Workers

Out-of-hospital high risk jobs include paramedics, substance abuse treatment center workers, occupational medicine personnel, visiting nurses, and child protective service workers. Additionally, abortion clinics and animal research labs are a common focus of dangerous extremist groups.

Occupational health centers are at particular risk because they commonly perform mandatory drug testing and fitness-for-duty evaluations. Staffers must be ready to defuse anger associated with disagreements over determining the degree of physical disability (e.g., Workers' Compensation evaluations) or time allowed off work for illness or injury.

Dangerousness Assessment

Neither medical training nor work experience substitute for the skills necessary to identify and manage violent individuals. Dubin reported 36% of assaulted psychiatrists retrospectively admitted to having moderate or strong intuitions, while interviewing the perpetrator, that the potential for violence existed but did not act on these instincts. With early implementation of security precautions, it was shown that fewer injuries and less property damage occurred. (Dubin, 1988)

Several clues may indicate an individual about to become violent. Use all your senses to identify key components of a danger assessment.. One may hear loud, pressured, profane speech filled with demands and inappropriate comments; see clenched fists or restless behavior; smell the presence of alcohol or other impulse-lowering drugs; or instinctively feel that someone is dangerous. (Physicians for Violence-Free Society, 1996)

Mental illness, especially paranoia, schizophrenia, mania, and borderline or antisocial personality, are highly associated with violent behavior. Patients with traumatic injuries may harbor unresolved conflict and should be watched care-fully. Gang membership is usually evident through clothing, tattoos, and language. System abusers, such as those attempting to obtain a prescription for unnecessary medications, may suddenly turn from pleasant to abusive when denied. Even our own behavior can be predictive. We must recognize when we are tired or over-stressed and modify our actions so that we do not put ourselves at unnecessary risk.

Risk Reduction by Verbal Intervention

It is human nature to become frustrated and angered during stressful, unfamiliar situations. Long waits for medical care are common in many settings, and as a result, patients and family members often fear their medical problem is not being taken seriously. Effective communication with those in the waiting room reduces frustration. Patient relations representatives improve client satisfaction with peri-odic status updates and basic amenities (e.g., blankets, refreshments, or use of a telephone). This ombudsman role is ideal for eager, mature volunteers wanting to help healthcare workers. (Wolford, 1995)

A period of mounting tension frequently precedes physical violence. (Dubin, 1989) Early use of verbal calming, nonaggressive gestures, and a display of genu-ine professional concern are effective preventive measures. (Rice, 1991)

To calm an agitated client, assume an advocacy role. Avoid disagreements, directives, rude remarks, and threats. Show respect and empathy, be a good lis-tener, and address realistic complaints. As well, exercise reasonable tolerance. Respect personal space, allow some venting, and ignore personal affronts. It is often necessary to set and enforce certain limits without appearing threatening.

Public service healthcare workers should always practice the following common sense precautions. Never unnecessarily divulge personal information. Wear comfortable clothes that allow rapid escapes from danger and avoid expensive jewelry which someone may attempt to steal. Consider self-defense training which teaches methods to free oneself from an aggressor's hair and choke holds. Lastly, utilize escort services or walk in groups to the parking lot, especially at night.

Never ignore overt assaultive or threatening behavior in hopes that it will not occur again. Passive negotiation ends with overt threats or assault, and an organized containment plan must be initiated. Don't try to be a hero. Always leave yourself an escape and summon security personnel once danger becomes imminent.

Checklist 14.2

Verbal Interventions to Reduce Violence Risk

✔ Give periodic updates to family and friends in waiting room

✔ Provide amenities such as blankets, coffee or use of telephone to patients, family or friends while waiting

✔ Display genuine professional concern

✔ Avoid disagreements, directives, rude remarks or threats

✔ Show respect and empathy, listen

✔ Allow some venting and ignore personal insults

✔ Set and maintain limits in low-key manner

✔ Avoid aggressive gestures

✔ Respect personal space

Physical Intervention to Prevent Violence

Emergency departments restrain about 4% of patients due to combative behavior, to protect them and the hospital staff from injury. (Lavoie, 1992) Only restrain someone when credible clinical evidence exists raising suspicion that the individual or others could be at risk of injury or death. Whenever possible, one-to-one observation should be utilized as an alternative to restraint (e.g., a cooperative person on suicide precautions and not felt to be a flight risk). Threatening behavior is the most common reason for restraint.

Checklist 14.3

Practical Tips to Protect Oneself

✔ Never share personal information unnecessarily

✔ Wear comfortable clothes

✔ Avoid expensive jewelry

✔ Consider self-defense training

✔ Use escort service or walk in groups to parking lots at night

✔ Recognize and respond to assaultive or threatening behavior

✔ Have an organized containment plan

✔ Ensure escape means at all times

✔ Summon security early

Remember that irrational patients are not always incompetent. Competent patients can decline recommended therapy and must be sober, fully oriented, and aware of the risks of medical noncompliance. In weighing the degree of incompetence against the gravity of the medical problem, for instance, a physician may allow a moderately intoxicated patient with a hand fracture to refuse a splint but the same patient may not refuse a laparotomy after an abdominal gunshot wound. While the absolute determination of competence is a legal decision, a physician must act on objective clinical criteria. Patients unwilling to cooperate with the medical evaluation, while suffering from impaired judgment and a potentially life-threatening problem, are considered to have given "implied consent" for treatment.

Physical restraint must always be performed in a manner that does not jeopardize a patient's well-being. A five person restraint team—four to immobilize the extremities and another to apply the restraints—is optimal.(Rice, 1991) Restraining devices are varied and usually institution- rather than situation-specific. It is important to search or undress all restrained patients and remove potentially dangerous items. Safe physical restraint comes with knowledge, experience, and teamwork. Chemical sedation commonly follows physical restraint in patients who remain agitated.

Once adequately restrained, the patient must be continually re-assessed to determine mental status, vital signs, distal extremity perfusion, and skin condition. It is also necessary to consider whether the reason to restrain (e.g., intoxication) has resolved. Competent patients, restrained for psychiatric or judicial reasons, may refuse medical treatment. Forcibly performing procedures or administering medications in such individuals constitutes battery. Documentation of restraint must be meticulous and describe the rationale, the method, the individuals involved, criteria when restraint will no longer be necessary, and re-assessments.

Checklist 14.4

Guidelines for Use of Physical Restraint

✔ Have convincing evidence of need

✔ Use alternatives when possible, such as observation

✔ Protect patient and others from injury

✔ Have procedure to ensure patient's well-being

✔ Have five-person restraint team

✔ Search restrained patients to remove potentially dangerous objects

✔ Continually assess mental status, vital signs, distal extremity perfusion

✔ Reassess need for ongoing restraint

✔ Have established rationale for termination

✔ Document rationale, procedure, staff, rechecks, and criteria for termination

---

Security Management Plan

Access control is a primary component of prevention and limits an employer's risk. In emergency departments areas of ingress should be attended by a security officer who scrutinizes every person entering. Just as in "community policing" strategies, all staff should participate in observing and reporting suspicious individuals. Staff, patients, and visitors must constantly display identification. Security doors (operating with a code or key card), metal detectors, and closed-circuit television cameras also control access to certain areas. Proper facility design incorporates such security checks and organized traffic flow in the building's architecture.

Alert procedures are the cornerstone of the management of assaultive individuals. Alerts can be initiated by calling a dispatcher, overhead paging, silent "panic" buttons, and even computer-initiated flags which identify known prior offenders. The expected security response and roles of various staff members must be outlined in policy form. Security procedures should be developed to control all conceivable hazards, including subduing combative patients, weapon screening and confiscation, hostage negotiation, bomb search and removal, and control of hostile gatherings. A recommended system uses three levels of alert.

Level 1

Level 1 is initiated when a hostage situation is in progress. In this situation a pre-existing hostage plan must be invoked. This involves removing as many patients or staff members from harm as possible, alerting the local police, and containing the situation. Ultimate control should be passed on to experts form the local police department.

Level 2

Level 2 is initiated when a violent act has taken place (e.g., overt threat or assault). One caveat is not to wait for a second overt act before establishing control. This usually results in physical restraint of the perpetrator. In selected cases, arrest or eviction from the facility may be the outcome for medically stable patients. Whenever a weapon is displayed in a threatening manner and not immediately surrendered, the situation should result in a Level 1 alert.

Level 3

Level 3 is initiated when dangerous activity is identified and there is a need for a presence while the situation is being assessed or while verbal interventions are being attempted. For instance with escalating uncooperative behavior utilize the security intervention of a "show of force" while verbal de-escalation and limit-setting is being attempted. Realize that in many circumstances behavior will persist or worsen, in which case a progression to Level 2 is needed.

Weapon Issues

Metal detectors are being used in some medical centers to ensure a "lead-free" clinical environment. This practice is supported by the American Medical Association, the American College of Emergency Physicians (ACEP), and the American Psychiatric Association. While all have a right to enter a medical facility, an individual may not refuse weapon screening if this is standard procedure.. Those in favor of metal detectors cite that staff and patients feel more secure. Those that oppose are concerned about possible negative connotations and violation of Second Amendment rights and antidiscrimination/equal access laws.

In a survey of 250 U.S. hospitals, only 1.6% were using metal detectors. (Ellis, 1994) Henry Ford Hospital ED reported one of the earliest experiences with weapons detection in the emergency department. They confiscated an average of one handgun per week and one knife every four hours—some type of weaponry was found on 3% of all screened. (Thompson, 1988)

Weapons screening protocols vary. Some institutions use a walk-through detector as in major airports. In other settings only "high risk" individuals are screened. In his article, Goetz reported a protocol which screened 0.4% of medical patients and 11% of psychiatric patients for weapons using a hand-held metal detector. For those searched, the overall recovery rate was about 17%. (Goetz 1991) It is necessary to screen all entering or develop a non-discriminatory policy based on objective criteria (e.g., those intoxicated, with a psychiatric complaint, or displaying threatening behavior are screened for weapons). The policy should also outline the search procedure, personnel roles, and the protocol for dealing with discovered weapons.

In general, illicit weapons should not be returned as there is no statutory obligation to return articles in violation of local statutes. By returning an item which places the patient or others at risk of injury, the hospital and healthcare worker(s) may be held responsible. Such tort liability even extends to legal weapons. While it is best to direct seized illicit materials to the local police, some institutions choose to avoid this issue by posting signs of the weapons search process and offering the use of lockers for those entering to store "personal effects" beforehand.

It is inaccurate to believe weapons are limited to patients and security personnel. A significant number of healthcare workers carry firearms for personal protection. Four percent of UCLA emergency medicine residency graduates admitted to carrying a gun to work for protection and 20% of healthcare workers in a southern U.S. trauma center admitted to carrying a gun to work for protection. (Anglin, 1994,) and (*Southern Med J*, 1995)

Incident Reporting

At one hospital, a review of 686 police calls for violent incidents—where 29 represented a significant threat to a staff member—none resulted in a formal hospital incident report. (Pane, 1991) Underreporting has been the norm, and reasons include denial that there is serious risk, acceptance that violence is not preventable, and the belief that victimization equates to poor job performance.

Incident reporting of episodes of hospital violence is integral to future prevention. ED directors can use the data to uncover and report occurrence patterns and measure the effects of preventive measures. Reporting demonstrates to staff and administrators that the problem is real and the costs are significant. Documented episodes of violence attributable to correctable deficiencies lay a foundation for potential negligence lawsuits, and this motivates even the most unsympathetic administration to take action.

Reporting allows patients with a prior episode of threatening or assaultive behavior to be flagged during subsequent visits utilizing the hospital registration computer system. Such a program at the Portland VA Hospital demonstrated a 92% reduction in violent behavior through early security interventions including police standby or "show of force", weapons search, and/or confinement to a certain part of the clinical area. (Drummond, 1989) Since the best predictor of violence is a prior episode of violence, reporting and computer alerting translates to prevention.

Legal Issues

In 1996, federal Occupational Safety and Health Administration (OSHA) published, "Guidelines for Preventing Workplace Violence for Health Care and Social Service Workers." The program outlines four main components:

✧ Commitment from top management

✧ Performance of worksite risk analyses

✧ Incorporation of necessary hazard controls

✧ Adequate staff training (OSHA, 1996)

The "general duty" clause (Section 5a of the Occupational Safety and Health Act of 1970) is used as a basis for citing employers if hazards of workplace violence are recognized and nothing is done to prevent or abate them. (Public Law 91-596, December 29, 1970; and amendments, P.L. 101-552, Section 3101, November 5, 1990) The monetary penalties incurred by a citation generally are not nearly as expensive as the government-ordered corrective actions usually related to improving security measures and educating staff.

Most Worker's Compensation (WC) agreements bar employees from undertaking civil suits after workplace injuries, however, employer liability may not be removed under these statutes when the injury is the result of an intentional act, for personal reasons, and unrelated to work. (Gagnon) New York State 1995/1996 Bill A09451 would amend WC and dictates that workers who are victims of certain types of violence are entitled to recover damages via civil lawsuits. Awards would then be much greater and highly dependent on the jury's interpretation of the victim's "deservability" and the "heinousness" of the hazard.

Hospital administration can be notified of potential dangers through reports of security and safety committee meetings, ongoing incident reporting, and excerpts from pertinent literature. In this way it is possible to avoid recurrences of violence incidents, and thus negligence law suits, by taking appropriate corrective actions.

State Laws and Regulations

Several states have passed stringent laws for violent acts against certain healthcare workers. These laws include Arizona Senate Bill (SB) 1150, California SB 587, Connecticut Public Act No. 94-62 and House Bill 5749, and Mississippi SB 2004. (Anshus, 1995) Another type of legislation directly addresses prevention and is exemplified by California Assembly Bill (AB) 508 which requires the following actions:

✧ Reporting of any assault in which an injury resulted or a weapon was involved

✧ Performance of a safety and security assessment of vulnerable areas of the hospital (e.g., emergency department, psychiatric wards)

✧ Development and implementation of a safety and security plan (based on the aforementioned assessment) which addresses physical layout, personnel duties, specific policies, and ensures that the recommendations of professional and government agencies are considered

✧ Development of a comprehensive education program for staff (Anshus, 1994)

A safety management plan, composed of the aggregate of individual related policies and procedures, can satisfy OSHA and JCAHO recommendations and legislative requirements. An effective plan begins with a mission statement supporting a zero-tolerance policy for threatening behavior. Described in their 1996 manual, the JCAHO standard, EC.1.6, requires an emergency preparedness plan describing how the organization will establish and maintain a program for all types of events that disrupt the environment of care. (Joint Commission on Accreditation of

Healthcare Organizations, 1996) The forthcoming JCAHO environment-of-care product, *Security: Keeping the Healthcare Environment Safe*, will detail further recommendations.

Education and Counseling

A comprehensive, annual safety training program for all employees should be in place and can effect a significant reduction in assault. (Infantino, Musingo, 1985] The program should include recognizing the previolent patient and methods of managing violence including defusion techniques and restraint procedures. Staff should be encouraged to complete incident reports on all episodes of workplace violence.

While attendees must include emergency and psychiatry department staff, security and safety officers, human resources managers, and administrators, it is recommended that all public service employees be trained through periodic in-services in the management and prevention of workplace violence. Program content, length, and training method should be adapted to particular needs. Inexpensive educational materials such as slides and lecture notes are currently available through some organizations (e.g., Physicians for a Violence-Free Society, 800-688-8678).

Critical incident stress debriefing should be available for those victims who elect to participate. Immediate group discussion of a violent incident has been shown to be effective in accelerating recovery. [Reigner, 1993] The staff assistance for employees (SAFE) program and the assaulted staff action program (ASAP) provide education (e.g., normal emotional response to trauma), incident debriefing, and referrals for on-going counseling. (Caldwell, 1991)

Conclusion

Healthcare workers are at risk of both homicide and assault. Not only is their on-the-job injury rate comparable to construction workers, but their occupation has one of the highest, if not the highest, injury rate. There are a number of interventions which can increase the level of security for healthcare workers. This includes a better security system and a plan to respond to different levels of threats. Healthcare workers need to be more skilled in assessing dangerousness and be aware of verbal interventions which reduce risk, as well as physical responses. Any violence prevention program needs to include staff training, incident reporting, and critical stress debriefing after any incidents.

Workplace violence management and prevention programs must overcome the cynics. Traditionally, medical staff have minimized the gravity of workplace assaults—a sentiment echoed in the common saying, "it comes with the territory." Many health care professionals do not appreciate the scope of the problem or are uninterested in the subject. Some administrators are unwilling to spend the amount of time or money required to institute a effective prevention program..

References

Anglin, D., D. Kyraicou, H.R. Hutson. "Residents' perspectives on violence and personal safety in the emergency department." *ACEP* reprint 47/1/54755.

Anglin et al. *Ann Emerg Med*, 1994.

Anshus, J.S. "Security in the ED: legislation paves the way." *Am J of Emerg Med*, 13(4):490-1, 1995.

Anshus, J.S., D. Boucher, K. Hubbell. *Making a Commitment to Security: Emergency Department Practices, Procedures and Treatment*. California Emergency Nurses Association and California Emergency Physicians Medical Group, 1994.

Caldwell. *Hosp Community Psychiatry*, 43(8):838-9, 1992.

Davis, S. "Violence by psychiatric inpatients: a review." *Hosp Community Psychiatry,* 42(6):585-90, 1991.

Drummond, D., L. Sparr, and G. Gordon. "Hospital violence reduction among high-risk patients." *JAMA* 261:2531-2534, 1989.

Dubin, W. R. and J.A. Feld. "Rapid tranquilization of the violent patient." *Am J Emerg Med*, 7(3):313-20, 1989.

Dubin, W. R., S.J. Wilson, and C. Mercer. "Assaults against psychiatrists in outpatient settings." *Journal of Clinical Psychiatry*, 49(9):338-45, 1988.

Ellis. *Am J Emerg Med*, 1994.

Flannery. *Hosp Community Psychiatry*, 42(9):935-8, 1991.

Gagnon, M. R. *Employee Liability for Workplace Violence*, The National Victim Center, http://www.nvc.org/

Goetz, R., J. Bloom, S. Chene, et al. "Weapons possessed by patients in a university emergency department," *Ann Emerg Med*, 20(1):8-10, 1991.

Infantino, J. and S.Y. Musingo. "Assaults and injuries among staff with and without training in aggression control techniques." *Hosp Community Psychiatry*, 36:1312-4, 1985.

Joint Commission on Accreditation of Healthcare Organizations. *1996 Comprehensive Accreditation Manual for Hospitals*, Oakbrook, IL, JCAHO, p.349. 1996.

Lavoie, F.W. "Consent, involuntary treatment, and the use of force in an urban emergency Department." *Ann Emerg Med*, 1992;21(1):25-32.

Lavoie, F., et al. "Emergency department violence in United States teaching hospitals." *Ann Emerg Med*, 17(11):1227-33, 1988.

Lusk, S.L. "Violence in the Workplace." *J Am Assn Hospital Nurses,* 40:212-3, 1992.

Pane, G., A. Winiarski, and K. Salness. "Aggression directed toward emergency department staff at a university teaching hospital." *Ann Emerg Med*, 20:283-6, 1991.

Poster, Ryan, 1994.

Public Law 91-596, December 29, 1970; and amendments, P.L. 101-552, Section 3101, November 5, 1990.

Reigner. "Escalating risk: Violence in the ED." *QRC Advisor*, 9(8):1-4, 1993.

Rice, M.M. and G.P. Moore. "Management of the violent patient: therapeutic and legal considerations." *Emerg Med Clin North Am*, 9(1):13-30. 1991.

The Sagging Safety Net: Emergency Department on the Brink of Crisis, Hospitals, Feb 20, 1992, pp.26-40.

Southern Med J, 1995.

Thompson. *Ann Emerg Med*, 17:419, 1988.

U.S. Department of Labor, Bureau of Labor Statistics, *Occupational Injuries and Illnesses in the United States by Industry*, 1993.

U.S. Department of Labor, Occupational Safety and Health Administration, *Guidelines for Preventing Workplace Violence for Healthcare and Social Service Workers*, OSHA, 1996.

Wolford, S. "Emergency department patient liaison volunteers: A cost containment and visitor satisfaction strategy." *J Emerg Nurs*, 21(1):17-21, 1995.

Wood, C.L. "Historical perspective on law, medical malpractice, and the concept of negligence, in medical-legal issues." *Emerg Med Clin of North America*, Nov 11(4):826-31. 1993.

Workplace Violence Prevention and Management, an educational slide presentation distributed by Physicians for Violence-Free Society, 214-590-8807. 1996.

Chapter Fifteen

❑ Early intervention after a violent event and reduction of trauma

❑ Range of physical and emotional responses to trauma

❑ Components of a post-incident response program

❑ Communication to better manage the post-incident reponse

❑ Implementing a post-incident reponse program

Post-Incident Response to Violent or Traumatic Events

Marilyn Knight, MSW

Case Study

Three men walked into an office of AC insurance company late Friday afternoon. One man pulled a gun and told the employees not to move and not to make any calls. As one man supervised the opening of the safe, another held a gun on the five women employees, and the third man escorted the women one by one out of the office down a back corridor. The waiting women heard gunshots from the back rooms. After the men left and the police finally arrived, they found the five women were all alive, tied up in five separate rooms. By this time, the company had five severely traumatized employees, and the vice-president wondered what should be done now.

Introduction

In spite of an organization's best efforts to protect its workforce and provide a safe, secure, clean and healthy work environment, accidents and tragedies may still occur in the workplace. If the tragedy involves a fire, chemical spill, or industrial or vehicular accident, most companies have disaster plans to deal with the physical restoration of their facility. However, few companies have well-developed strategies to assist with the restoration and recovery of their workforce. Often there are no plans in place to assist the employees who have survived, witnessed, or have been injured by the event, short of addressing their physical injuries.

When accidents or tragedies happen, they are experienced as a "traumatic" event or "critical incident" by the employees, the organization, and employees' families. Depending on the magnitude of the event, even the greater community in which the business operates may be affected. Americans witnessed the expanding circle of impact of a traumatic event on April 19, 1995, when a terrorist bomb exploded at the Alfred P. Murrah Federal Building in Oklahoma City, Oklahoma. Americans everywhere were impacted by the trauma of that event.

Post-Incident Crisis Response Intervention

Post-incident crisis response intervention is a means for reducing the impact of trauma on those individuals affected, as well as restabilizing the organization after a traumatic event. The process of developing such a crisis response program is becoming a priority in progressive organizations and corporations today because it is consistent with " mission statements" and Total Quality Management philosophies which affirm the "value" and the individual worth of the employee as integral to the organization. Moreover, the deployment of a crisis response intervention team is a manifestation of loyalty and a commitment to the safety and wellbeing of employees who have experienced trauma while at the worksite. While there are many things that must be done in the aftermath of a critical event, this chapter will deal with organizational responses to aid those people victimized by exposure to trauma. In the midst of a crisis, there is far too much at risk to rely merely on ad hoc responses.

Providing an immediate post-incident response has numerous benefits for the organization. One, it allows an immediate response and begins re-establishing control of a traumatic situation often characterized by lack of control. This effectively begins an event closure while providing support and stability to the individual "victims" impacted. Onsite intervention establishes and sets an expectancy of recovery by acknowledging and normalizing the pain and reactions of those persons impacted by the trauma. They no longer feel quite so vulnerable or out of control and at the mercy of the crisis event. The act of an onsite response allows the organization to take immediate control of the situation. Providing crisis debriefing, education, and information about the kinds of reactions and responses "normal" people may have in response to a critical event "normalizes" reactions they may be experiencing. It also establishes and provides an opportunity for impacted employees to participate with their peers in a natural support group to begin the healing process.

Through participation in a group intervention and discussion of the event, they are able to recreate the event in a safe, secure environment. This allows them to begin processing the event on cognitive and emotional levels, to explore the impact of the event on them personally, and to be able to recognize many of the reactions that they may be having as similar to those that their co-workers are experiencing. By providing assistance to those individuals who were exposed to the trauma, it demonstrates loyalty to one's employees, customers, clients, and the community.

The availability of an onsite post-incident response also provides an opportunity to assess the severity of the impact of the crisis on the employees, the company, the customers, and the community in which it occurred. This allows the organization to begin addressing the concerns of those various entities, and to begin mitigating the trauma and reducing the risks in terms of worker compensation claims and litigation.

The Nature of Critical or Traumatic Events

It may be useful to identify and to define some common terms and concepts that we will use when discussing traumatic events or "critical incidents". A critical event is defined simply as any event that is outside the range of one's everyday experience or expectations and that would be distressing to almost anyone. It is usually sudden and unexpected, and it temporarily overwhelms our normal coping abilities and may interfere with normal daily functioning.

There are primarily three types of critical events as defined by their source. They are natural phenomenon, technological disasters, and man-made disasters. Natural disasters would include hurricanes, floods, tornadoes, wind storms or other phenomenon generally referred to as "acts of God." Recall the trauma of the Midwest that we all witnessed in the news reports of the devastation of homes and lives when the Mississippi River flooded its banks and in Florida after Hurricane Andrew. Technological disasters are also referred to "as acts of omission" such as fires, chemical releases, explosions, etc. The Three-Mile Island and Chernobyl meltdowns are classic examples of technological disasters. Lastly, there are critical incidents that are man-made, either intentionally or by accident, which may also be referred to as "acts of commission." Included among those would be industrial accidents, assaults, robberies, rapes, threats or acts of violence, and organizational crises, such as downsizings, mergers, acquisitions, layoffs, and plant closings. A crisis event caused by human error or intent is more difficult for people to cope with in the long run than natural disasters because people see these as being "avoidable." However, in the initial stages the psychological reactions to all critical events are essentially the same.

Posttraumatic Stress Disorder

There has been considerable interest in and study of the impact and consequences of such events on the individuals who experience them, as well as on the organizations within which the event occurs. There has been a corresponding interest by professionals from a multitude of disciplines including mental health, legal, organizational development, unions, risk management, Employee Assistance Programs, and medical and workers' compensation insurers on assisting workers who have been exposed to workplace tragedy. The object of such interest pertains to how to return employees to their optimal pre-incident functioning. This has been accompanied by a significant interest in identifying the most effective methods of assisting people to cope with and to recover emotionally and psychologically from exposure to trauma. (Hillenberg and Wolf, 1989)

Much of the knowledge base and interest in the effects of trauma on individuals has been generated as the direct result of the study of the long-term effects of exposure to trauma by combat veterans. (Figley, 1985; Kaplan and Sadock, 1994; Williams, 1987) Kaplan and Sadock (1994) trace the development of what is now known as Post-traumatic Stress Disorder from the American Civil War when combat veterans developed what was then called "soldiers heart." Through each successive war that the United States has been involved in, the syndrome, with its consistent constellation of symptoms, has been known by various names. Among them are "shell shock" from the World War I era veterans, and "battle" or "operational fatigue" of World War II and Korean Conflict era soldiers.

However, it was in response to this constellation of symptoms in a large percentage of Vietnam War veterans, and the recognized similarities of the syndrome within noncombat, nonmilitary personnel who had been involved in or exposed to traumatic events that led to the development of the psychiatric diagnosis that has come to be known as Posttraumatic Stress Disorder (DMS-IV, 1994). Study of the effects on the survivors of concentration camps (Wilson, Hazel, and Khana, 1988), hostage situations, and victims of other acts of violence has also contributed to our current knowledge base and understanding of exposure to traumatic events. According to Kaplan and Sadock (1994), there is a correlation between the severity of the traumatic event and the development of the syndrome. It has been found that in the most severe instances of trauma, more than 75% of those individuals exposed to the trauma develop Posttraumatic Stress Disorder Syndrome.

Reactions to Trauma

While there is great variability in how individuals are psychologically affected by trauma, there are some consistent types of reactions and responses that normal, healthy human beings experience when confronted with an abnormal crisis event. People may experience changes or symptoms cognitively, behaviorally, emotionally, and physically. Cognitively, they may experience memory problems, difficulty concentrating, intrusive images, or diminished problem-solving skills. Behaviorally, response to a crisis may result in changes in eating or sleeping patterns, self-imposed isolation or withdrawal, increased use of drugs or alcohol, or heightened startle reflex. The full range of emotional responses may occur in the aftermath of involvement in a traumatic incident, including anxiety, grief, guilt, depression, fear, and panic. Physical manifestation of the crisis response might include nausea, intense fatigue, headaches, intestinal upset, muscle cramps, and shock symptoms. Still, it is important to remember that this list of reactions is not a complete and recognize that individuals experience a critical incident in their own unique way . Some individuals may experience symptoms immediately; others may have a delayed onset of reactions.

Factors That Affect Reaction to Trauma

Each individual's reaction to a critical incident will vary depending upon various intensity factors. Individual reactions may be influenced by one's perception of the event and one's direct relationship to or involvement in the incident. Other stressors in the person's life, their stress management skills, and the level of social support they receive both at work and at home play important roles in how an individual reacts to a traumatic event. Previous exposure to or involvement in other critical events, the availability of crisis intervention services after the event, and other individual characteristics may all be determinants in how an individual will respond to trauma. The reactions and the process one generally goes through in recovering from exposure to a critical event may be viewed as occurring in distinct sequential phases. This correlates strongly with the findings of Elisabeth Kubler-Ross (1969) and the reactions and stages she identified among people responding to impending death. Kubler-Ross's work on the individual's personal incorporation of the information, and how they come to terms with the trauma of death and dying is very similar to the resolution all people must achieve in their quest to recover from exposure to trauma, regardless of its source.

First Stage: Crisis

The initial reaction of any individual exposed to something that is far outside the norm of their everyday experience is often one of shock, disbelief, denial, and numbness. They respond in ways similar to our ancestors when confronted with an apparently life-threatening situation; their "fight or flight" survival response mechanism is automatically triggered. There are a number of physiological reactions that occur when this happens. The body begins to pump adrenalin and experiences a desire to relieve itself of excess body fluids via perspiration, urination/defecation, or vomiting as it prepares itself to become a finely tuned fighting machine or to flee the challenge. One's senses may become acute or distorted; heart rate and respiration increases.

First Stage Reactions

Emotionally, there is an intense feeling of vulnerability and lack of control over the situation. People involved in a critical incident report a perception of a life-damaging threat, one that shatters their assumptions about how the world operates. People in crisis situations may hyperventilate and usually experience intense fatigue once the crisis has passed, which is a function of the physiological response to the increased adrenalin in the system and a biological need for the body to rest after having been so stimulated.

Second Stage: Impact

As the initial crisis reaction subsides, the second stage, or "impact stage," begins. In this stage, the full impact of the event enters the person's cognitive awareness. During this period people often feel overwhelmed with cataclysms of emotions over which they feel they have no control. People refer to this phase as feeling as if they were on an emotional roller coaster, experiencing a wide range of often divergent and conflicting emotions and being helpless to control their reactions or stop the roller coaster. Emotions during this time may range from fear of a repetition, nameless unknown fears, powerlessness, grief, guilt, rage, confusion, alienation, fear of being alone, intense sorrow, and preoccupation with death. Exposure to a critical event shatters one's sense of safety and security, creating a heightened degree of "free floating" anxiety and vulnerability. This makes it difficult for individuals to accurately test reality. This results in a significant reduction of the physical space in which a person can feel safe. This diminished safety zone may make it difficult for employees to return to work or even to leave their homes.

Second Stage Reactions

Anger is often a reaction to a traumatic event. Anger stems from the fear, sense of helplessness and resentment over how the event altered the person's world. However, if one is allowed to deflect that anger rather than get in touch with it and understand it in the context of it being a normal natural reaction to trauma, they may have more difficulty overcoming the event and may experience more long-term negative effects. Therefore, it is important that the crisis intervention provide information educating the person as to the source of their anger and "normalizing" that reaction for them while attempting to defuse the anger to facilitate a more rapid recovery.

Dealing with the Urge to Blame

Immediately after the event, there is also a tendency to attempt to assign blame or responsibility. This is a function of people attempting to discover how and why the event happened so as to avoid a repetition and regain a sense of mastery over their world. An organization frequently responds by attempting to assure people that they "did everything that could have been done" and otherwise reacts to any accusations leveled at them. Post-incident response intervention is useful in ameliorating this blaming/defending cycle, which is counterproductive to the healing process. While there may be responsibility in some way for the event, the post-incident response should not concern itself with that issue. The goal of the intervention is to facilitate healing and recovery, not to tear down or destroy. Therefore, it will always be in the best interest of the individuals and the organization for the intervention to refrain from engaging in the need to assign blame, but rather refocus the energy on recovering from the incident and away from dwelling upon the negative aspects of it. However it is important to understand that this will happen and what it indicates. Primarily, assigning blame or responsibility answers the question "Why?" which, in turn, begins to alleviate the individuals sense of vulnerability so that they may begin to regain a sense of mastery over their world.

Awareness of Vulnerability

A traumatic event is particularly destabilizing in that it challenges some of the basic assumptions upon which we base and live our lives. These assumptions are extremely powerful although we rarely verbalize them and may not even be aware that they exist. For example, most of us assume that children will outlive their parents. Therefore when a child dies, it is very traumatic for us because it violates one of our primary assumptions about the way the world operates. Similarly, we assume that we will go to work, do our jobs, and go home. We assume that our co-workers will do the same. If we didn't have those assumptions, we would not make plans for after work, or plan vacations, join ball teams, or golf and bowling leagues. When a critical incident occurs in the workplace, when someone dies, is seriously injured, or is threatened with death or serious injury, it forces us to confront our shattered assumptions about the way the world operates, and we develop an increased awareness of our personal vulnerability.

Final Stage: Event Closure

In the final phase, the emotional roller coaster levels out, and we try to facilitate an event closure. People begin to reconstruct meaning in their lives, regain a sense of safety and security, and come to terms with the existential and interpersonal losses that they experienced. Primary goals and challenges for those impacted by a critical event are to re-evaluate their personal strengths and vulnerabilities. "Victims" often emerge from a trauma feeling sadder but wiser, realizing how fragile life is, and are forced to confront new choices regarding this heightened awareness of the fragility of life and seek new satisfactions. Positive outcomes may result from this self- examination in the form of a newfound appreciation for life and resetting of one's priorities about what is important in their world.

While most people tend to recover from trauma over time, there are those persons who become emotionally and psychologically paralyzed by the event. They become secondarily traumatized by their own reactions to the event and may never fully recover. They are the people who develop Posttraumatic Stress Disorder. Early intervention in the aftermath of a crisis, with a focus on providing emotional support and education about the nature of trauma and the recovery process, speeds up the recovery process significantly and limits the potential for debilitating long-term effects.

Identifying "Victims" after the Incident

Whenever a critical event occurs at one's workplace, it will be to greater or lesser degrees, a trauma for everyone since it happened to their work "family." Our relationships at work are much like our nuclear and extended biological family. Thus, the entire workplace should be seen as the target for intervention.

Helping individuals recover from the psychological impact of workplace critical incidents and facilitating reconstruction of their lives is a tremendous challenge. Identifying and prioritizing of individuals to receive post-incident response interventions and the types of intervention services that are most appropriate depends on many factors related to the incident itself and the variability of how people are affected by that traumatic incident.

It is hard, if not impossible, to predict which individuals will have intense reactions to a critical incident. There are a variety of factors which may influence the degree of trauma or dysfunction a person may have. One factor is where on the location on the "range" of human experience was the event for a particular individual. Previous exposure to traumatic events may "innoculate" the individual to be more prepared to handle the current painful event. For example, after one of the plane crashes in Michigan, airport crisis response workers noticed different degrees of traumatic reactions among first responders to the crash site. Those officers who had "field" experience from road patrol or were evidence technicians at numerous gruesome crime scenes, seemed to demonstrate fewer traumatic reactions than officers who worked "inside" and had little exposure to traumatic scenes.

Intensity Factors

Other factors that influence the magnitude of a traumatic reaction is whether or not there was an abrupt contrast of the environment, such as would occur with an explosion. How much warning there was of the impending disaster and how much opportunity for effective action a person had to attempt some control also affect intensity. The amount of traumatic stimuli in the form of sounds, smells, and sights present may contribute to the individual's subjective experience and may also provide clues as to what types of stimuli may function as "triggers" to provoke them to relive the experience. The time of day that the event occurs and the duration of the event are additional intensity factors.

Given that there is no way to predict who may experience post-incident psychological problems, it is imperative to quickly identify all the potentially impacted individuals and provide crisis services in a consistent uniform manner. The intervention response team will need to "triage" victims based on their involvement, role and what they witnessed during the incident. The individual's functional work group should be taken into account as well as their role within the organization. For example, supervisors and managers should be dealt with separately from non-supervisory personnel. For organizations that are intent on the "jointness" process, this may be difficult to deal with initially. However, supervisors' and managers' outlooks, as well as responsibility and liability exposures are different and unique, and it has been found to be a good idea to address their reactions independently.

Triage

When triaging the victims, it is much like envisioning the concentric circles we get when we throw a pebble into a pool of water. There is a ripple effect of ever widening circles of victims. The post-incident response should direct its intervention activities toward the victims as a group, starting from the trauma core and working outward.

The first or inner circle of impact is going to be those individuals injured, surviving, or witnessing the incident. The next circle would include employees who came to the scene immediately and the first responders to the incident. While the first responders are generally charged with taking control of the scene, rescuing or providing services to those who were injured, they are also subject to the impact of trauma around them.

After these two groups, the circles expand to encompass the immediate work group of the individuals who were directly involved in the incident, then other shift employees, friends or co- workers of those impacted, etc. Organizations will want to consider other company locations, especially any location that has experienced a critical event at that worksite since the current trauma may precipitate a "reliving" of the earlier trauma in those other locations.

Depending on the scope and magnitude of the critical incident, it may be necessary and advantageous for the company to provide, or assist in providing, intervention services to the community in which it is located. Mass or large-scale disasters have the ability to traumatize communities as well as the organization in which they occur. This is especially true if the community closely relies on or identifies with the company itself.

Rationale and Cost Effectiveness of the Post-Incident Program

In addition to the impact on the individuals who experience a critical incident, a crisis may effect the viability of the company or even the entire industry. Consider the damage, albeit temporary, to the makers of Tylenol and the pain-relief industry after the Tylenol product tampering crisis or the impact of Three-Mile Island and Chernobyl on the nuclear power industry. Even if a crisis is not sufficiently damaging enough to threaten a company or industry's survival, it may result in uncomfortable scrutiny by the public, the media, and the government. The current and future image and goodwill of the organization may be severely jeopardized.

Equally as important, but much more difficult to assess, is the human cost resulting from having been involved in a traumatic incident. This can be quite significant. These costs to the organization usually manifest themselves through increased litigation, sick leave, absenteeism, accidents, increased use of drugs and alcohol, workman's compensation claims, and reduced productivity or quality of service. The costs to employees in human pain and suffering is impossible to measure.

During times of great pain and tragedy we are challenged personally, spiritually and organizationally to reach out to one another and help each other deal with the suffering that takes place. Companies may perform this service for their employees by developing and utilizing a Post-Incident Response Program. Employees who have experienced workplace trauma and received post-incident support report feeling "cared about" by their employer and demonstrate greater feelings of loyalty to their employer. They view their employers as progressive and proactive.

Such post-incident intervention has hastened the recovery period because employees, prepared for the kinds of reactions they may have, are less likely to become debilitated by them. Having an organized, systematic approach to respond to traumatic events when they occur in the work environment ensures that the response will be timely, effective and coordinated.

Benefits of Early Intervention

Data on financial costs offer additional pragmatic reasons for post-incident intervention. In the past decade, there has been increasing study of the psychological and occupational consequences of workplace trauma and attempts to identify more precisely the costs associated with them. An obvious ethical consideration in any research project of this nature is the issue of withholding treatment. Therefore most of the studies in this area have been retrospective, correlational studies based on artifactual data. However, the results of those studies make a compelling argument for every organization to have a post-incident response program. In their study of 200 cases of individuals impacted by a traumatic, event Friedman, Framer and Shearer (1988) found significant disparity in the costs between early intervention and delayed intervention. Figure 15.1 graphically displays the financial variances in average costs for time lost from work, treatment cost, litigation, rehabilitation, and disability costs.

In just one of the real life examples cited by this study, an early intervention program that cost a total of $5,834—versus a projected average cost of $43,400 had a delayed response occurred—saved and estimated $37,600 in that one case alone.

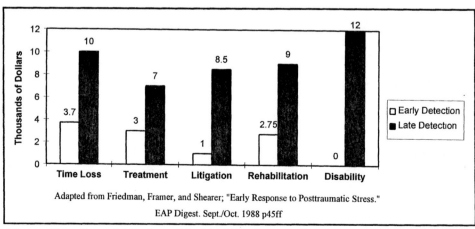

Adapted from Friedman, Framer, and Shearer; "Early Response to Posttraumatic Stress." EAP Digest. Sept./Oct. 1988 p45ff

Figure 15.1: Cost of delaying critical incident intervention

This study is consistent with other findings including that by Jeffrey T. Mitchell (1993) in his comparison of the impact on emergency services personnel in the aftermath of two airline disasters. The San Diego airline crash in 1978 and the Cerritos plane crash in 1986 had striking similarities in a number of ways including the number of emergency personnel involved in the responses. However, the Cerritos disaster had a comprehensive coordinated post-incident response intervention to help the emergency services personnel deal with the personal impact of the experience while the San Diego disaster, eight years earlier, did not. In the one-year period following the respective crashes, 29 of the 300 emergency service workers who responded to the San Diego accident left their career fields, yet only one of the 300 Cerritos emergency service workers left their occupations. There was also a 31% rate of increase in utilization of mental health benefits by the emergency service workers who responded to the San Diego disaster in the first year post-incident compared to a corresponding 1% increase in utilization rate of mental health services by the Cerritos emergency responders. The dramatic differences in these two areas alone reinforce the effectiveness of early intervention to assist people who have been involved in traumatic events and may be experiencing intense stress reactions.

There has been considerable interest in and study of the role of stress (Selye, 1980) in mediating between the mind-body response to traumatic stimuli and the role of stress in precipitating illness and disease. Stress-related claims typically cost two times the amount for claims for physical injuries, and account for approximately 14% of all workman's compensation claims for "occupational disease" according to the National Council on Compensation Insurance (McCarthy, 1988). Interestingly, Jenkins' (1996) discussion of stress indicates that it may play a dual role in the phenomenon of workplace violence in that it may be both a cause and an effect agent. The literature takes many approaches in the question of identifying predictors of violence. While it demonstrates that there is very little empirical data in this area or any definitive measures that may be relied upon with any degree of accuracy, it is generally accepted that stress may precipitate aberrant behaviors that are not characteristic for an individual. Therefore it may even be possible that stress reactions from exposure to trauma in the workplace could lead to additional trauma for that organization in the form of a violent episode.

Government Regulatory Activity

Violence and violent crime in American society has continuously escalated since the 1920s (Selby, 1984), an era that was characterized by crime, violence, and bloodshed. As simply a microcosm of the larger society perhaps it should not come as a surprise that a major societal focus during this decade of the 1990s has been the violence that is occurring in the workplace. Rarely does a day pass that the media does not report on an incident of violence in a workplace somewhere. A recent publication by the National Institute for Occupational Safety and Health (Jenkins, 1996) reports that an average of twenty workers are murdered and another 18,000 assaulted every week at their workplaces in the United States. Statistics of this magnitude and concomitant media coverage of these acts of violence has created a new era of fear for American workers who now worry about being killed or injured while on the job. Employers, too, are concerned about violence in their workplaces. There is a heightened awareness of security precautions, litigation exposures, and uncertainty about how to prevent violence from erupting in their workplaces. There is considerable interest in and proliferation of programs and philosophies on how to prevent, predict, manage and respond to potential violence and how best to create an organizational response that is swift, caring, and effective in its prevention intent. While a significant focus is on how to prevent, intervene, and defuse a potentially violent situation, another crucial element that should be prioritized is the appropriate organizational strategies to deal with the impact of threats or acts of violence on employees, organizations, and the community. Thus, Post-Incident Response activities to assist those individuals impacted by the event are an excellent means for reducing the impact of trauma on the individuals affected, as well as for restabilizing the organization.

The Occupational Safety and Health Administration (OSHA) has recognized the importance of responding to those persons who have been victimized by exposure to violence or potential violence and has included post-incident response in its guidelines for creating a comprehensive violence prevention program (OSHA, 1996) In its recently published *Guidelines for Preventing Workplace Violence for Health Care and Social Service Workers*, OSHA describes post-incident response as "essential to an effective violence prevention program." (U.S. Department of Labor, 1996) OSHA previously recommended a post-incident response program as an abatement measure to reduce the impact of trauma on employees at an organization cited for failure to provide a safe workplace under the OSHA General Duty clause 5(a).

In addition to the fines and lawsuits from government or regulatory agencies, there are many other legal and financial consequences that may result from failure to prevent or adequately respond to traumatic events or critical incidents that occur in the workplace. Organizations may experience an increase in disability and workman's compensation claims with resultant increases in premiums. It may also witness a decline in performance and productivity, resignations or worker turnover, employee anger directed at the employer, and low morale. The negative publicity and perceptions of the organization may do irreparable damage to its reputation and ultimately its profitability. There may be an increased utilization of medical benefits for extended psychological treatment/rehabilitation or misdirected medical care by those individuals impacted by the event.

Establishing a Post-Incident Response Program

Service Providers

Developing a Post-Incident Response Program requires many considerations. Chief among them is whether or not the organization has the internal resources and/or wants to assume the responsibility for conducting all of its crisis response activities in-house. Some advantages to providing crisis response services in-house are the obvious cost effectiveness of utilizing personnel who are already on the payroll as well as considerations of confidentiality and the fact that the organization would be able to maintain complete direct control of the intervention process. Company personnel would be intimately knowledgeable about the organization's culture, its history, its personnel, and its internal politics. However, these same factors may be just as powerful a rationale for utilizing independent, external crisis resources, particularly considering problems of internal politics and familiarity with other company personnel.

An alternative may be to use neutral external providers to deliver the actual interventions to employees. Additional benefits to using external crisis responders are that they most likely will have more expertise and experience in responding to critical incidents. Also it might be more disruptive and ultimately create more stress for the organization to have to do without the skills of their staff who are removed from their regular positions during the post-incident response. A final consideration is that regardless of the involvement of the company personnel in the actual incident, the fact that they are members of the organization will mean that the incident will be experienced to some degree as a crisis by them simply because it occurred within their "work family". This may make them not only less objective, but also more vulnerable to additional traumatization by vicariously reexperiencing the event through their efforts to assist their co-workers.

This author has found it most advantageous to create a team composed of internal and external crisis resources. An external resource is generally most effective in providing the actual on-site interventions to employees in conjunction with supportive and active participation of pre-identified and trained internal liaisons from the organization. Equally important to the decision of utilizing an external provider is identifying that provider and developing a relationship with them prior to an incident occurring which will require their services. It is very important to carefully scrutinize the credentials and references of the external crisis resources before engaging them to be the providers of services to an organization.

Planning

One of the first tasks in establishing a post-incident response program is to determine who are the core stakeholders and who will "own" the program within the organization. Responsibility for program development, budget, design, and opera-

---

Checklist 15.1

Components of a Post-Incident Response Program

✔ Who delivers the program

✔ Stakeholders

✔ Program owner

✔ Response team

✔ Definition of critical incident

✔ Identification of local providers

✔ Procedure for system activation

✔ Contact list with telephone numbers

✔ Response sequence

✔ Communication material, handouts

✔ Overall communication strategy

✔ Information packet describing post-incident responses

tion of the program must be defined. Included in the development and design will be setting up the entire system, the structure, the onsite protocols, procedures for program implementation, and deployment of resources after a critical incident. During the planning stage, it will also be necessary to identify the department or individuals who will have the ultimate responsibility for activating and assisting with the post-incident response should an incident occur and a deployment be required. Since these persons may not be the same, it is advisable to have some representation of the response team on the core planning committee.

Another consideration that needs to be taken into account when developing a critical incident response program is to define what will constitute a critical event for the organization. Keep in mind that the nature of various work environments, the organizational dynamics and the types of work performed will result in different types of trauma or critical events for different industries and work places. For example, the stress and trauma that ordinarily exists in an emergency services organization would create a significantly different perspective of what constitutes a critical event from that of a manufacturing facility. Identify, at least in general terms, the types of predictable incidents that will precipitate a response. This list will not be exhaustive as it is impossible to foresee everything that could possibly occur and many situations will need to be evaluated on a case-by-case basis. In this planning period, the persons who will make the preliminary assessment of the incident to determine whether or not it falls within the deployment parameters for a post-incident response need to be identified. Criteria for making this preliminary assessment should be developed. Lastly, the procedures for response deployment and the final authority to activate the response mechanism need to be clearly defined.

The plan should include a resource list of local providers who have an expertise or familiarity with the dynamics of a critical incident, the critical incident response activities and posttraumatic stress reactions, so that they might be available for follow-up with particularly distressed individuals. Included among local crisis resource providers would be clergy, mental health professionals, community crisis intervention agencies, and appropriate support groups. Such responders should demonstrate previous onsite crisis management experience and supply a list of references. The need for familiarity with local resources, as well as the ability to provide linkages between the impacted employees with the appropriate referral resources, is another aspect of the benefit of having a company representative actively participate with the response.

Activation Response

Essential to a Post-Incident Response Program is notifying response personnel that a critical incident has occurred. Therefore, consideration must be given to a mechanism for reporting or identifying the need for a post-incident response. Options may be an 800 reporting telephone number, a call to the personnel director, security department, or health and safety officer. Once the system and its structure have been determined, this information should be disseminated to all managers and supervisors within the organization as well as to union representatives and health and safety committee members, who may be among the first people to become aware of a traumatic incident.

Once notified, the persons responsible for making the preliminary assessment of the incident will need to verify a consensus among themselves as to the most appropriate response to the specific critical event. The response options may include one-to-one crisis counseling, large-scale defusing, or formal critical incident stress debriefing sessions. The format for critical incident stress debriefing in the workplace is an adaptation of the model developed by Mitchell (1993) for alleviating traumatic stress among emergency service workers. This team will also have the responsibility for contacting the key decision-makers within the organization who have the authority to authorize deployment of the post-incident response resources. Once key decision-makers approve and authorize a response, the next step will be to contact and deploy the crisis response group to deliver the crisis intervention services to the impacted employees. Onsite strategies and timeframes for the intervention should be determined.

Identify key organization personnel who will need to be contacted in the event of a crisis. Compile a roster of these individuals with current telephone numbers. Be sure to include home telephone numbers, pager numbers, and cellular phones, as well as their work numbers since they may need to be reached during their nonwork hours. Review and update this list and phone numbers regularly. Should a post-incident response be activated, identify the chain of command for immediate and strategic decision-making during the intervention process.

It is important to identify a media liaison, preferably someone internal to the organization who will be responsible for handling all communications with the media. That person should have specialized training and skill in dealing with the media so that, in the aftermath of a crisis, the organization and its workforce are not further traumatized by negative or inaccurate media reports about the event. Everyone involved with the onsite crisis response team should know who the Media Liaison is and how to contact them at all times. All requests for information from any external source should be directed to the media liaison.

Communications

There will be a number of communications that will need to be disseminated during the onsite response. Establish guidelines for onsite communications during a deployment of the post-incident response. Part of the planning process will be to compile a post-incident response information kit. Samples of the various print materials generally published during a crisis response should be developed and kept in this kit so that when an incident occurs, the prepared handouts and materials can be customized or modified to address the particular event.

Contained in the kit should also be handout literature that identifies crisis reactions that normal, healthy people may have in response to a traumatic event. This handout should be given to individuals who participate in the crisis intervention as well as be made available to other employees throughout the organization who may not be available to participate. The purpose of this literature is that it helps reinforce and "normalize" any reactions or responses that employees may have relative to their exposure to the critical event. Having this information in written form will make it possible for them to refer back to it at a later time should they experience a delayed onset of symptoms or need reassurance that the reactions they may be having are indeed normal. This handout should also list a crisis team phone number so that distressed employees can more easily be linked to helping resources.

There should be informational literature for employees to take home and share with their family members describing the kinds of reactions and responses that are normal and natural after exposure to a critical event. This information should educate family members about critical incidents, the kinds of reactions their loved ones may be experiencing, and what types of support the family can provide to help facilitate and expedite the recovery process. This will be very useful in helping to provide an informed support system for the employee within his or her own family and social network.

In conjunction with the triage process and the setting up of individual and group interventions, will be the need for ongoing communication between the crisis team and the supervisors and employees. It should be determined during the planning stages how that will be handled and by whom.

Rumor control statements should be developed and disseminated during the onsite response activities. A rumor control statement gives a simple, factual account of what happened. Studies have demonstrated, that people prefer to get information from their own supervisors or from their own organization. It is preferable to communicate incident facts to the workforce through the organization's own internal communication system rather than allowing employees to learn new information about their own workplace from the television, newspapers or other public media, if at all possible. In these rumor control statements, avoid speculation or premature discussion of responsibility. Refrain, too, from disclosing personal information about the individual(s) involved in the incident. Schedule regular intervals to disseminate informational updates about the event, the status of any employee who may have been injured, and the company's post-incident response activities. Maintain the communication schedule even if there is no new information. If there is no new information, state just that, but continue to provide informational updates from authorized sources. Recall that nature abhors a vacuum. The absence of reliable information will create a vacuum which can lead to destabilizing rumors. The proverbial grapevine will pick up grains of truth and create its own story around those small morsels of information. To prevent this from happening and as a restabilizing technique, release facts as they become available through your own internal communications system and network first, then through the public media. Establish a rumor control hotline where individuals within the organization may call to get accurate, updated information regarding the incident and also where they can find out information about the location, types of crisis services, and activities that are being provided. Specify who will be in charge of rumor control activities and create a feedback loop between the crisis team and the rumor control person so that as rumors and speculation develop, they may be addressed and dispelled quickly.

Publish a schedule of the crisis response activities and identify employees by work group who will be expected to participate during particular time frames. If the incident resulted in any fatalities, the organization should publish memorial biographies of the deceased. A memorial biography serves several purposes in that it demonstrates to employees that the organization does not trivialize the loss of a member of its "work family." It also provides additional information to co-workers about the deceased.

Goals of Post-Incident Response

The primary goals of the post-incident response program are to provide safety and support to employees affected by the trauma and permit them to recreate the event within a safe setting so that they may explore its personal impact on them. This process of ventilation of their intense emotional reactions, having those reactions validated by their peers and the crisis team and re- experiencing the event helps serve the purpose of normalizing those crisis reactions, thereby reducing the potential of secondary traumatization or more intense symptoms.By providing employees with education and awareness of the types of reactions and responses that they may experience in the next few days, few weeks, or few months, they will be better equipped to deal with possible post-trauma reactions should they experience them. Otherwise, individuals who experience delayed onset of symptoms, not realizing these are normal, often begin to second guess themselves and question their own sanity, wondering whether or not they are going crazy or losing their minds. Advance awareness and understanding that they may have these reactions, prepares them to more readily cope with and accept these reactions in the context of normal stress responses to the crisis event that they experienced. This awareness and understanding facilitates a more rapid recovery.

Another important goal of the onsite intervention is to assist individuals develop coping strategies to deal with the aftermath of the trauma. The crisis response team might assist the affected employees in the identification of coping strategies that they have effectively utilized in the past in dealing with other crises in their lives. They may learn new coping strategies from their peers by sharing and discussing coping mechanisms that others use in dealing with difficult situations. The crisis response intervention activities may help individuals cope by reframing the myriad kinds of losses they experienced into a positive sense of growth and new meaning. It is an appropriate time to begin to predict and prepare them for the changes that may have been created as a result of the event and to identify available personal support systems.

A follow-up plan should be developed for all individuals who participate in the crisis intervention activities which provides linkages and encouragement to seek additional help if they are continuing to have distressing symptoms. Follow-up activities continue to assure everyone that problems are being addressed organizationally and that they are, personally, going to get better.

Onsite Activities

Upon notification that a crisis event has occurred, the company liaison to the crisis team should begin to compile the facts regarding what happened. Among the facts that are relevant to the intervention are a description of exactly what happened, who was involved, the number of people injured and the nature of their injuries, approximately how many people were involved or witnessed the incident, where the incident occurred, when the incident occurred, and any additional information that may be known about the event. Ancillary information that may be very useful and should therefore be gathered are details of any previous critical incidents, both at that location or in that particular community. The onsite liaison should also accumulate general background information regarding the particular location. Among information that will be particularly useful is the local population of that particular facility, the number of shifts it operates, their start and stop times, any unique production or cultural issues regarding the organization and the availability of personnel to participate in the crisis response activities.

As soon as a preliminary assessment of the incident has been made, the company liaison should start a time log of the post-incident response activities and maintain this log throughout the entire intervention. Crisis response team members should also maintain an activities log listing and identifying their activities and rationale for such activities throughout the crisis intervention procedure. This is important for internal quality assurance and continuous quality improvement of the response program. This activity log will help coordinate and define the activities of the entire team and ensure that the crisis response follows defined protocols and guidelines established and approved by the organization.

Before beginning any actual intervention activities with individual victims, it is important that any questions or concerns personnel may have or "barriers" to the crisis response activities be resolved. Once the crisis response team arrives at the incident location, schedule a meeting with those management and union leaders who have ultimate responsibility for the personnel and/or the physical site involved. Although those local leaders may be aware of the crisis response program, it is important, particularly during these times of stress immediately following a crisis, to reiterate the goals and objectives of the crisis response program and answer any questions they may have before beginning crisis activities with any of their union members or employees. The crisis response team should visit, if possible, the site where the incident occurred so they may better understand and relate to descriptions or information that may be shared during the intervention process. Familiarity with the site may also be helpful in assisting those people exposed to the trauma with identifying significant sensory perceptions that they may not immediately be aware of, such as powerful odors, loud noises, or other unusual sensory reactions that may be trigger events for them. Also review whatever incident summaries, photographs, newspaper articles, or known facts related to the event which are available. It is important at this juncture to reassure participants that a crisis response intervention program is not part of an investigative process nor is it an operations critique.

Once on site, the crisis response team should establish an operations center and locate a secluded room where the interventions with impacted employees will take place. Something to consider when establishing the operations center is accessibility by the people who will be coming in for the intervention. Ideally, the operations center that the crisis intervention team will operate from and the crisis intervention center where "victims" will be counseled or debriefed should be located relatively close to the workforce and to one another, yet out of view and nondisruptive to normal organizational operations. This will assure some degree of privacy and efficiency. At the very least, the crisis team will require one room large enough to accommodate up to 20 employees seated comfortably in a circle or preferably around a table. The table should contain boxes of tissues strategically placed so that it is not difficult for anyone to unobtrusively reach out and take a tissue should they experience intense emotional reactions when discussing the event. Having tissues handy will reinforce the notion that it's normal and natural to have intense emotional reactions in this setting. Refreshments of some kind should be provided which will encourage socializing among peers before and after the interventions. This socializing is not wasting time, but is therapeutic in that it facilitates natural bonding and support-group formation that may be relied upon long after the post-incident response team has departed.

In addition to this large room, there should be at least one other room that will function as the operations center. The operations center should have a telephone with a number that can receive incoming phone calls. The telephone number of the operations center should be distributed throughout the organization so that individuals wishing to communicate with the crisis response team, or supervisors or union representatives who want to send employees to participate in an intervention or set up additional interventions, would be able to contact the response team.

Depending upon the magnitude of the event and the size of the response team, a smaller third room, to be used for one-on-one crisis counseling or smaller intervention groups, would be helpful.

Once the above tasks have been completed, it is time to begin scheduling the interventions with the various individuals who were significantly impacted by the trauma. Initiate the first contacts and interventions with those individuals who were most immediately affected and were triaged as the primary "victims" of the incident. Then continue to expand the scope of the crisis intervention to encompass as many of the identified "victims" as is feasible as quickly as possible. To accomplish its goal of setting an expectation of recovery, it is important that the post-incident response intervention

Conclusion

The use of crisis intervention teams and post-incident response programs for employee populations has been gaining acceptance in work environments because such crisis assistance after traumatic events is consistent with concerns for employee well-being. In addition, the implementation of total quality cultures suggests that organizations should focus, not only on productivity, but also on responsiveness to its people in the work environment. Helping employees after work-site critical incidents by deploying crisis response teams and offering crisis intervention assistance reflects a sensitivity to employees, is a demonstrated cost-effective strategy to reduce litigation, human suffering, and potential worker's compensation or disability claims, and maintains a responsible public relations posture after negative events.

Currently, crisis response programs are used by a variety of retail, health care, and nuclear facilities; manufacturing, transportation, and utility companies; unions; and government entities. Such crisis response programs are seen as a "win-win" strategy since they serve the mutual interest of management, the union, employees, and the company.

References

Azrin, N.H., T. Flores, and S.J. Kaplan. "Job finding club: A group-assisted program for obtaining employment." *Behavioral Research and Therapy* 13:17-27. 1975.

Brenner, M.H. *Mental Illness and the Economy*. Cambridge, Mass.: Harvard University Press. 1973.

Feather, N.T. and P.R. Davenport. "Unemployment and depressive affect: A motivational and attributional analysis." *Journal of Personality and Social Psychology* 41:422-436. 1981.

Fedrau, R.H. "Easing the worker's transition from job loss to employment." *Monthly Labor Review* 107:38-40. 1984.

Figley, Charles R. (Editor). *Stress Disorders among Vietnam Veterans: Theory, Research and Treatment*. New York: Brunner/Mazel. 1978.

Foster, B. and L. Schore. "Job loss and the occupational social worker." *Occupational Social Worker Today* 5:77-97. 1990.

Friedman, R.J., MD, PhD, M.B. Framer, PhD, and D.R. Shearer, PhD(cand.) MFCC, CEAP. "Early response to posttraumatic stress." *EAP Digest* September/October 1988.

Jannotta, J. "Stroh's outplacement success." *Management Review* 76:52-53. 1987.

Johnson, Kendall. *Trauma in the Lives of Children*. Claremont, CA.: Hunter House Inc. 1989.

Kates, N., B. Greiff, and D. Hagen. *The Psychosocial Impact of Job Loss*. Washington, D.C.: American Psychiatric Press, Inc. 1990.

Lauer, Robert H. and Jeanette C. Lauer. *Watersheds: Mastering Life's Unpredictable Crises*. Boston, MA.: Little, Brown and Company. 1988.

Leana, C.R. and D.C. Feldman. *Coping with Job Loss*. New York, N.Y.: Lexington Books. 1992.

Leana, C.R. and J.M. Ivancevich. "Addressing the problem of involuntary job loss: Institutional interventions and a research agenda." *Academy of Management Review* 12:301-312. 1987.

Mitchell, Jeffrey T. and H.L.P. Resnik. *Emergency Response to Crisis*. Bowie, MD.: Robert J. Brady Company. 1981.

Raphael, Beverley. *The Anatomy of Bereavement*. New York, N.Y.: Basic Books, Inc. 1983.

Raphael, Beverley. *When Disaster Strikes*. New York, N.Y.: Basic Books, Inc. 1986.

Slaby, Andrew E. *AfterShock: Surviving the Delayed Effects of Trauma, Crisis and Loss*. New York, NY.: Villard Books. 1989.

United States Government. *Role Stressors and Supports for Emergency Workers*. Department of Health and Human Services. No. (ADM) 85-1408. Printed 1985.

Williams, Tom. *Post-Traumatic Stress Disorders: A Handbook for Clinicians*. Cincinnati, OH.: Disabled American Veterans. 1987.

Index

PC #	ENVIRONMENTAL TITLES	Pub Date	Price
585	Book of Lists for Regulated Hazardous Substances, 8th Edition	1997	$79
4088	CFR Chemical Lists on CD ROM, 1997 Edition	1997	$125
4089	Chemical Data for Workplace Sampling & Analysis, Single User	1997	$125
512	Clean Water Handbook, 2nd Edition	1996	$89
581	EH&S Auditing Made Easy	1997	$79
587	E H & S CFR Training Requirements, 3rd Edition	1997	$89
4082	EMMI-Envl Monitoring Methods Index for Windows-Network	1997	$537
4082	EMMI-Envl Monitoring Methods Index for Windows-Single User	1997	$179
525	Environmental Audits, 7th Edition	1996	$79
548	Environmental Engineering and Science: An Introduction	1997	$79
578	Environmental Guide to the Internet, 3rd Edition	1997	$59
560	Environmental Law Handbook, 14th Edition	1997	$79
353	Environmental Regulatory Glossary, 6th Edition	1993	$79
625	Environmental Statutes, 1998 Edition	1998	$69
4098	Environmental Statutes Book/Disk Package, 1998 Edition	1997	$208
4994	Environmental Statutes on Disk for Windows-Network	1997	$405
4994	Environmental Statutes on Disk for Windows-Single User	1997	$139
570	Environmentalism at the Crossroads	1995	$39
536	ESAs Made Easy	1996	$59
515	Industrial Environmental Management: A Practical Approach	1996	$79
4078	IRIS Database-Network	1997	$1,485
4078	IRIS Database-Single User	1997	$495
510	ISO 14000: Understanding Environmental Standards	1996	$69
551	ISO 14001: An Executive Repoert	1996	$55
518	Lead Regulation Handbook	1996	$79
478	Principles of EH&S Management	1995	$69
554	Property Rights: Understanding Government Takings	1997	$79
582	Recycling & Waste Mgmt Guide to the Internet	1997	$49
603	Superfund Manual, 6th Edition	1997	$115
566	TSCA Handbook, 3rd Edition	1997	$95
534	Wetland Mitigation: Mitigation Banking and Other Strategies	1997	$75

PC #	SAFETY AND HEALTH TITLES	Pub Date	Price
547	Construction Safety Handbook	1996	$79
553	Cumulative Trauma Disorders	1997	$59
559	Forklift Safety	1997	$65
539	Fundamentals of Occupational Safety & Health	1996	$49
535	Making Sense of OSHA Compliance	1997	$59
563	Managing Change for Safety and Health Professionals	1997	$59
589	Managing Fatigue in Transportation, *ATA Conference*	1997	$75
4086	OSHA Technical Manual, Electronic Edition	1997	$99
598	Project Mgmt for E H & S Professionals	1997	$59
552	Safety & Health in Agriculture, Forestry and Fisheries	1997	$125
613	Safety & Health on the Internet, 2nd Edition	1998	$49
597	Safety Is A People Business	1997	$49
463	Safety Made Easy	1995	$49
590	Your Company Safety and Health Manual	1997	$79

Electronic Product available on CD-ROM or Floppy Disk

PLEASE CALL OUR CUSTOMER SERVICE DEPARTMENT AT (301) 921-2323 FOR A FREE PUBLICATIONS CATALOG.

Government Institutes
4 Research Place, Suite 200 • Rockville, MD 20850-3226
Tel. (301) 921-2323 • FAX (301) 921-0264
E mail: giinfo@govinst.com • Internet: http://www.govinst.com

GOVERNMENT INSTITUTES ORDER FORM

4 Research Place, Suite 200 • Rockville, MD 20850-3226 • Tel (301) 921-2323 • Fax (301) 921-0264
Internet: *http://www.govinst.com* • E-mail: *giinfo@govinst.com*

3 EASY WAYS TO ORDER

1. Phone: **(301) 921-2323**
Have your credit card ready when you call

2. Fax: **(301) 921-0264**
Fax this completed order form with your company
purchase order or credit card information.

3. Mail: **Government Institutes**
4 Research Place, Suite 200
Rockville, MD 20850-3226
USA
Mail this completed order form with a check, company
purchase order, or credit card information.

PAYMENT OPTIONS

❏ **Check** (*payable to Government Institutes in US dollars*)

❏ **Purchase Order** (this order form must be attached to your
company P.O. <u>Note</u>: All International orders must be pre-paid.)

❏ **Credit Card** ❏ VISA ❏ ▨ ❏ ▨

Exp.___/___

Credit Card No. _____

Signature _____
Government Institutes' Federal I D # is 52-0994196

CUSTOMER INFORMATION

Ship To: (Please attach your Purchase Order)

Name: _____

GI Account# (*7 digits on mailing label*) _____

Company/Institution. _____

Address _____
(please supply street address for UPS shipping)
_____

City: _____ State/Province: _____

Zip/Postal Code: _____ Country: _____

Tel: ( ) _____

Fax: ( ) _____

E-mail Address: _____

Bill To: (if different than ship to address)

Name _____

Title/Position: _____

Company/Institution: _____

Address: _____
(please supply street address for UPS shipping)
_____

City. _____ State/Province: _____

Zip/Postal Code: _____ Country: _____

Tel. ( ) _____

Fax ( ) _____

E-mail Address: _____

Qty.	Product Code	Title	Price

❏ **New Edition No Obligation Standing Order Program**
Please enroll me in this program for the products I have ordered. Government
Institutes will notify me of new editions by sending me an invoice. I understand
that there is no obligation to purchase the product. This invoice is simply my
reminder that a new edition has been released.

15 DAY MONEY-BACK GUARANTEE
If you're completely satisfied with any product, return it undamaged
within 15 days for a full and immediate refund on the price of the product.

Subtotal_____
MD Residents add 5% Sales Tax_____
Shipping and Handling (see box below)_____
Total Payment Enclosed_____

Within U.S:	Outside U.S:
1-4 products: $6/product	Add $15 for each item (Airmail)
5 or more: $3/product	Add $10 for each item (Surface)

SOURCE CODE: BP01